"Both foreshadowed destination and a point of departure, *Scary Monsters* is a significant staging post in Bowie's career. Adam Steiner's erudite book communicates the thrill of an artist meeting the times, and his past, head on."
—**Graeme Thomson**, author of *Themes for Great Cities: A New History of Simple Minds*

"Adam Steiner's analysis of one of Bowie's most charismatic yet strangely elusive albums is as compelling as it is rich in detail. It sent me straight back to the record, as the best writing on music always does. This is a fresh and vital addition to the lengthening bibliography on David Bowie's extraordinary career."
—**Michael Bracewell**, author of *Souvenir*

"Bowie's writing on *Scary Monsters* is so dense and complex in meaning, it deserves this highly literate book which presents in-depth analysis of the album lyrically and musically, and of the multitudinous influences on Bowie which helped shape it. I particularly appreciate how *Silhouettes and Shadows* is so vividly set in the societal context of the day; the horror and terror of Britain and America under the influence of those two very scary monsters, Thatcher and Reagan."
—**Nacho Video**

"Adam Steiner's *Silhouettes and Shadows* is the mindbendingly fascinating story of an album and its maker at the peak of his career."
—**Arsalan Mohammad**, host of David Bowie: Albumtoalbum podcast

"Steiner gathers together much significant research—covering areas of Bowie's recording career that have been previously overlooked."
—**George Underwood**, artist

SILHOUETTES AND SHADOWS

the Secret History of

DAVID BOWIE'S

SCARY MONSTERS

(AND SUPER CREEPS)

ADAM STEINER

Backbeat
Books

Essex, Connecticut

Backbeat Books

An imprint of Globe Pequot, the trade division of
The Rowman & Littlefield Publishing Group, Inc.
4501 Forbes Blvd., Ste. 200
Lanham, MD 20706
www.rowman.com

Distributed by NATIONAL BOOK NETWORK

British Library Cataloguing in Publication Information Available

Library of Congress Cataloging-in-Publication Data

Names: Steiner, Adam, 1973- author.
Title: Silhouettes and shadows : the secret history of David Bowie's Scary
    monsters (and super creeps) / Adam Steiner.
Identifiers: LCCN 2022056356 (print) | LCCN 2022056357 (ebook) | ISBN
    9781493065646 (paperback) | ISBN 9781493065653 (ebook)
Subjects: LCSH: Bowie, David. Scary monsters (and super creeps). | Rock
    music—1971-1980—History and criticism.
Classification: LCC ML420.B754 S75 2023 (print) | LCC ML420.B754 (ebook)
    | DDC 782.42166092—dc23/eng/20221123
LC record available at https://lccn.loc.gov/2022056356
LC ebook record available at https://lccn.loc.gov/2022056357

((((For Hugh \ oguH))))

Contents

viii   *Contents*

Just >>> Press >>> Play

Every time the tape clicked into play, the spool running away with itself; I heard it *hear* it twice, sound chasing sound after the echo of the reel. The music turned over in the brain as Bowie counts down 1,2,1,2,3—then all hell breaks loose—shards of grinding, angular guitars and thundering drums—looking from the top of my mind, above my head—don't look down—thoughts poised to leap over the edge into nothing. Journeys demand nostalgia, words as a roadway, for places you've been and places that you have only imagined, never to arrive. My first car was a cherry-red Rover Metro, a tiny car of the people like a Mini or a Volkswagen Beetle sitting at its own end of the spectrum; it was transport without class, flux stripped of style. Never mind—it got me places, all over in fact. Driving, like music, brings freedom; together, they take you somewhere else entirely. Because it was an older car, I bought up cassette tapes that soon filled the glove box, which contained nothing but a fine old pair of blood-red leather driving gloves. They were my granddad's and became part of the inheritance, his hands working through mine. They were made in the town of Yeovil in southwest England where he chose to live, its football team nicknamed "The Glovers." The town was famous for aircraft production, manufacturing Spitfires during World War II. My grandfather left Vienna at the end of the 1930s, escaping somewhere through the mountains into the Czech Republic, they said; he eventually reached Haifa in Palestine and went on to join the British navy in Egypt. In the space of a few short years, he became a refugee, a veteran, and then an immigrant in retreat from the terror of a darker time that is not my story to tell. I scoured charity shops and the internet for old tapes, but my first Bowie album was, of course, a *Ziggy Stardust* thirtieth-anniversary reissue, then a *Low* and *"Heroes"* double CD and then I stumbled on an original 1980 *Scary Monsters (and Super Creeps)* cassette for fifty pence, maybe a quid. This album soundtracked many journeys. Even then, the format already seemed like an anachronism. You listened through side A and turned over to side B; it wasn't a skipping-and-flipping tape deck in the car (everything was manual). Listening habits have changed since, first a vinyl revival, now the second coming of CDs; we change, the music doesn't. But where everyone else had a CD player and an MP3 plug-in, I was at first resigned, then gradually absorbed into slow listening in real-time. I worked through the tapes, bootleg Zeppelin *I–IV*, ABBA's *Visitors*, the Smiths' *Meat Is Murder*, music from before I was born. *Scary Monsters* was full of angry, feverish melancholia—sad, mad and strange—it sounded like the future arrived to fulfill an alternative present. As exhilarating as the music was restless, the Doppler effect of the car's tin can shell was tied to the speed of the road, chased along motorways, echoing out the gaps of multi-story car parks like a brutalist de Chirico painting, winding down nocturnal single-lane country roads with no passing places and dead ends in alleyways sunk subterranean by the night sky, littered with broken bottles, scrub grass, and the humming glow of the streetlight caught the rain, making it fall in slow motion like snow. I remember doors closing slowly like each street was a narrowing corridor, false memories slamming shut with a metallic clang, loose glass shaking the scenery. Idling, waiting with nowhere left to go, bleeding out passive energy, it was only after a half-handshake through an open window that I knew I was in the right place; as quick as we were in, we were out. I heard Bowie slurring out, "These pees-uz ah brokaaaaiiiinnnee." I was still trying to gather myself up—exhausted from the night after last and whatever came before that—mishearing seemed truer than the original, singing only to me. If I had looked up to see where I was going, the windshield half-blind beyond the glass, a ragged wave of mountains dipped in snow just a few miles off like the imitation of a landscape. Back and forth again, pushing remembering into forgetting (or trying to), but I already knew the way. Sheer repetition back and forth to the hospital for the same shift night in day out, seeing to people who had done terrible things and had terrible things done to them. I seemed to have been stuck for hours, waiting, but there was no traffic—the road was empty. Then the car beside me was ablaze, no one inside, just wild flames, all the windows were down; I hope they got out, if there ever was anyone? I blinked at the fierce heat as I passed, forcing sweat onto my brow in November. Crossing over into the other lane, the road markings sunk meaningless as they warped into the blubbering tarmac, white lines fade to black. It felt odd, going the opposite way but the right direction. Bowie drawled of ashes sucked back to Earth, another handful of dust; his slurring tone felt like the tape was melting in the deck, my head still burning. But as bad as things ever got, the music stayed the same and stayed with me. I heard it differently every time; lyrics shifted meaning, lines running through my head, my hands and feet twitching in response to jerks of the guitar string or slamming drums to create fresh muscle memory, paranoid, tense, vulnerable, still breaking; an explosion of sound hooked me out of myself and helped me draw the days back from the nights, to see the future in the now.

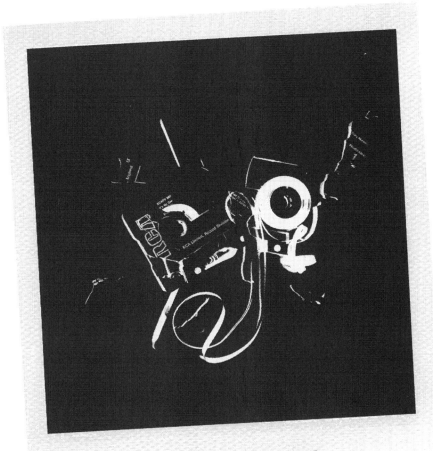

SIDE A

Fragment #123

A little piece of me, a little piece of you. Tore your suit in two, two halves of the hole. Ripping our shreds to shreds, lines of blood, twisting out human thread. They do the motions of difference, i can't fake it, make it, taking it all off, all of the time, nothing but a nakedness—still you can witness that, can't you—and still no closer, no further. Over the sea of heads, up out to the exit flow, just to get some, a little something. Whatever you can spare, I'll have it anyways, something you can take away, but not with your hand. And always. Wear it like love-mark, prideful scar, kiss on the cheek I won't wash, until someone new takes my heart off me

Here Comes the Fear

(1979, 1980, 198?)

And with each waltz
Like the last
The dance is made new

—Florian Dietrich, 1880

All Clear 1980
Personal—eyes only
Tragedy Converted
Into comedy
Indifference
Complete lack of
Task
To be 67 by 1990
To win a revolution
By ignoring everything
Else out of existence
To own personal copy of "Eraserhead."

—"Thoughts on the New Decade," David Bowie,
Melody Maker, January 1, 1980

Staring down the barrel of the 1980s David Bowie faced an uncertain future that blurred feelings of optimism with old reflexes of fear and dread. Jumping off from his golden era of music, Bowie had enjoyed a breathless run of eleven studio albums across a ten-year sprint. In the 1970s, Bowie lived by distraction, recording one album ahead before the last one was even released; the further he accelerated forward, the greater the weight of musical history accumulated behind him. Shifting from struggling singer-songwriter, glam superstar, (plastic) soul man to krautrock crooner and arch-experimentalist, Bowie had already lived several lifetimes of creative reinvention. By 1980 he should have been confident and secure in his career, but his internal critic continued to edge him into a deeper sense of doubt and self-questioning. Bowie would have to draw on new reserves of energy to keep pushing himself onward, to relentlessly merge old forms into something different, managing to exist outside of the mainstream while producing a consistent flow of hit singles to support each album. Faced with the great unknown of the imminent new decade Bowie felt like he was starting all over again.

The 1970s had been a time of political, cultural, and social extremes; many now hoped that leaving behind that long, dark decade and arriving into the 1980s would be like looking back to another country, captive in time. Bowie would compare the close of the era to the tumultuous 1920s, a waypoint to mark the beginning of the twentieth century's descent toward a long, dark night, suggesting that he was heading toward the divided confusion of the new 1930s. But it was within—or perhaps against—the 1970s that Bowie had come into his own as a catalyst to revolutionize the popular imagination, subverting everyday reality and making transgression his safeguard against forced normality.[1] Still echoing the fallout of Bowie's most self-destructive phase, *Scary Monsters* would straddle eras, as much an artifact of the 1970s as an album out of time. Bowie was forced to live under the shadow of his earlier brilliance and now felt the weight of it bearing down on his future.

Bowie's list of predictions for *Melody Maker* suggest a (purposefully) scattered mind: glib, subversive, and slightly at odds with itself. But masquerading behind a playful disregard for the counting of years remained a fierce sense of purpose. Bowie stood poised to make an album that would drive his career forward, an affirmation of his songwriting talent with a forward-thinking sonic edge that had marked the "Berlin Trilogy." For Tony Visconti, "[*Scary Monsters*] sums up the whole era from *Space Oddity*; it wasn't our original intention but we realized that we had ten tracks which were all very commercial, and encapsulated one period or another. Like the title track was back to the Ziggy days, and "It's No Game" was like a *Low* kind of feeling." *Scary Monsters* (2007) would come to be the album that crowned Bowie's

1970s while heralding the emerging new sounds of the 1980s that would be so indebted to his musical legacy.[2]

From the heights of glamour, the trajectory of *Scary Monsters* soon runs downhill into the very real pressures of modern life exposing the cracks within democratic society. The songs are forceful and urgent, strong-arming the listener to attention; the close-listening experience involves a kind of deep immersion with Bowie whispering pain and despair as much as he screamed self-loathing and horrific outrage, where the race to the top was in fact heralded by a vicious struggle on the way down. *Scary Monsters* sees Bowie rise up from the ashes of his most confessional music since *Low* to become the definitive exorcism of his greatest struggles and highest lows.[3]

In the mid-1970s, Bowie's music had already become a high-wire art form; his songs speak to a lasting sense of psychic damage, a time Bowie described as: "Demons of the future [were] on one's emotional plane." He would recount nosebleeds, near-fatal overdoses, and random blackouts like a power-cut to the brain. And before that, days spiraling into weeks of lost time, his jaw ached from endless talk; the next day he couldn't remember a word he'd said, speaking with ghosts, disappearing further into himself. In the song "Golden Years," Bowie's call to run to the shadows marks a retreat into his own private space, an anonymous, self-contained darkness, but a darkness he thought he could control (Doggett 2011). Many years later, Bowie would repeat his claim that the era was largely a blank slate for him, a painful feeling that came on like the hangover's echo of the previous night he could not fully articulate or remember. It stayed with him long enough for Bowie to claim that by 1980 he was "different person," having shed not only the Thin White Duke but also the deeply troubled "David Bowie" persona of the 1970s; he was no longer wandering under the balance of the lightning strike, cocaine blindness, and fire burst of orange hair, hazardous elements jostling in mercurial (im)balance, undermining the possibility of a stable mental outlook.

Charles Shaar Murray gave a notoriously harsh review of *Low*, demanding better, brighter music over what he considered to be indulgent self-regard. Murray later explained that he himself was crawling out of a deep hole of speed abuse, the record holding up a dirty mirror up to his own condition: "*Low* appeared to be an actual sonic incarnation of post-speed-addiction breakdown." This sentiment chimed with Bowie's own experiences put onto record: "I may have been living through a breakdown and not knowing it."[4] *Low* was cathartic and enervating for Bowie, who was trying to get clean physically and mentally, but the deeper repercussions of his period of addiction continued to be felt, rippling across time.[5] It seems fair to say that if

Station to Station reflects the all-too-brief "up" phase of cocaine use, then *Low* is the inevitable comedown.

Always known for his discipline, artistic rigor, and punctuality, Bowie's work in the studio during early 1980 suggested he was back to full fighting strength, as David Mallett remembers it: "He was disciplined upright, the first time I met him in England we went to see *Amadeus* at the National Theatre." At first glance, Bowie's diligence to the task of making an album in a mere couple of months suggested that while he had achieved a new state of grace and mental security, creative work had become a business. But the barely restrained anarchy of the songs on *Scary Monsters* bucks that interpretation. The year 1980 marks the point at which a series of long-suppressed shocks that cut through Bowie's 1970s had compounded into a mass effect on his psyche; the brittle ferocity of the music and fragmented lyrics reveal a man permanently on the edge, still haunted by the darker moments of the recent past. This inner vulnerability would resurface a few short years later when demands of global fame and success brought new pressures to bear against an already fragile veneer that cracked as soon as it was forced.

> Where there is discord, may we bring harmony.
> Where there is error, may we bring truth.
> Where there is doubt, may we bring faith.
> And where there is despair, may we bring hope.

> —Margaret Thatcher, 1979

Bowie's internal conflict doubled as a reflection of the times: where the distance between desire, dreams, and reality came into stark relief; as dark shapes began to emerge from all corners, new hopes soon coalesced into nightmares. The 1979 election of a new British Conservative government helmed by Margaret Thatcher aimed to overturn the stagnation of the previous prime minister, James Callaghan, and deconstruct the recovery of postwar years dominated by the Labour Party. The 1970s had seen Britain stagnate under a cycle of strikes, inflation, and power cuts until it began to feel that society was in retrograde. With Shakespearean verve, the period was branded the "Winter of Discontent"[6] and ran from late 1978 into February of the next year with striking public-sector workers demanding higher pay increases with the then-Labour government held to ransom by union power. Thatcher's remarks after becoming the new prime minister in May 1979 liberally paraphrase St. Francis of Assisi; her rendition would come to be stricken by vicious irony when her later political actions overturned the sentiment of her words.[7]

The background to the late 1970s rise of punk was soundstaged by news footage of uncollected rubbish bags piled high in the streets; in graveyards, mounds of frozen earth awaited bodies that had been left unburied, and everywhere, rats crept out from their hiding holes; the abiding stench added to the overall air of decline. Dylan Jones stated that the scenes of detritus piled high across the capital provided Conservative critics with a "bombproof political metaphor" of the city turning into a giant rubbish heap; the detritus of a once-great empire ruined before its time.[8]

In the run-up to her general election victory, Margaret Thatcher fed on this paranoiac energy, name-dropping dystopian visions, made popular by artists and musicians like Bowie. She warned of imminent disaster if a more authoritarian government was not brought into power alongside secret fears of a socialist coup: "When rule of law breaks down, fear takes over . . . criminals prosper, the men of violence flourish, the nightmare world of *A Clockwork Orange* becomes reality."

Thatcher's rise was a revolutionary revival of the old order's warped neo-classicism: to return Britain to a mythical imperial greatness while establishing a "classless" society not unlike the model of American democracy, claiming to look to the future while being duty-bound to tradition. What might have seemed like a bright new beginning radically changed the nation for far beyond the 1980s. Operating under a dictatorial air, the idea of progress that was on offer represented one woman's very personal and private vision for the United Kingdom. Not since the English Civil War had the country been so drastically altered and deeply divided. As the head of a country that in her party's words was literally "not working," Margaret Thatcher was emboldened to declare a mandate to revive the stalled nation, fast becoming the new "sick man of Europe."[9] Along with many other declarations of a lawless and weakened country in which people were afraid to walk the streets, she declared her own scorched-earth policy. The postwar consensus politics of reconstruction and recovery, along with the scaffolding of social infrastructure and the welfare state, were kicked away like the walking stick from an old man. Old-fashioned ways of doing business were seen to be clogging up growth, sparking mass financial deregulation and the rise of reckless insider trading across the cattle market of the international stock exchange, birthing the future monster of the amoral *American Psycho* yuppie, born to excess tech-fueled and greed driven; these were the rebel entrepreneurs, iconoclastic risk-taking captains of new industry, not dissimilar to Bowie's own 1970s reputation.[10]

This promised a great leveling of the social order in creating equal opportunities (for prosperity) built around Thatcher's ideal citizen checklist presupposing that everyone wanted the same things: sovereignty, wealth accumulation, private ownership—a singular national identity for all. A regression to "little England" bourgeois values, enforced sameness, hard Conservatism with a big "C," a small-state government enforced by big-state iconoclasm—this was tyranny by another name. Her defining message became to prioritize individuals over collective ideals of communities, leading her to declare: "There is no such thing as society."[11] Many took her words to heart and looked inward to the self, the rest be damned. But as more people learned to enjoy the fruits of ghost wealth, spending money (credit) they never had, the economy would continue to expand to dangerous levels of instability.

> Money doesn't mind if we say it's evil, it
> goes from strength to strength. It's a fiction,
> an addiction, and a tacit conspiracy.

—Martin Amis, *Money*

Speaking in 1977, Bowie described himself as a social observer. But instead of focusing on specific events of the past he tried to capture the energy of the imminent present, his albums became a living performance. Having completed the artistic revolution of the Berlin Trilogy, 1979's *Lodger* album divided critics and fans between grudging acceptance and deepest adoration.[12] Bowie's final call on the closing track, "Red Money," unites the album as a grouping of "planned accidents"; as Bowie yelps, "Project canceled" to angular, convulsive funk rock, the record is written off as an autodestructive exercise, another exploding ticket to nowhere, the infectious document that must eat its own words. Chris O'Leary hears Bowie's natural evasiveness come full circle, devouring its own tail; the abortion of the process becomes its own catharsis revealing Bowie stung by the malaise of the twentieth century's "nervous disease." Spiked with fresh uncertainty, *Scary Monsters* is still tangled up in the same hesitancy and divided struggle of *Lodger*. According to Greil Marcus (1979), the songs of *Lodger* "all speak for a future in-the-present in which one must protect oneself from the world, from other people and from one's own visions, desires and fears," combining the shock of brute reality and more private internalized horrors.

The end of 1979 marked a new year zero from the weight of Bowie's previous decade, *Lodger*'s rational conclusions born out of irrational experimentation, moving with scattered purpose(s) with Brian Eno's Oblique Strategies cards as disruptive agent. *Lodger*'s contrary overlapping styles veer between brilliantly constructed verse-chorus songs and a more jagged clash of ideas, suggesting both anticonformity and a confirmation of "being David Bowie" (Kardos 2016). Nonetheless, the album and its forebears expressed Bowie's conscious process of "reeducation" in the avant-garde, to free himself from songwriting orthodoxy and rekindle the ability to surprise himself.[13] *Lodger* becomes another one of Bowie's "boundary moments" (O'Leary 2017) but remains a murky watershed that was neither an absolute failure nor a reigning success—the record is just that, a self-contained artifact. This process became the scorched-earth position that allowed Bowie to clear his head and make a new start with the great escape of *Scary Monsters*.

In his self-enforced exile to America and later mainland Europe, Bowie was largely absent from England for the brief explosion and even shorter fizzling out of punk.[14] Less a movement than a short-term affect, it became a grassroots avant-garde rejection of the body politic tied to monarchy, church, and state. The Sex Pistols' cry of "no future" would seem prophetic echoing down the decades; if not entirely fulfilled, it would be met by the true struggle of Thatcherism yet to come.[15]

Bowie emerged blinking into the cold light of 1980 to find a new Britain. The election of a Conservative government seems to be the moment of first blood, sparking his renewed interest in the growing discord reflected across society: "*Scary Monsters* always felt like some kind of purge. It was this sense of: 'Wow, you can borrow the luggage of the past; you can amalgamate it with things that you've conceived could be in the future and you can set it in the now'" (DeMain 2003). This fed directly into Bowie's continued fascination with postapocalyptic scenarios, always jumping the gun toward a "greatest hits" of the worst-case scenario.

At a time when Cold War hostility remained eerily present, *Lodger*'s "Fantastic Voyage" made a glamorous ballad of coldly satirizing the drama of waiting for the bomb to drop, reaching mutually assured destruction as an act of bad mood.[16] "Five Years" was a prediction of intergalactic disaster, "Drive-In Saturday" its aftermath,[17] and "Diamond Dogs" the new world built out of the ruins of societal breakdown. Alongside this the drama-documentary genre of speculative "what-if" films, *The War Game* (1966), *Threads* (1984), and *When the Wind Blows* (1986) tried to show the real horror of nuclear fallout.[18] Greil Marcus (1979) called "Fantastic Voyage" a song "about the coming depression, general entropy, rampant criminality and vague resistance. It's singularly ill-written and musically empty; the horrors it means to summon up never coalesce into a threat."[19] But at least fear was something to believe in; to hold life close as a precious thing that could be snatched away at any moment, in seconds, minutes, hours, Bowie could already see miles ahead, it's just the waiting that kills you.[20]

On *Young Americans*, we find Bowie living through someone else's nightmare, dragging a premonition of a long winter in America, decline stretching far beyond 1975, a stuck clock symptomatic of economic collapse, domestic struggle, and civil unrest feeding on the dark energy of a Richard III thief in the White House.

We have to wonder if the prophecy building of "Aladdin Sane (1913, 1939, 19??)" and its expectation of future war is also present in *Scary Monsters*; if Bowie had never expected to live beyond the 1970s, he was now holding tight a few short years before the real terror of 1984. But as fast as Bowie could record his albums, they were already history in the making, singing in past tense about the present; he remained strangely alert to where culture might be heading next; his rising concern was of the world falling apart before decade's end.

Elsewhere in 1980, there were already signs and symptoms of what Bowie seemed to fear most. President Reagan inherited extreme "stagflation" with the prime rate at almost 20 percent until 1982, which he tried to alleviate through deregulation and tax breaks while making massive cuts to public service spending—the birth of "trickle-down" economics—which saw the poorest left behind to scrape what they could from the heels of the rich. This served only to push the United States deeper into national debt and recession as defense budgets ballooned to catastrophic proportions; the home front was made to suffer under the ideological aegis of national security to guard against imagined terror networks and the Red Menace of Communist influence, causing many economists to warn of another cyclical recession comparable to the economic crash of 1929 and the Great Depression that followed.[21]

In his draft lyrics for *Scary Monsters*, Bowie warned of future clashes with Iran, perhaps alluding to the hostage crisis of November 1979 where fifty-two U.S. staff were held at the embassy in Tehran for 444 days, sparking nightmare visions of the fall of Saigon, and eventually released in January 1981. And later, on April 30, 1980, Arab gunmen seized the Iranian embassy in London, this time in protest against the Iranian revolutionary government of Ayatollah Khomeini. This sparked a rescue operation by thirty British Special Air Service troops who stormed the building and rescued almost all of the hostages unharmed, with the rescue watched live on television by millions of people at home. For many, this cycle of events expressed the underground chaos of Cold War disruption that would continue with the shadow play of puppet governments, dictatorships, energy crises, CIA-backed coups, and failing international relations as Western democratic states struggled to hold their world together.[22]

Laurie Anderson's farsighted 1981 anthem "O Superman" dragged the great superpower of the United States of America down to earth with sardonic dark humor. Voicing an airline hostess, she offers "smoking or non-smoking" seating, an offhand reference to the first abortive military rescue attempt of the U.S. hostages in Tehran, when a helicopter and a cargo plane collided in midair, killing eight servicemen, a shocking event on the domestic front that Anderson referred to as a time of "techno-humiliation" for U.S. military superiority. In her song, the consequences of overreliance on technocratic governance was brought home "crashing and burning."

From his review of *Lodger*, Jon Savage noted "a small projection from present trends, call it Alternative Present if you will," in Bowie's music. This granted him the perspective of an advanced future tense, seeing through the everyday atrocity with a knowing inevitability. Everything seemed to be fast-forward, in free fall, accelerating toward the hyperreal technocratic state chained to the conspiracy theories of the military-industrial complex—the hunger for progress driven to a fever pitch at the bleeding edge of now. Viewed through the twisted prism of a thwarted political climate, everywhere Bowie looked, the world seemed full with clear and present dangers of terrorism and foreign conflict—some imagined, others very real made manifest in the political rhetoric of Reagan's "evil empires" and Thatcher's "enemy within."[23] This weaponized language became just cause for witch hunts to root out the freaks, radicals, and rebels on the domestic front, to normalize "war all the time" against one common (invisible) enemy after another—all for the preservation of Western conservative supremacy.[24]

Scary Monsters is infused with the same spirit of paranoiac doom-ridden rhetoric chattered among the political classes and media bombardments; Bowie's lyrics are flush with violence, broken bones, and damaged lives cut short. Where before Bowie heard warning shots fired overhead, they now rained down as friendly fire from loose cannons and assassins, all with the deadly intent of the sniper picking off undesirables.[25]

Where so many people's inner lives hinged on daily uncertainties, the songs of *Scary Monsters* find Bowie setting himself against an unhinged global picture. His lyric notes express burning ambiguity mired in contradiction; for once, Bowie seems afraid to make the first move: "Half of me freezing, half of me boiling, I'm nowhere in between," Bowie wrote on his sketch sheet. "A reactive person . . . too much data, possible events." Chris O'Leary hears the album as a singular "horror documentary," the reel caught in its own teeth; phrases tumble out of him, spooling endlessly, turned over and over in a frantic mind as if overhearing oneself from another room: a wild terror, fresh heartbreak, psychic collapse.

The inevitable neoliberal triumph of the decade would be confirmed in 1989 by American academic Francis Fukayama, who claimed that after the collapse of European communism, the democratic West had been victorious and arrived at the "End of History," after which it seemed impossible for other political realities to ever fully take hold as citizen-subjects remain inescapably grounded by mutual values and "common sense" and loyal to the populism of the free market. This fed into Bowie's own weird and eerie predictions for 1980 as it rapidly (de)evolved toward the inevitable conclusion of postmillennial Britain.

A vividly alarmist record, then, *Scary Monsters* shows Bowie certain that things are only going to get worse. Unable to contain the growing terror—he is powerless in the struggle to find solid ground from which to take a stand and arrest the sensation of reaching terminal velocity—his real fear is not knowing when or how the end will happen. One reviewer for the *New Musical Express* (*NME*) would perversely mark *Scary Monsters* as Bowie's "realist" album with fear as an infectious social disease: "This is a time in which the intelligent person does well to be afraid."[26]

On the final track of 1979's *Lodger*, "Red Money," an adapted version of Iggy Pop's (for once) more restrained "Sister Midnight," Bowie exploited deep enunciation in his singing; more like a rant, hiccuping through his vowels words tumble out from the sky, falling into silence. Like the falcon and the falconer, he could no longer hear himself above his own noise, yelling the title line louder and louder like an act of self-revenge. Like his long-coming divorce, Bowie offered up cash for blood and flesh by the pound. Sinking deeper into doubt, he makes one last statement of the need to grow into the realpolitik edging in around us: "So much responsibility/It's up to you and me." As earnest as he might be, his cry of the heart lands flat.

Scary Monsters shines a harsh and unyielding spotlight of recrimination and doubt on both Bowie and the listener. He is too heavily saturated in his own climate of fear; it runs through the record like the word "hate" through a stick of Brighton rock. His troubles cast long shadows: awkward, jilted, freakish, and deranged—this is Bowie backed up against the wall of his futurism that will not hold.[27] He can only go on with his best foot forward toward the abyss.[28]

Where he had previously tried to gauge the mood of the nation and failed, Bowie now let the tone of his music do the fighting talk. Spiky, jarring, but also vulnerable, the state of things Bowie envisaged now seemed reflected in his own body politic—brittle, self-regarding, and edgy. The songs of *Scary Monsters* are part cathartic excess and an outpouring of suppressed rage; somehow their ideas survive in the airless vacuum. Bowie makes us complicit specters witnessing our own execution, a grasping mouth with a plastic bag drawn tight over the head, reaching out too late from a lapse of conscience as the black cloud closes in.

Tired of seeming to be the outsider looking in, passing commentary on a planet that in many ways had always seemed alien and foreign to him,

Bowie discovered a newfound need to reconnect with other people though still focusing on himself as introspective subject. Chris O'Leary noted that the David Bowie of 1980, whether by accident or design, found himself most at home in a "society of one." The rising atomization of the individual remained at the heart of Bowie's music for several albums, charting humanity's growing separation from common cause. In 1997, Bowie observed of himself, "Thematically I've always dealt with alienation and isolation in everything I've written."[29] Putting himself into the mindset of loneliness as a place to write from, where small universes bloomed inside the mind, this act of self-distancing would increasingly become a shared disconnect. As Bowie watched the real-time heat-death of common mutuality, it seemed to confirm that alienation was simply a new expression of freedom (from others), so worldly concerns became centered around transactional analysis, individuals weighing the needs of their own lives against the invisible many. The decline of the nuclear family, rising divorce rates, and the carve-up of land and homes into real estate spoke to private interest trumping collective responsibility, with each Englishman raising the drawbridge of his or her own castle. This confirmed the entitlement of a round-waisted petit bourgeois middle class, championing the climbing of the social ladder and the accumulation of "new" money to escape their past and avoid working-class associations, kicking the rungs out beneath them as they went higher.[30]

Bowie's situation remained unique. He was one of the "children allowed to grow tall"[31] that Thatcher expounded as the virtuous path to identity and self-creation. Bowie fought his way into the position of cultural Übermensch, coupled to the deep narcissism that came with it. Although this rise was not granted to him by birthright or other institutional bias, Bowie's native talent, risk-taking, and physical attributes took him further than most musicians in spite of his limited formal education and class background that seemed destined to set him up as another indifferent citizen doomed to a white-collar office job. With greater success, he became part of the problem of the isolated individual, detached from society, sparking his later need for personal and creative reevaluation.

For much of his career, Bowie maintained a mobile lifestyle he called "nomadic" as if setting down roots would cause him the pain of suddenly being stuck. His records offered the musical hints and sensational atmosphere of a global travelogue as part of their mystique, jumping from London, Tolworth,[32] Japan, Africa, New York, Los Angeles, Berlin, Indonesia, Paris (or maybe hell), and Amsterdam. In parallel with this physical state of flux, Bowie continued to pursue a compulsive sense of artistic freedom. Despite owning a house in Switzerland and the placeholder vignettes of New York, Kenya, and Kyoto on *Lodger*, Bowie would claim that there was no single city he felt at home in; he remained a citizen of nowhere. Perpetual movement made him happy as the alien stranger wherever he went; able to live a life of luxurious escapism, he became the constant émigré by choice rather than desperate and terrifying necessity.[33]

Shuttling between American isolation and later European exile, he grew into the idea of the jet-set, thirty years after the term was invented. In some respects, Bowie became the tacit conservative, an early tax exile, and, like most artists, left-leaning but fiercely individualistic, liberal but always edging toward self-centered libertarianism.[34] There remained an empathetic humanism in his work at odds with his often quiet reserve, unwilling to speak on many social issues, along with his status as a handsome, wealthy, and highly influential white man living in hotels across the world as he pleased. But by 1980, Bowie was seeking to interrogate the state of the nation and reconnect with the broader "English character" that he still carried within him and could play up to so well. Inevitably, he drifted into his hometown of London in early 1980, the voyeur in him sourcing the latest records and scanning the headlines with horrified excitement.

Writer and journalist Jon Savage,[35] who began as a music fan and became the man-on-the-ground chronicler of punk, noted the perilous times of 1980 in which Bowie had arrived. Still popular, it was as the glam rock entertainer that mainstream audiences and casual radio listeners valued him most. But now even his most outlandish tendencies had been absorbed into the new subculture. Bowie was no longer himself; he was "us," standing at odds with the unsettled mood of the times, while the most radical of new musics that emerged in the brief renaissance of post-punk would gradually become less confrontational, more acceptable, and unthreatening as the decade wore on or otherwise remained underground as nonconformist subversion, somehow ruining the party: "In the face of increasing hardship and political polarization, arty posing and homosex—inextricably linked too often thanks to Bowie's example—are definitely seen to be out: the former as a childish luxury, the latter as a definite social disadvantage as dog eats dog."

This closing expression used by Savage was prominent in newspaper headlines of the time, a direct response to Margaret Thatcher's harsh survivalist tone of governance that preached every man for himself under the guise of individual responsibility. As the state increasingly washed its hands of its duties, dismantling the framework that supported the poorest and most vulnerable members of society, this misanthropic attitude would feed the wider atmosphere of dissent that nonetheless dragged the Conservative government into the 1990s and gave Ronald Reagan two presidential terms in the United States while disaffection began to eat away on both sides of the special relationship. As Bowie would later sing on "Because You're Young," he would find so many people of the new generation to be deeply unhappy, caught somewhere between being born and dying—either way—their life seemed to mean nothing to them.[36]

> If imagination's the lifeblood of the people
> and thought is our oxygen, then his job's to
> cut off our circulation and hers is to make sure
> that we all stay dead from the neck up.

—Jonathan Coe, *What a Carve Up!*

By 1980, Bowie was a man in a better place but stranded on the precipice of new directions. Emerging from a period of mental turmoil and addiction, he had become the star who fell to Earth. Bowie fought hard to extricate himself psychologically and financially from the Ziggy Stardust years and to finally break free from the management of Tony Defries, arguably the man who, more than any other, helped make Ziggy—and Bowie—a living icon.[37]

Bowie told Lisa Robinson of *NME* in 1976, "To cause an art movement you have to set something up and destroy it." His use of cause, yielding effect, is interesting. Ziggy sparked his own short but brightly lived clan for people to join, but Bowie had to kill his icon to fulfill the powerful vision of "Rock 'n' Roll Suicide." So the "Ziggy experience" became something of a death cult, the image to mourn; the records hear the lost voice returned from the grave. Years later, after reading a *Sunday Times* article about the history of surrealism, Bowie would admit that he saw some sense in the argument that "all revolutionaries should be shot by the time they reach thirty."

It was no accident that at the final gig by the Spiders from Mars on July 3, 1973, Bowie performed his booming solo rendition of Jacques Brel's "My Death." At the song's end, he began his disappearing act, trailing away its final line into nothingness, "behind that door, there is . . ." People cried out, "Me, *me!*," seeing themselves in the empty space as Bowie stepped back from the dimming stage lights and into the gloom of the wings.[38] The cause, the spark, the martyr, "Ziggy" served his purpose and alongside the financial boom of *Young Americans* established Bowie as a commercial contender, brimming with star quality ripe for the U.S. market, though he remained conflicted in how he was seen by his fans, the music industry, and himself.

While Tony Defries took Bowie to a new professional level, he also stage-managed his own sociopathic performance, maintaining a careful veneer of success at Bowie's expense, while pushing him toward financial ruin. Bowie's MainMan contract made him responsible for every cost that his career demanded: from the globe-spanning travel of cars, ships, and trains to hotels for his growing entourage, which soon included the obligatory hangers-on, alongside the running costs of MainMan itself, from offices and staff to cocaine and paper clips. Bowie was neither wholly artist nor partner but really a silent investor. On the coke-fueled U.S. tour in late 1974, turning from Diamond Dog into a Philly Dogs soul revue, Bowie would see a vision of himself from the early Ziggy shows on television after which he attempted to throw himself out of the window; all of his problems had converged to a singular point of self-destruction (Doggett 2011). The blue meanies of his nightmares began here, eventually sparking all his anxieties of the naive artist being ripped off by Tony Defries as both champion and super creep.

When he was due to release the delayed *Young Americans* in 1975, Bowie decided that to go global, it would have to be from a position that benefited him the artist first and foremost. But getting out of his old contract in 1974 would prove doubly costly. Defries pressed for a settlement, forcing RCA to reckon with the further stalling of Bowie's career and potential losses, but the price paid would be heavy. The deal struck demanded a fifty-fifty split with MainMan of all earnings and future royalties on his back catalog, to date, including pre-Defries recordings with the Decca label. The true sting in the tail was that Bowie's contract with MainMan still had seven and a half years to run (until September 1982), after which Bowie would be forced to pay 16 percent of his gross earnings to the company for albums of 1972–1982, in perpetuity. But Bowie had won his freedom, renewed support from RCA, and the vision of a new career aimed at entering the world stage.[39]

The fallout of this period continued long after Bowie quit MainMan, triggering a traumatic period of addiction, no doubt brought on by the stress of the legal battle that saw Bowie weighed down, in debt, and directly under the control of new financial masters via loans from RCA. In the song "Always Crashing in the Same Car" from *Low*, Bowie speaks of addiction like a car without a steering wheel, the hapless driver doomed to go over the edge— "it could only end one way," written after Bowie went driving circular laps around a multistory garage in Berlin, repeatedly ramming into the car of a dealer he thought had burned him, the track's spiraling pattern saw Bowie watching himself as he continued to repeat his own worst mistakes, until, in a neat metaphor, he ran out of gas.

Bowie's drug recovery was slow and gradual, a long up-and-down process of getting his system clean. He remained worried about scraping through after some serious scares, passing out and hemorrhaging blood from the nose, at times sucked down into a low mood that trapped him between the clock, the bed, and the ghost traces of marching white lines. Speaking about abandoning the fame and trappings of his Ziggy persona with all of its baggage, Bowie said, "I changed because I wanted to move forward. I just hoped the

DIAMOND DOGS TOUR — 1974

Tired, emotional, sick with Soul — Bowie gives it his all

audience would come along. For me, it wasn't the smart thing to do; it was the necessary thing to do." Bowie's time in Berlin was never the entirely clean living rehabilitation that he presented (he was sometimes found staggering around the streets drunk on German pilsner), though he claimed the albums of that period to be largely drug free.[40] Certainly, *Scary Monsters* deals with the aftermath of this process: the shadow imagination of Ziggy, the stark ghost figure of the Thin White Duke, and the idea of "David Bowie" beginning to escape himself.

While Bowie quickly moved on from his early career in a short space of time, *Scary Monsters* was an album tied to the (recent) past. On *Lodger*'s relentlessly catchy "DJ," Bowie had playfully mocked the "living nostalgia" of pop music's adherence to formula, but with his new chart-conscious outlook, he struggled to pull his new album together from an entirely blank slate. Straddling past and present, he drew on lost demos, scraps of old songs, and uncompleted projects; ideas that had never gone away were rehashed or, on another reading, reinvigorated. As much as he was self-deprecating about the idea of a legacy from his 1970s, Bowie seemed wrong-footed and on uncertain ground, forcing him to first look back in order to go forward.[41]

In 1979, he spent time reviving alternative versions of his old songs and rerecording others. Like many of his cover versions, Bowie's choices can seem random, often preferring the more obscure song that he thought deserved renewed public interest (such as "Wild Is the Wind" on *Station to Station*), while *Scary Monsters* was futuristic in sound it still clung to a Bowie-esque world.[42]

Bowie recorded a stripped-back version of "Space Oddity" with Zaine Griff, who had just completed an album produced by Tony Visconti. The minimalist arrangement took the song back to its heart with Bowie on twelve-string guitar: "Having played it with just an acoustic guitar onstage early on I was always surprised as how powerful it was just as a song, without all the strings and synthesizers" (MacKinnon 1980).[43] Leah Kardos (2016) notes Bowie's deep connection to the signature style of John Lennon's solo music, "minimal, vulnerable, visceral," without the sonic scenery he would express more with less. The new version of "Space Oddity" becomes a strange act of remembrance for the song that helped to get Bowie's music career started. In 1980, it was more than ten years old, a creative lifetime for the racing mind of Bowie and something of an anachronism to the high-art period begun with *Station to Station*. Clearly, Major Tom was still on his mind—he never truly went away—waiting in outer space. With "Ashes to Ashes" arriving just a few months into 1980, Bowie hurled him into a new and final revision of history.[44]

Bowie had a masochistic streak toward his own past, afraid that if he ever paused long enough for the dust to settle, it would be ossified as a "legacy." He became Caliban as cannibal; much of his older work, unfinished fragments, or recurring lines were resurrected and hurled forward, merging introspection and autobiography into the present. When it came to repurposing musical motifs and even spare lines, abandoned song titles were turned into new lyrics for a different track to become jumping-off points toward a freer association of ideas.

On *Scary Monsters*, there is a suppressed rage that mourned, mocked, and sampled the Bowie mythology, dissecting the beautiful corpse, still living. The faint and resigned "woah-ah-oh" line that ushers in the pre-chorus of "Ashes to Ashes" is heard again on *Tonight*'s "Loving the Alien," reaching strange heights of self-awareness but also managing to sound new and different, standing entirely in its own right. Elsewhere, Bowie blogger Neil Anderson points out that Bowie's 1999 song "Pretty Things Are Going to Hell" revisited the youthful spring of "Oh You Pretty Things!," like "Changes" in reverse, backward growth that interrogates images of the past. The sheer magnitude of Bowie's back catalog meant that he was weighed down by the number of songs and the refraction of images, forcing Bowie into a confrontation with his many selves. As Greil Marcus noted, "Right at this point, then—the verge of the '80s—Bowie should be ready for a major new move, or a major synthesis."[45]

I felt I was on the cusp of something absolutely new. There were no absolutes. Nothing was necessarily true, but everything was true.[46]

—David Bowie

"When we began *The Man Who Sold the World*, David and I jokingly said, "Let's make this our *Sgt. Pepper's*." Tony Visconti and Bowie would continue in this same spirit with every album that followed since their first collaboration. Summoned to New York in early 1980, Visconti leapt at the chance to produce a new Bowie record. In 2007, he remembered Bowie arriving for their recording sessions as he always did, somewhat unprepared with just the very intimations of thoughts and sounds, "just a few chord progressions and some rough lyrical ideas." But secure in the knowledge that once work began these would be fully realized as living, breathing songs, Visconti would not be disappointed as Bowie worked from a deeper creative incubation that would be expressed in what seemed like pure spontaneity. This allowed

Bowie to approach each record with a fresh and open mind, keen to embrace or discard what worked best for each track, building a song outward without being tied to the weight of preconceived ideas. In 1978, Bowie told *Melody Maker* that it was only after he had completed an album that he could hear it properly: "For me, listening to *"Heroes"* is quite as new an experience as any other listener."

Tony Visconti's choice of New York's Power Station studio was no accident. A former Con Edison power plant, it was transformed into a top-end studio by Tony Bongiovi, cousin of Jon Bon Jovi (O'Leary 2020a). Based on the design of Motown's Hitsville studio, where Bongiovi had worked for some months, in the spirit of industrial espionage and healthy competition, he had mapped out the exact measurements and technical specifications of the legendary recording studio. Visconti was excited by the level of technical sophistication the Power Station offered, with Pultec tube (valve) equalizers, going through the input and output of the studio's twenty-four recording channels (a total of forty-eight); this ensured a powerful, rich sound that was not possible in other, less well-equipped studios: "Every channel went through a tube amplifier. So we would get these warm, fat sounds, which thrilled us to no end (2007)." The powerful equipment stage-managed by Visconti gave the album a classic "old modern" sound that remains fresh to this day.[47]

Visconti and Bowie dug in for a longer, more considered recording process: "We decided to give ourselves the luxury to think of every possible thing we could do. That was the premise. And we took ourselves very seriously." Noting that the role of the producer often required him to make hundreds of creative and technical decisions each day, Visconti points out that Bowie was keen to experiment and discard approaches that weren't working—more parts were left out than included.

The producer would later compare *Scary Monsters* to the more urgent and vital intensity of the Beatles' *Revolver*; thankfully free of the nostalgic whimsy and kitchen-sink drama of *Sgt. Pepper's*, it remains a leaner, sharper, and harder record despite having a less-focused track listing. Visconti noted that *Sgt. Pepper's* took the Beatles nine months to record and, *Revolver* nine weeks, about the same timescale as *Scary Monsters*.

By comparison, *Low* and *"Heroes"* took around five weeks to record, relying more on the lightning strike of improvisation with Bowie sometimes singing the lead vocal in the control room or simply ad-libbing in the vocal booth in search of a melody. Bowie would often write lyrics at the last minute, spiking them with immediacy and capturing the moment where myriad ideas implanted by heavy reading were suddenly ignited by the emotive power of the music. This added urgency demanded a tightrope balance between the mood of the moment set against the reach for a strong technical performance often captured in one or two takes (O'Connell 2020).[48] The process behind *Scary Monsters* was more focused and exacting: "We spent four weeks at The Power Station in New York and another five weeks at my own Good Earth Studios in Soho, London. There was a two-month gap between the sessions of rhythm tracks recording and overdubs and vocals, as David said he needed more time to write the lyrics and melodies. . . . This was a departure from procedure" (Visconti 2007).

Bowie would riff with much enthusiasm on Julian Jaynes's 1976 book *The Origins of Consciousness in the Breakdown of the Bicameral Mind*, which seemed to encompass the near-schizoid operations of the divided and crisscrossing hemispheres of the human brain. Exploring the "other" side of the dualist puzzle, where the subconscious mind or soul operates beyond mere physicality, outside of the purely rational jurisdiction of logic, truth, and goodness, it allowed for the necessary embrace of chaos.[49] Bowie acknowledged that his own intuitive sense of music making relied on feeling, discovering what worked well rather than knowing where a song would definitely end up: "I related to that tremendously because I've often had that feeling very strongly with myself that . . . well, it's like what Dylan said about the tunes are just in the air. I still believe in that kind of naive approach to writing. I leave the cerebral stuff to the Enos and Fripps of this world. Because I'm far more tactile in my approach to what I do. I think it's probably why we work together so well."

Bowie's considered spontaneity meant that he only had a rough vision for how a song should (or could) sound and encouraged his musicians to explore various methods to reach it: for tracks to mutate in the process with each experiment reinforcing the direction to follow. This allowed for flexible song structures, speaking to Bowie's 1960s upbringing in a more open-ended, less goal-motivated counterculture, a lazy aestheticism that required creating art for its own sake. Bowie draws on the naive discovery of ideas: imperfect narratives without neat resolutions from his early reading of Jack Kerouac's *On the Road*[50]—the free-form, long-distance, wide-screen vision of bop-prosody in which he prioritized "first thought, best thought"—but also carried out substantial revisions, reaching for a more vital and authentic expression of the first feeling he was chasing—a method that became an exploration of freedom itself. Bowie told ABC News that by 1980, he was working on "pure barbaric impetus. A lot of it is pure instinct for knowing that I've found something that I hadn't found before."

Bowie had again chosen to work with the "DAM Trio" rhythm section.[51] After the creative breakthroughs of *Station to Station*, further united by the bond of the Berlin Trilogy, the group instinctively knew when a take was feeling "right" and had tight professional musicianship—the pure moment they were all reaching for. Bowie has said that he sometimes worked on a system of "drawing" the music, trying to explain the shape of the sound he imagined. Elsewhere, Carlos Alomar remembers Bowie working intuitively, directing the DAM Trio to pursue a certain feeling in the music, explaining that Bowie always "knew what he wanted once he heard it," aiming for a new perspective of more pop-oriented songs. After Bowie had selected the final arrangement idea, the band would refine the song's structure, making sure to leave dynamic gaps and spaces in which others could solo or layer overdubs to enrich the song's texture. Alomar said, "I wanted to make sure that this album had me, George and Dennis being totally forceful. I wanted songs with defined beginnings and endings that had signature lines, with complexity. But we also left holes for other players, and for David to shape his melodies" (DeMain 2003).[52]

The band's dynamic overdubs weave in and out of the main tracks, creating cohesive tracks with stronger, harder breaks between the sections, allowing Bowie to return with a closing chorus or outro. Alomar would acknowledge Bowie's direct contributions as a musical director if not as an arranger in his own right: "To David's credit, he was a great listener, and had an innate sense of which pieces would fit together, like a jigsaw puzzle. When you put that puzzle together, you end up with *Scary Monsters*."[53] Bowie demonstrated his independent sense of orchestration putting together *Diamond Dogs* in 1974. Brian Eno, who was also at Olympic Studios mixing *Here Come the Warm Jets*, remembers Bowie going back and forth between his white Perspex guitar, mellotron, and synthesizer, restlessly creative and energized. Glenn Hendler points out that Bowie's sampling method at this time involved assembling songs from pieces of tape, best realized in the audio collages of the "Sweet Thing" triptych.

Scary Monsters would cast a wide arc, uniting many of the best elements of Bowie's sound developed over the preceding decade, a partial return to *Low* and its "mood of downbeat retrospection within a progressive musical framework" (Hewitt 2016) but minus the disruptive agent of Brian Eno. Testament to the evolving power of the DAM Trio, the bootleg album of outtakes and demos from the New York sessions *Vampires of Human Flesh* (*Scary Monsters* working title) reveals a rawer, punky, and funkier edge to the songs than even the live versions played onstage years later. We can imagine Bowie's first instruction to his band for "It's No Game (No. 1)": to "play like a British punk group." Stripped to the bare bones without Robert

Fripp's guitar and studio effects, we hear more of the dynamic strength of the song structures along with Roy Bittan's piano and Lynn Maitland's backing vocals, songs that run and run without overstaying their welcome.[54] Bill Cummings noted the dynamic influence of Joy Division's "She's Lost Control" with Bowie consciously absorbing ideas from the post-punk groups that inspired his Berlin period.[55] In this spirit, the overall sound of the record is more caustic and immediate than the 1980s sound that would follow in its wake.

Robert Fripp has said that *Scary Monsters* was an effort by Bowie to "take his work in rock and roll seriously," aligning this to the intense mood of New York. No longer afraid of flying, Bowie embraced the city like a constant and wayward lover edging toward his neoliberal future just as the era of sociopaths, flaming vanities, and ritual hate was in the ascendant.

Bowie often portrayed himself as resolute Englishman abroad, and New York suited him well. His love for the city grew organically from his early reading and overall fascination with America, with New York defined as its cultural capital, becoming fixed in his young myth of self-creation. First visiting America in January 1971, Bowie was struck by the overwhelming self-image of the place; a mental door was kicked open: "I didn't believe it till I came here. From England, America merely symbolizes something, it doesn't really exist." Much later, the film *The Man Who Fell to Earth* became an experiment in seeing America as an outsider making their home there, the vastness that harbored its infinite microaggressions and excesses living with the constant threat of violence fueled by the dominance of money (and the lack thereof). The gun in the till, the hostile takeover, the alien Jesus thwarted, corrupted and crucified—in this interpretation, blood is both the price and the real-world cost of "America."

After the glacial waiting room of Switzerland, returning to New York for recording seemed to give Bowie a shot of adrenaline, thriving on the eclectic and chaotic energies of a city permanently on the edge. Bowie rented an apartment in the Chelsea area, settling there permanently many years later as a semilegal alien.[56] Emotionally as well as geographically, he would move farther away from his birth city of London as his career progressed across tours, new international homes, and different studios, though a part of him would always remain there.[57] Bowie absorbed the authentic "street" vibe of New York as it got under his skin, explaining that he loved the city's sense of urgency: "Wherever I'm writing, that place tends to make itself very known, either in the atmosphere or sound" (DeMain 2003).

New York in 1980 was symptomatic of Bowie's current interest in the darker corners of urban life: young love, the madness of crowds, cocaine culture(s), the underground gay scene, ghost exits, and trend-driven imitations; he approached all of this with eyes and heart wide open. Bowie described his return to the city in a 1980 interview for French TV: "After an absence of a few years, settling in New York longer than a month; the influx of the general paranoia, high jet-set fashion, and abject poverty, all had an awful lot to do with input that went into *Scary Monsters*. Again being thrown in at the deep end to come back to New York with all of its terrors and delights." Amid a rising tide of violent mob crime, police corruption, and the beginnings of a crack cocaine epidemic, New York was also a city in the grip of a private recession. Facing bankruptcy alongside budget cuts and depopulation with a million people leaving by the end of the 1970s, it seemed emblematic of the wider state of the nation that Ronald Reagan would continue to engender.[58] The gap between the wealthy people living in penthouse towers looking down on the street and a landscape of crowded housing projects, buildings burned down for insurance money, and emptying apartment blocks seemed to widen each year. Fulfilling J. G. Ballard's vision of flawed modernity—the wider rot expressed a Western democratic system in sharp decline—the *Diamond Dogs* dystopia inched ever closer. On *Scary Monsters*, dubbed by *NME*'s reviewer as "Fears of a Clown," he could see what was coming around the corner: a crumbling relationship between the citizen and the social contract, another center that could not hold.[59]

But compared to gloomy downbeat London of the late 1970s, the final ebb of a long and difficult decade, New York's electrified air was full of drama and new possibility, as intoxicating as it was edgy. A major part of Bowie's cultural thaw following his European exile involved the keen listener moving out from the studio and back among the audience: "hanging out with David Byrne, catching bands at CBGBs and concerts by contemporary New York composers Steve Reich and Philip Glass, performing art music with John Cale, and importantly, reconnecting with John and Yoko" (Kardos 2016). It was in this milieu that a two-way influence could be widely felt (also with Devo, Television, and Talking Heads) as the post-punk evolution was slowly overcome by the overlapping pop edge of New Wave.[60]

Both London and New York would become characters living through Bowie's songs. As Bowie told Sir Tim Rice (1980), "As I was writing a New York album [*Scary Monsters*] seemed the perfect collective title for the bits and pieces I was writing." Chiming with "synchronicity" for his later role in *The Elephant Man*, the city was a place where demons became real and nightmares found new daytime shapes. Elsewhere, Bowie referred to the title track "Scary Monsters" as a "piece of Londonism." Forcing his most English brogue, Bowie slipped back in time to his all-round entertainer impression of Anthony Newley.[61] Bowie provides vocal winks and nods: "as you do"/"know what I mean"; laying it on thick, he repeats himself, dropping casual day-in and day-out expressions, but alongside the seeming normality, he places the fantastical grubby weirdness of abuse, drugs, and ruined lives to paint a sad and tragic picture of the everyday subculture.[62]

Fully embracing his own "Englishness," *Scary Monsters* would stand as a kind of homecoming from Bowie's more "continental" European phase, rediscovering the emergent capital city that would become unreal concrete in the 1980s, wiping out the old London that by the 1960s of Bowie's teens was already fading fast and withdrawing into the new center of tourism hell. Although the album seems equally divided between twinned Anglophone poles of inner-city tension, this adds to the album's frictive power of culture clash: London's bustling streets winding down into crypts of ancient plague pits, austere Hawksmoor churches[63] carving invisible ley lines beneath the street, the spare light sucked into myriad arcane passages; New York seemed permanently modern and growing upward straight out of the twentieth century like it had always been there, the cold shoulder of skyscrapers trying to outdo one another as the new ruins of old slums were torn down and resurrected as tightly packed housing projects cut through with giant expressways and striding bridges. The sonic register of *Scary Monsters* bounces between the tight, compacted human crush and the far-reaching visions absorbed into darker places, two cities made interchangeable with a sound that is utterly modern, hip, slick, and front-loaded with intensity.

Embodied by the staggering, wayward Pierrot figure of "Ashes to Ashes," *Scary Monsters* as an album shows Bowie trying to regain his balance with no small sense of desperation to keep things contemporary and interesting. Angus MacKinnon (1980) would consider Bowie's position as a self-confessed outsider working within the music industry to be both blessing and curse, under which he suffered "lacerating self-analysis" demanding constant reexamination divided across zones of past/present/future tense. Bowie confessed to these deeper anxieties on "Teenage Wildlife," confronted by the rising tide of young hopefuls following in his wake that already threatened to eclipse him as yesterday's news. MacKinnon noted, "It must have been exhausting to be David Bowie. You could tell that it weighed heavily on him."[64]

Through his music, Bowie tried to reassert an inner identity, the man behind the music, sick with his own shadow, haunted by characters he had created that threatened to overpower him. While personal expectations were heightened, there was renewed pressure from RCA to deliver a more accessible album that could return Bowie to the sales heights of *Young Americans*.

Moving through the sea changes of punk into post-punk, the 1980s would become the era when several musical moments overlapped before reaching the kickback reaction of pop music merging New Wave and electronic synthesizer music. An early pioneer of synth sounds, John Foxx of Ultravox, remembers the keyboard, synth, and sampler being as revolutionary as anything punk produced, the new technology creating "violent extremes of sound" constructing whole songs alone or providing overdubs, from "lyrical beauty to sonic mayhem." Much broader than bands simply sticking to their lane, the culture opened the floodgates of press-invented groups and movements born of anti-art manifesto journalism, extroverted styles, critical theory, and easy labels from which Bowie was keen to distance himself. Post-1979 would find David Bowie trying to shed the attachments of his earlier career; where before he could be copied, masqueraded, and in the most straightforward ways imitated, he now pushed against the past to realize a more postmodern Bowie that existed outside of the personal history that always threatened to drag him backward.

In describing the direction of the new album, Carlos Alomar could have been talking about *Let's Dance*: "Scary Monsters was a new awakening. The intention was up-tempo, high-energy songs. It was to hit them right between the eyes" (DeMain 2003). The album sits at the peak of Bowie's most accessible and immediate writing: short, sharp songs in praise of pop and rock traditions, pieced together by studio musicians but endlessly adapted and altered by studio production. In the days before digital recording, Bowie and Visconti would reach for better and better takes, knowing that once they had recorded over the last tape, there was no going back, fighting alongside one another for the best of the best: "We were pushing the boundaries further than we ever had with this album."

THE MAN WHO FELL TO EARTH — 1976

Transition / Transition — Stage to Screen to real life

Fragment #87

you ain't all trade tho are ya

never done nothing

no bettr or worse than any of them   [in voices, then]

what's surviving if it's not getting ahead   [get ahead of yourself]

what's voices if they don't give you answers?   [don't go]

                                    [please, stay here, don't go]

can't ask for more from nothing

                                    [don't open the door]

nothing from everything   [do NOT open the flamin' door]

always knew "never" would mean leaving, better out

than in . . .

better off

dead   [SHUT IT]

It's No Game (No. 1)

I'm Pierrot, I'm Everyman. What I'm doing is
Theatre and only Theatre. . . . What you see on stage
isn't sinister, it's pure clown. I'm using my face as a
canvas and trying to paint the truth of our time on
it. The white face, the baggy pants—they're Pierrot,
the eternal clown putting over the great sadness.

—David Bowie, *Daily Express*, 1976

A click-clack-hissing static whirr of a tape reel pulses into life among the
winding volley of Dennis Davis spinning a heavily phased football ratchet
over his head. There is the faint touch of a live guitar string (contact), a
warped robotic voice counts in the song, and the band lurches into action.
"It's No Game" begins with Tony Visconti miking up his twenty-four-track
Lyrec tape deck, rewinding briefly, and then, by his invisible hand pressing
"Play," opening the album in earnest—Bowie breaks into his long shout "Silhouettes and shadows!," throwing the shape of huge open vowels that echo
down the spine of the album's sonic signature.

From the first drumbeat, the producer had applied his harmonizer
effect, hurling us headlong into the wonky fun-house-mirror world of *Scary
Monsters*. With off-kilter forces standing at odds to the listener, screaming
underwater or down the length of a subway tunnel, shouting out to no one
in dead space, we enter with Bowie into a strange and freaky place the other
side of reality. The meta-music introduction to *Scary Monsters* frames the
album as a deus ex machina, a machine after God. Visconti lifts the lid on the
recording process, and we are there in the studio with the live band, outside of
standard time, songs compressed into a series of splintering moments.

Almost immediately, the ear is struck by Robert Fripp's "lumbering robotic dance," the pendulum of heavy guitar that lends the song its swinging fists. Hearing the visceral and frantic distortion marching tight with the drums, Tony Visconti would reflect that the song was "a tip of the hat to the opening of Taxman," calling back to the Beatles' *Revolver*: equal parts melodic, experimental, and anarchic.

Fripp becomes one of many signature players on the record despite appearing on only half the tracks.[65] After disbanding King Crimson in 1974, Fripp offered himself as a hired-gun guitar player: "a small, independent, mobile and intelligent unit." Tonally, his guitar echoes the shock and awe in Bowie's voice—across the album they dance about in harmony and discord, ground down by their own screwed-too-tight intensity. At times, Fripp seemed to work against the songs; his guitar pushed high in the mix, becoming confrontational for many listeners. But perhaps that was the point. When he steps out to allow the rhythm tracks to breathe, it sometimes leaves dead air in his wake, but this anarchic conjunction brought a whole new level of overbearing power to the songs.[66] Bowie too stands out as a person tired of holding back, lending full force to his phrasing, a dive-bomber swooping through octaves and chewing through his lines, like eating a mouthful of broken glass. Visconti described Bowie's voice full with "blood-curdling passion" as his vocal acrobatics give full vent to his inner bile. This sets the stage for the album: impassioned but powerless, cold but fierce, wrestling with inner anxieties—the sound of nails bitten down to the quick, broken fingers (you cannot write, hold on, touch, or feel), he cried out in pain but no one listening.

Bowie pays tribute to the primal scream expressionism of Lennon's 1970 album *Plastic Ono Band*, where his acid tongue vocalized his inner pains across the tracks "Working Class Hero," "God," and "Mother" (Kardos 2016).[67] Reaching a point where art and autobiography converged, Lennon scorned the weight of his public image bound to a false identity and emotional insecurity. Speaking on a 1979 BBC show where he was invited to deejay, Bowie found something resonant in the raw but graceful melancholy of Lennon's "Remember": "I think, a really despondent track . . . erm . . . he'd left his band, and he was doing his first solo album. . . . I found it rivetingly depressing, I really enjoyed playing it to myself."[68] Emotional exhaustion is now marked by an exaggerated rage brought on by years of bitter experience. The year 1980 suggested a new world but with the same old problems. Even with a renewed sense of social awareness, Bowie is poised at the cusp of outrage but fails to act—the two parts of "It's No Game" parody the contradiction and inertia of the protest song.

From the start, Bowie spars vocal lines with a female voice speaking in Japanese. This sense of combat gives each speaker someone else to push against. Bowie asked a language professor friend, Hisahi Miura, to translate his lyrics into Japanese and at first tried to sing them himself, but the phrasing didn't work out. Instead, a friend of Tony Visconti's, the actor Michi Hirota,[69] was drafted in. Visconti said, "He tried and tried, squeezing some words here and stretching some there, but our collective knowledge of Japanese was useless in how to sing it." The original translation was deemed to be too literal and too straight. Hirota worked through the text to find a more poetic angle, and on hearing her reading, it was decided that she should recite it aloud on the record. Instructing Hirota to take on the character of someone from an Akira Kurosawa film, Bowie spurred her on: "Say it like a man!" She allowed the natural aggression of the words and phrasings to flow through her, matching Bowie's own histrionics.

Hirota uses the masculine accent of gendered Japanese, finding a tone somewhere between an angry adolescent and a domineering older man. Instead of becoming an empowered woman, she is respected only when she makes herself into a vehicle for the masculine voice. For Bowie, Hirota's mode of expression manages to deconstruct cultural clichés, taking a wrecking ball to "the whole very sexist idea of how Japanese girls are so very prim. She's like a samurai the way she hammers it out. It's no longer the little Geisha girl kind of thing, which really pisses me off because they're just not like that at all." The "performance" is self-consciously double-sided, the sound of a geisha-type girl putting on the strong voice rather than undergoing a complete transformation. She is wearing the mask, speaking in half-truth, and both sides know it; nonetheless, it is surreal and disarming. Hirota's words walk a knife-edge between tension and passion; along with Bowie, she abandons edgy chic for bravura manic hysteria—setting the tone for the album's excesses of volume and emotive force, pushing everything into the red.

As with all acts of translation, some aspects of the native tongue are lost, while new meanings are gained, granting a second sight to Bowie's lyrics. When he sings, "I am barred/From the event," the Japanese version presents heavier consequences for the spectator:

> *ore wa genjitsu kara shime dasare*
> I have been excluded from reality[70]

This lyric streaks across the personal divide to capture multiple perspectives: "I am barred *at* the event"/"I am *bored after* events"/"I am *born of the* event." I cannot help but hear that Bowie's spectator is both bored at the world and bored of himself—"He's as estranged from political life as from an emotional one" (O'Leary 2020a).

The spectator stands held at a distance behind broken glass; he tries to look away, only to confront himself again in reflection. The song emerges from a blank-faced silhouette; it is only the shape of a person blindly watching the shadows play below. This is Bowie pushing back at a world that feels both fake and painfully real, sparking a constant wound in his consciousness. Now the reels of horror show images wind back around again, events unfold secondhand, and, playing catch-up with the aftermath, he is already late to the game.

In a Politico interview, Simon Critchley observed, "What you have in Bowie is a kind of post-revolutionary situation—the revolution has happened and it has led to a kind of disaster, now and we find ourselves in that situation, how do we cope with that?" (Fossett 2016). Bowie looks in vain for the righteous moral of violence "where people have their fingers broken"; in the name of an idea, he cannot reconcile the end with the means.[71] Bowie as director frames the double shot of broken syntax, "couple against target"; his aim is to throw off his audience: are these fellow bystanders or civilians caught in the crossfire, the parentheses of a crisis? This clash of viewpoints is one of the first examples that shows Bowie reaching to find new meaning(s) in fragmentation that reflect the brokenness of the times.

But the story is already old news, with the chorus of "It's No Game" borrowed from an early Bowie song, "Tired of My Life," written when he was just sixteen years old—it bears all the marks and growing pains of adolescence between the existential dreaming and nihilistic fury of a teenager. Talking about "Width of a Circle" in a 1972 interview, we hear Bowie (now twenty-five) grappling with the same feelings just a couple of years after "Tired of My Life" was first demoed. "I used to have periods, weeks on end, when I just couldn't cope anymore. I'd slump into myself . . . I felt so depressed, and I really felt so aimless, and this torrential feeling of 'what's it all for anyway?'"

Although only a few of the original lines are carried over, the hopeless mood of the earlier song is intensified on "It's No Game (No. 1)": "I don't believe but I'm trying to decide/Which game is best for me, which can I bear." This is life paraphrased as a game, where the rules now seem meaningless but with real consequences at stake. The line "Pull the curtains on yesterday/And it seems so much later" of the earlier song now becomes "Draw the blinds on yesterday." The Japanese translation gives a more literal version of blindly bottling things up, to "put a lid" on yesterday, hoping it won't erupt.[72] Everything gets scarier when you know that tomorrow is already too late.

Bowie throws off time and pushes back against the day, trying to make the world disappear.

But for the sixteen-year-old Bowie writing "Tired of My Life," there is not yet such a thing as yesterday;[73] he is too young to have experienced true regret, and his life has yet to run (Tanaka 2021). By 1980, Bowie was thirty-three and had packed more living into the previous fast and shell-shocked decade than many would manage in a lifetime.[74] This mood of preternatural exhaustion and emotional burnout resonates in both versions of "It's No Game."

There is an echo of earlier defiance coming back around. Now Bowie is forced to deal with the same kind of embattled situations as an adult. Having once told an interviewer that his attitude in the studio to the critical reception of *Low* was simply to "pull the blinds down and fuck em all," instead of seeking outside approval, Bowie pushed harder and further in his own creative direction. It's interesting to hear this hard-won sense of independence continued on *Scary Monsters*. It speaks to both artistic resilience and self-care to keep a distance from toxic influences while not being completely deaf to criticism. The strength of Bowie's most successful songs would fix on the microcosm of the individual "you" before zooming out to the macro-state of humanity to become genuinely universal, where deeper concerns could connect with both the casual listener and the freakishly obsessive fan.

In his scrawled lyric notes for *Scary Monsters*,[75] Bowie reels off various statements, wrestling an internal argument to echo the playful sarcasm of his fractured 1980 All Clear list:

"These are the last days"
"A world of TV and drugs"
"Let's write about events of international import"

In these lines, Bowie is reflecting the current (and future) state of things as he sees them, but he is neither leader nor martyr pointing the way—never a follower; even the "I" of authorship is erased—these are statements taking aim at anyone with a pulse. Pointing the bloodied finger both at "us" and himself, we are absorbed into the well-meaning majority who say all the right things but fail to follow through on our moral principles; even in his self-righteous hysteria Bowie manages to sound sincere.

The tone of Bowie's draft ideas reveal some affinity to his close friend John Lennon, a searching musical kinship but stopping well short of Lennon's call-to-arms songs of social concern in which he tried to state plain and unequivocal support for causes such as antiwar protest, class struggle, and feminism that everyone could appreciate. On the songs "Gimme Some Truth," "Power to the People," "Working Class Hero," and "Imagine,"

Lennon openly used his fame as a platform to reach as wide an audience as possible, displaying his personal struggle with "utopianism and realism, politics and aesthetics, celebrity and genuineness" (Maekla 2005).[76] Although Lennon often sang truth to power against institutional corruption and wrongdoing, he realized that it was the acts of lone individuals, as much as collective protest, that could incrementally effect global change. Clearly, Lennon's concerns chimed with Bowie's own experiences: "the shrieked, bellowed lines in 'Pt. 1' as Bowie's attempt at the righteous zeal of 'Instant Karma,' the catharsis of *Plastic Ono Band*.[77] It's no coincidence that 'Pt. 1' is sung by an Englishman and a Japanese woman" (O'Leary 2020a).

But while Lennon remains direct as ever, Bowie filtered his own political concerns through his more diffuse artistic point of view. His mistrust of the value of protest and dissent spills over into caustic rejection of broader artistic claims to highlight greater moral and ethical truths: who is telling it, who is it for, and, as Lenin demanded, who benefits?[78] In his lyric notes, Bowie spits at do-gooder singer-songwriters, the ranks of which he once belonged to: "Pricks will write songs about it and tell you 'it's the truth.'" Like Lennon, Bowie bears a deeper cynicism over the power of music to hold humanity to account or drive genuine change. To paraphrase the former Beatle, change must always come from within the individual. It cannot be made to happen because someone else tells you to. This steers him further toward abstraction; he is invested in the words of his lyrics but not yet taking sides on the battle lines.

In punk, Bowie must have foreseen the short-fused, live-fast-die-young aesthetic of a movement with no real direction, burning bright before getting caught up in self-awareness. Punk was always the revolution betrayed, as freedom of expression became conditional on an increasingly narrow orthodoxy of ripped jeans, leather jackets, safety pins, and swastikas—fashion clichés that eclipsed all meaning. Where the Sex Pistols righteously imploded, "punk" fucked itself via the pub rock shortcomings of the Clash, who decried the heroes of Bowie's generation, "no Elvis, Beatles, or Rolling Stones," while they riffed on their own four-bar blues, guitar solo as sub-two-minute pop wonder.[79] In a few short years, their adoption by the fans in the United States saw them become a stadium rock band, reaching their peak limitation. Bowie saw this numbing spectacle, refracted in a draft lyric, "I hear The Clash and I don't react," a hollow-hearted rebellion more about pop power than protest.[80] At the very least, Bowie fed on similar anger as energy, driven by moral outrage that tried to reconnect with deeper ethical concerns, perhaps trying to beat the punks at their own racket in 1980.[81]

"It's No Game" stands as Bowie's own "Sign of the Times" (1982), but where Prince made a spirited and explicit rundown of the rotten-to-the-core social, political, and environmental extremes of the 1980s, Bowie generalizes to the limit, toying with abstraction. He is the eternal spectator standing at his high window, far above the action.[82]

Who is the vague watcher of Bowie's song? Starring, ostensibly acting, in *The Man Who Fell to Earth*, Bowie was the protagonist Thomas Jerome Newton, the musician-as-actor hiding behind the alien, itself concealed beneath a human disguise. Bowie complained that by wearing the mask of Newton, his face ached from lack of movement and expression, caged in near-silence he became "the ice-man cometh" holding close to his own alienation, everywhere besieged by the death of affect. In the play *Lazarus*, Leah Kardos (2022) noted that, like Major Tom, Bowie was so closely identified to his myths that seeing Newton on film or onstage was also seeing Bowie, as epitomized in the *Station to Station* and *Low* album covers. Perhaps thinking of Bowie, the director Nic Roeg aptly called Newton someone who was in society but couldn't find his place within it; once again, he is defined by his position as a man apart.

At the end of the song, Fripp's angular riff goes falling up the stairs in a blind rage, trapped in a tremolo tailspin eating its own spleen. As Bowie tries to draw a stagey curtain closed behind him, he tears the blinds down, ripping the song in half like the front page of a tabloid. The mask has slipped, and the persona is shattered—Bowie screams "shut up" at his band, at himself, a very human cry pressed close to the ear. Fripp's guitar slows with Bowie still yelling at his subconscious; the furies leave him only temporarily, just to return again in the next song. In a final blast of aggressive self-destruction, Bowie's distorted and broken voice cut off almost mid-sentence. As Debra Rae Cohen says of the track in her 1980 album review, "It's an ugly, disturbing moment. *Scary Monsters* is full of them."

Fragment #XX

I sit with a glass in my hand, in my hand the glass sits, sitting I like glass
Waits its turn, sip by precious sip, fear of running
fear of running out
the sun runs a knife under the door,
daylight to bleach the vampire
clutching the glass, perched on a shadow,
spilt honey casts a mood across the floor
can't we do something about thisconstantdaytime
Sparkling neon winking at me like it knows something

Someone left something on the carpet, please don't look. It's nothing.
    Shapes I can't count. The scars
of nothing. I've been here too long. Drawing
patterns in the carpet with a cane, my leg
Is fine, it only hurt once I started carrying up the cane.

The sun shines all
day sits in his shade, the sky is a foreign landscape
even then its 100 degrees of hell,
My private hell
slivers chased through the blinds, collected razor blades of sunshine cutting
    my hand
Suggest sunglasses. See his teeth, suggests "no sun"
might as well be behind glass, he said witness to a fall,
I ask who,
answers—"me".

pick him up by the bones of his shoulders and shake, shake rough love back
   into blood
anger reminds the comatose, slapping frozen blue skin, breaking the ice,
   no change.
Got to get him out of here.

Ground is falling up at me the walls falling away, it's a cardboard city
   trying to stand
Put its shadow over me, the whole aspect is gone, far gone
Like a smile
Washed away in so much rain

CAPTIVE PRESENT TENSE – 1980

Bowie stands backed-up against the wall of his futurism

Up the Hill Backwards

(Cameras in Brooklyn)

"Up the Hill Backwards" is both a confirmation and a confrontation with the violent extremes of apathy. It begins in dogged, ragged rhythms of Tony Visconti strumming a wildly tricky acoustic Bo Diddley shuffle in 7/4 time.[83] As he keeps the pace through gritted teeth, the rhythm section marches a clunky stop-start groove, distorted tom fills jump in like starting pistols, the snare sparks into life, then falls off in static. The drum time of the track is stretched out by Visconti's production, like Dali's melting clocks; the world goes slipping underneath your feet, and we search in vain for something to hold on to.

Thick and fast, the short, sharp shock of half words are blurted out, the band feints, then jumps back in, tripping over itself before being arrested back into a lock-tight rhythm. You hear the tightness of Davis and Murray's playing holding down the scrambled-eggs beat as the song wobbles under its own weight of dysfunction, threatening collapse. Bowie remembered: "Dennis was so open. He was almost orgiastic in his approach to trying out new stuff. Dennis is crazy, an absolute loony man, but he had a lot of his own thoughts on things, and he would throw us all kinds of curve-balls" (Budofsky 1997).

Several writers noted Bowie's use of fragmented time signatures, making disparate elements—that shouldn't work—come together into a much edgier piece of music than the song's lyrics might suggest. "Up The Hill" crackles, snaps, and pops on this creative tension. The verse lines arrive as a sigh of relief, sharpening the contrast between the coolly chanted lyrics, drum fill breaks, and angular guitar setting the track as avant-garde pop within a rock format. Bowie finds a midpoint at which the sound of a song breaking down becomes its own kind of meaning in a riot of abrasive textures and self-contradiction.[84]

Robert Fripp's first few notes are bent high, inching into the song's verse, an exercise in poise and a (sudden) lack of restraint when he surges forward with needling tremolo guitar lines pointing toward his forceful precision playing across the album. Again, Fripp brings forth the improvisational power first heard across *"Heroes"* in 1977 when, after stepping off a plane, he walked straight into Berlin's Hansa Studios, plugged in his guitar, and played along to the album's title track before hearing a single note. The verse of "Up the Hill" lulls us into a false sense of security, suggesting that everything will be okay until the sharp-edged guitar threatens to strong-arm the song into 3/4 time, Fripp shifting gears at his own pace above when the middle-of-the-road chorus of voices float away with themselves off into the clouds.[85]

Fripp remembered Bowie's bizarre instructions that somehow came to suit the song's conflicting moods: "The sessions began around midnight; I said to David, 'Any suggestions?' David said, 'Think Ritchie Blackmore.' I knew exactly what David meant. So my playing was nothing like Ritchie Blackmore, but I knew what David meant—that was a direct piece of advice." Perhaps reaching for the antithesis of the lugubrious Deep Purple guitarist, Fripp's guitar lurched half drunk, pushing and pulling with the band as its own worst enemy, a hymn to maladjustment. Fripp mentions in an interview that he sometimes asked Bowie for chords but ultimately it was the creative freedom to experiment that encouraged him to give such off-the-wall performances, sounding as subconscious as they do effortless in speed, tone, and measure of force. Fripp pointed to this feeling of sudden spontaneity: "Here is the map for the terrain—go." His rare ability to destabilize and enrich the work of his fellow musicians seems to unmoor the song, taking it toward strange new territories.

For his part, Bowie alluded to even more retrospective rock influences, such as the laid-back bluesman B. B. King and the furious, twanging riffs of Chuck Berry, 1950s rock and roll springing forward from Bowie's earliest interest in music, where, in his most recent work of dark soul and krautrock minimalism, they had been suppressed or diverted.[86] Bowie once suggested that his whole idea of getting into music was influenced by critic George Steiner and his postmodern take on the future of creative culture *In Bluebeard's Castle*, leading to Bowie's pluralism of styles that arose from the new era of art school freethinking and postmodernism: "Fuck rock 'n' roll! It's not about rock 'n' roll anymore. It's about: What is content, and how do you distance yourself from the thing that you're within?" From the start, Bowie was grappling with how to take music to different places and to remove the "artist" from his art. Entering the 1990s, Bowie arrived at the home point of deconstruction: the theory that absorbed and eradicated the idea of absolutes, reducing all major aesthetics to ground zero with each attempt. So it is here, when "Up the Hill Backwards" suggests a middle-of-the-road trajectory, the steering wheel is yanked from the hands of the driver, threatening to run the whole song off a sharp cliff.

Fripp's guitar bursts become increasingly unhinged, breaking away from the verse's gentle incline: "The liberation of the rhythm section—eventually denies the lyric's fatalism. It's making common cause against the void, loudly" (O'Leary 2020a). Bowie described the track as "a very odd piece of music," noting the sharp turnaround hinted at but never fully delivered in the lyrics: "On first hearing, it sounds as though it's a very shrugged, almost cynical, there-is-nothing-we-can-do-about-it attitude, which is thrown at you on a very MOR-voiced track, so that it sounds like very much the epitome of indifference."

The sing-along vocal melody marks the start of Bowie's casual nursery rhyme phrasing with the swing of Jack and Jill going back and forth, employed elsewhere on "Ashes to Ashes." As far as the song's progression gets toward its limit, like the lurch of Sisyphus's boulder gone wrong—everything ends back at the start, or perhaps it never even moves in the first place—this is entropy as slow death—the illusion of progress.[87]

This idea of "commitment" appears again after "It's No Game (No. 1)" and its eruption of internal conflict, with "indifference" sitting at the center of Bowie's 1980 All Clear list for the start of the new decade. These growing power struggles "give ["Up the Hill Backwards"] another kind of switch: it has far more power than it would first seem. In fact, it has a very strong commitment, but it's disguised in indifference." The built-in cynicism of the lyrics is counterpointed by the ferocious guitar playing of Fripp that seems to evoke Bowie's anger at an increasingly narrow way of thinking, to be exorcised in the flames of white-hot guitar noise.

Just a few years later, Bowie talked about the video for the song "Let's Dance" as a continuation of the gauntlet thrown down by "Up the Hill Backwards" between empty talk and a real commentary on human empathy. Bowie would admit that the visual element of "Let's Dance" carried a far stronger message than its "nebulous" lyrics: "There is an undercurrent of commitment, but it's not quite so straightforward." Music video director David Mallett explains that the closing statement of the nuclear blast in the distance, which results in the children ritually destroying the red shoes, is based on the 1948 movie *The Red Shoes*.[88] Bowie said, "It's a one-to-one thing, yes, but the danger, the terrifying conclusion is only intimated in the piece. It is not apparent what exactly the fear is that they're running from. There's an ominous quality about it, quite definitely. That was the dance song that has all the trappings of old disco music, but it's almost like the last dance."[89] We also hear the coming warning of "Fashion"—to avoid thought is to let ourselves be set up, driven to living by others' ideals.

> When Love is gone, there's always Justice,
> And when Justice is gone, there's always Force.

—Laurie Anderson, "O Superman" (1981)[90]

By 1980, Bowie was in a strange emotional space. The new era that awaited him already seemed wanting for compassion and empathy as an antidote to end-of-days good times. The "Summer of Love" of 1967 was truly extinguished by the 1970s, and in spite of his own benign career struggle in that naive decade, the springboard of "Space Oddity" had enabled Bowie to become one of the artists who helped to kill it off. In place of positive vibes and community spirit, people were looking for the new forms of escape: the male right to sex and a feminist backlash, cocaine outpacing psychedelics and in turn being dusted down by crack and heroin, with street violence as a means of direct communication. Bowie noted how self-interest boomed into a vicious rat race toward the "death of love." This was J. G. Ballard's death of affect, the free-fall loss of empathy, and emotional stuntedness that entitled people to pursue wealth generation as a divine interest.

So it was with the long-awaited end of David Jones's marriage to his wife Angie on February 8, 1980. Made official while Bowie was on an alpine skiing holiday with his son Joe, the court ruled for a settlement of $500,000 to be paid to Angie over ten years, along with the obligatory gag clause about their relationship.[91] They met for coffee, spoke a few words, and parted with a brief kiss—never to meet again. Following the holiday, Bowie and Angie's son, Joe (formerly Zowie, later Duncan), over whom Bowie retained sole custody, returned to his private school Gordonstoun in Britain.[92] Graeme Thomson noted Bowie's newfound happiness as a single father; reconnecting with his son seems to have encouraged a new sense of responsibility, forcing Bowie to consider more the world around him that his son's generation would later come to inherit.

It is now well documented that only a couple of years into Bowie's marriage with Angie, an open relationship was established, with both husband and wife sharing multiple partners. Already living in separate rooms on tour and in different residences back in the United Kingdom, the couple were literally passing one another in separate lives. When Bowie sings, "We're legally crippled," he delivers a stinging indictment on the powerlessness of romance, where the law meets matters of the heart, no doubt reflecting on his recent years of emotional pain and uncertainty in the latter half of the 1970s. Each in their own private world, kicking and screaming, fighting back to the top, in their separateness, the ex-couple were forced to help themselves—both trying to pretend that everything was okay.

No doubt, after nine years of marriage and many adventures, it was a bittersweet breakup; although separated for much of that time, Angie was nonetheless a formative part of Bowie's early career and one of his greatest champions. Angie has often claimed that she was meant to be "next" for her own pop career to follow after Bowie. As loud and brash as she was charismatic and magnetic, it's hard to see how she would have become a popular musician or singer; more likely, she would have been a celebrity in the modern mold. Perhaps Bowie knew this all along, and so his promised support never arrived.

Many in Bowie's circle from the early days have referred to Angie Bowie's extreme neurosis as one aspect of her ability as a tireless promoter, to constantly push Bowie and herself forward. Bowie would say that life with her was "like living with a blowtorch" always on full flame, spoiling for attention or a fight. But like Tony Defries, love or loathe her, Bowie could not deny that Angie's early encouragement, networking, and moments of inspiration had helped him become Ziggy Stardust rather than simply remaining David Bowie, just another struggling singer-songwriter. Elsewhere, on 1977's "Be My Wife," Bowie had expressed the anguish of a thwarted marriage, seeking a replacement to share his life with, but after he had announced the "death of love"[93] on "Up the Hill," the marriage was truly consigned to the past. It was as much a good-bye as a fresh beginning for new loves that might be realized in the future.

The lost track of the album that might be reflective of Bowie's divided emotional state was given the working title "Is There Life After Marriage." Actually a rhythm track for a cover of Cream's "I Feel Free," Bowie had rehearsed the song with Mick Ronson and the Spiders from Mars; now jammed out by the DAM Trio, it was completed only with 1993's *Black Tie White Noise* album.[94] Given Bowie's recent divorce in 1980, the title is a punning play on freedom in contrast to the lifetime commitment of marriage; the phrase is attributed to the self-proclaimed "stately homo" and wit Quinten Crisp and as a knowing, sarcastic feminist slogan of the era. It is possible that Bowie thought that the sentiment expressed might be taken too literally as schadenfreude, and he chose another cover song, "Kingdom Come," a track of spiritual exile and deliverance, instead, highlighting another fork in the road between the album's often fractious moods.

Equally, Tony Visconti would refer to 1980 as one of the unhappiest years in his personal and professional life. He was also going through relationship difficulties with his then wife Mary, and they would soon part ways. After Bowie invited him to New York, Visconti was forced to choose between his family and his work. Already considering separation, he and his wife agreed that it was better for Visconti to go and record with Bowie. In his autobiography, he recounts that his personal stress levels were brought to a head when he realized the band had only just started jamming in the studio a few days before he arrived.[95] In spite of the challenging emotional times they each shared, Visconti and Bowie seemed to enjoy the mutual support of the studio environment, separate from the challenges of real life. Alongside Bowie, Visconti immersed himself in the work as a means of escape; music was to prove both a form of creative therapy and an outlet to vent personal pressure.

Bowie would neatly drop in the lyric "I'm ok/you're so-so," a glib response to the 1969 self-help book *I'm OK—You're OK*, written by Thomas Anthony Harris. Branded as an accessible and practical guide to how psychiatry and transactional analysis[96] can change your life, its runaway success rightly or wrongly marked the book as offering (the right) answer for a quick emotional fix.[97]

Harris simplifies our emotional spectrum to four codependent states where individuals are either "okay" or "not okay" in relation to one another. In order to live, love, and work happily alongside others, we exchange "strokes," words or actions that yield emotional impact as a kind of game. As we mature through life, we must balance progressive ego stages (parent, adult, and child) with the aim that most of our transactions become situations where both parties are mutually "okay." In this balance, we become a mentally healthy and emotionally rounded individual, overcoming childhood trauma and negative influences of social adjustment and psychological damage. Perhaps Bowie is mocking Harris's overly simplistic approach to human relationships—that two people can simply trade on extreme positions of being in a good or a bad emotional place. To reach polarized states of well-being, the state of things is merely "okay," a flattened-out lifeline. On paper, the song is one long smile of sunshine, putting the upbeat side of the world face forward—until Bowie flips it over on its head, the song's cheerful brain weather unravels in self-doubt, and we sink into the acid burn of Bowie's withering tone.[98] With the power of foresight, Bowie was in on the joke that the ubiquitous self-realization bible had now become. The song remains a caution against looking for all the answers in one place.

Bowie's deadpan verse exploits day-to-day banality to pave over a slow and steady breakdown. Alienation begins to seep in around the conceited narrator, emotionally stunted, and he is held adrift in longing for some greater connection with the wider "we" who might understand what he is going through, but Bowie's words only seem to echo his dissatisfaction. This is pushed further in the three-way backing vocals of Bowie, Visconti, and Lynn Maitland; like a Greek chorus without the drama, they push the sickly saccharine agenda that all things will eventually return to their even keel. The stacked chorus voices carry the song, surrounding Bowie as a callback to *Young Americans*, the concept album dealing with mid-Nixon depression, another sarcastic revelation, chanting Hare Krishna and reciting the Sunflower Sutra at the prolonged wake of the American dream.

However, there is some therapeutic weight to Harris's psychiatric learning; he identifies three points of struggle at which people realize the need to make changes that alter the future direction of their lives:

- One is that they hurt sufficiently. They have beat their heads against the same wall so long that they decide they have had enough. . . .

- Another thing that makes people want to change is a slow type of despair called ennui, or boredom. This is what the person has who goes through life saying, "So what?" until he finally asks the ultimate big "So What?" . . .

- A third thing that makes people want to change is the sudden discovery that they can.

Harris evokes similar challenges faced by Bowie in his ongoing recovery as he struggled to escape the shadow of the vampire castle in Los Angeles still standing tall behind him. Bowie mocks the feel-good doctor's approach to forced happiness on "Ashes to Ashes," wishing well but meaning something quite different; playing on the clipped English phrase "I hope you're happy,"[99] Bowie laces it with the bitter irony of the Chinese proverb, "May you live in interesting times," as much a curse as a casual invitation to random acts of the future. When Bowie sings "It'll be alright," it is with the half-hearted resolve of a man long suffering from diminished expectations; regardless, "Up the Hill" lingers just a little too long on self-satisfaction, resigned to greater forces that he can neither control nor understand.

For Bowie, the idea of becoming a better person as citizen who simply conforms to societal expectations offers limited appeal. Instead of a bleached-blank life, Bowie's major project was to try to become more than oneself, to push against limitations. Across *Scary Monsters*, true satisfaction remains elusive, an open noose hanging as a question mark. "Up the Hill Backwards" burns with Bowie's inner resentment of middle-classness, to be willingly absorbed into the flow toward shared mediocrity and a morality of tedium:

KYOTO — 1980

Swallowed in the commuter's scream

"I have this great long chain with a ball of middle-classness at the end of it which keeps holding me back." The daily grind rolls into a collection of minor grievances, another one of those "things that gets up your nose,"[100] a gross expression for sweating the little stuff driven by social friction to generate political sway. These are people already dead above and below the waist; suffocated under the mindless platitudes of "Thank you so much, you're welcome, have a nice day," they just don't know it yet.

The principle of books such as Harris's mutated into the broader concept of the well-being industry of self-care and "feeling good" and shifting priority toward an amped-up pleasure principle. The 1980s took this to its nadir with monstrous hedonism for its own sake, addicted to selfishness, the ultimate "product" for the increasingly narrow "me" generation. Their inheritance becomes a loveless world spinning off into indifference as an unformed collective of emotional refugees fighting one another to get ahead, killing yourself just to feel "okay."

In his original lyric notes, Bowie would sing "Skylabs are falling," Skylab being the space satellite that fell to Earth in 1979, which Chris O'Leary calls "an all-purpose symbol of American decline," a national disaster that cut too close to the bone, as when Laurie Anderson would refer to deaths of U.S. troops during the Iranian hostage crisis. Bowie shifts from disintegrating space stations to the more down-to-earth line "sneakers fall apart," exposing an uneasy mind where nothing feels built to last. Lifting the lid on this deep mood becomes like gazing into the gray-skinned universe of stone-cold coffee held inside a styrofoam cup. Bare feet flapping on the pavement, Bowie finds an inherent cheapness to life he can't shake, caught within the modern monoculture. He jauntily sings of witnesses falling (past windows?), numbed to suicide; the victim and the bystander are united seeing each other in free fall or a flashback to Los Angeles—the return of daytime monsters.[101] Even with your feet firmly on the ground, the world's ceilings must inevitably come crashing down on our heads.[102]

Where "Space Oddity'" invested its optimism in the stars as waypoints to greatness offering deliverance from Earth, it meant nothing (and everything) to the downbeat family man of "Repetition," who channels his inner rage and frustrations into workaday abuse. Glued to the TV, watching a constant feed of anarchy at the bottom and high-rising success above, he gets the sense that he is being overtaken by history in the making. So he complains about his wife, tells her she can't cook, finds fractures in all the little ways she held him back; man can go to the moon but he remains a stay-at-home spectator. We revisit the character years later as "Johnny" in 1997's "I'm Afraid of Americans," a blank-eyed gawker blindly sucking on a Coke. Just like Warhol, the obsession with branded "USA" products provides the riches of the poor. "Repetition"-era man blames lack of education for his situation, where Dylan's "Subterranean Homesick Blues" sees the narrow funnel of the system preparing people for the world of work, clocking in and out one day after another.[103] Where "Boys Keep Swinging" begins with the pleasures of male youth, "Repetition" ends with masculine crisis, the pain of being a man.

Bowie was in full and fine voice across *Scary Monsters*, his often-erratic vocalization pitch-perfect, as wild and deranged as each song needed him to be.[104] Bowie stretches normal speech patterns to the breaking point; crooning violence into your ear, screaming love and solidarity into a void, he makes baritone drawls swing into heightened states of anger to reach full euphoric flight. Studio engineer Chris Porter speaks of Bowie as a truly unique performer, at one point chatting in the mixing room, then stepping into the recording booth as a different person, transformed into the "David Bowie" of the popular imagination: "He was just about the best singer I've ever worked with. He sings from his soul, from his spirit. My job was to step to the side when he was doing great" (DeMain 2003).

You hear this commitment in his singing, playfully overemoting, leaning on the power of his naturally loud vocals. In *The Last Five Years* documentary, we hear the raw take of Bowie recording the track "Lazarus," the sound of a breathless Bowie, gasping before his next cue. Visconti points out that despite being very ill at the time, Bowie was not fighting for breath; he had simply worked himself up into a feverish state ready to deliver each line. Elsewhere, he was a great mimic, which perhaps explains the characterization in his singing; an excellent recording exists of Bowie "doing" the voices of Iggy Pop, Sinatra, Lou Reed, and others, sounding eerily like the real thing. This well-rehearsed form would continue to *Let's Dance* and the rest of the 1980s, but with Bowie denying himself the freedom of chance and experimentation, his final taboo broken after 1980 would be to bend toward conformity and compromise.

"Up the Hill" bears the influence of "It's No Game" and its fierce attack—life is not an exercise in second chances, and we cannot always trade our way out to escape deeper problems. Bowie is calling out the hypocrisy of personal development guides when desperate people are poor, angry, and fighting for their lives as the city collapses down around them and the world beyond it burns.

The attitude of "Up the Hill" is fueled by Hans Richter's book *Dada: Art and Anti-Art*, an examination of the fin de siècle Dada movement, an era of dramatic cultural and political upheaval. Richter sees existential crisis occur when the individual is confronted with the gift of infinite escape, dream, and illusion, like a rabbit in the headlights—the tyranny of risk and possibility becomes no freedom at all. Dada's broad trajectory flows from Zürich in 1916 via Berlin to Paris in 1922, by which time it was absorbed into the more populist form of a formal surrealist movement:[105] "Berlin Dada presents all the symptoms—good and bad—of a neurosis." Richter then provides a hit list of factors that marked the early 1900s as the beginning of an increasingly complex and fragmented century, the great break with the old order and the birth of modernism, moving beyond the neatness of rational humanism. This new temper of seriousness demanded the equally extreme and extroverted artistic response of Dada's playful reshaping of reality. Emerging from World War I, "four years of senseless slaughter in which many friends had died on both sides," to the rise of global communism and the collapse of the German government, Richter found "the inconclusiveness of the revolution that was being fought out on the street-corners at that very moment" meeting with "the spirit of opposition, so long suppressed." It is here that the infighting among artistic movements and political radicals become parallel and sometimes clashing struggles. Bowie lifts a choice line, almost wholesale, from Richter's text for "Up the Hill Backwards":

> And finally the vacuum created by the sudden arrival
> of freedom and the endless possibilities it seemed
> to offer if one could grasp them firmly enough.

Richter exposes the terrific and terrible void of new opportunity with people rushing eagerly forward, tripping over themselves, to fill the vacancy with something meaningful. It is both the cause and the symptom of a desperate people who don't know what to do with a sudden explosion of liberty—because they've never had it before.[106]

Richter's thoughts express the existential hinge at the heart of Bowie's song; we are free to do anything but often remain inhibited either by state controls and economic situation, or by tunnel vision around which we build walls of "cant" for ourselves: better to complain of our situation, as if we were powerless to act, denying our fear to grasp life by the throat. It was Bowie kicking through these imaginary doors to pursue the creative freedom that so defined the breadth of his career. In the previous track, "It's No Game (No. 1)," all "free steps to heaven" had been exhausted, suggesting that true freedom lies in taking control over one's life rather than coasting along, harried by gatekeepers, expecting new opportunities to be made for us.

Nobel Prize–winning economist Bengt Holmström said in a 2018 interview, "People think that creativity comes from freedom. That's a fundamental misunderstanding. Creativity comes from obstacles, limitations and questions." His view suggests that finding something to be in opposition to, even if it is an element within yourself, gives us renewed power of resistance—on *Scary Monsters*, deviance becomes liberty.

Richter's response to the dynamics of early twentieth-century European culture was to keep himself separate and somewhat aloof from changes that would come to seem like an inevitable electrified shift: "The whole atmosphere was hysterical, convulsive and unreal; artistic expression could hardly have taken any other form." Like Bowie's distant observer in both parts of "It's No Game," Richter hears echoes of history recurring, "the sound of the streets, the sinister sounds of discord that we had so hated during and after the war and were to hear, more frightening still, in later years." Before the deluge of the Great Depression and World War II, the 1920s would prove to be the nascent beginnings of a more modern world driven to extremes of art and culture clashing with the limits—and growing demands—of technology and big business combined. At a social level, the song seems to attack notions of political progress; we ascend and develop, move up the hill, but we're doing so ass-backward, with one eye always looking to the past, not where we are going to next.

Elsewhere, Bowie borrows a line from the preface of Friedrich Nietzsche's *Twilight of the Idols*: "there are more idols than realities in the world." It is from here that Nietzsche advocates the mode of thought of "philosophizing with a hammer." Far from an intellectual remove, he demands that we test the heroes of our culture and their ideas, by force of inquiry, trying to find out whether their bodies resonated "hollow" or "sound," weak or strong, lacking the conviction of the courage they presented to the world. This stress testing is as much a gauge of personal character as artistic quality. Those lacking true resolve, the naive youth too full with passionate intensity that Bowie later describes in "Teenage Wildlife," are just more butterflies to be broken on the wheel of life, in this case one-hit wonders and genre bands churned out by the music industry grind. The false idols of culture only generate attrition of the real, seeking routes of short-term escapism—in this world a guide to self-help is no help at all.

Nietzsche's earlier book *The Birth of Tragedy* offered the idea of Apollonian and Dyonisian natures, reason, and chaos as the dueling natures in humankind delivered through classical Greek drama. This feeds directly into *Scary Monsters'* mixed moods of ecstatic depression, hysterical anguish, and crying laughter. As he entered the 1990s and the work of *1. Outside*, Bowie increasingly found himself drawn toward a more primal view of life, perhaps drawn from his earlier work. In 1980, society is not falling apart; rather, it is following an inevitable crash course toward hard rationalism, the post-God spirituality of neopaganism. Death, sex, and art are the true forces of human evolution—a time in which we have everything to fear but are too afraid to look inside and ask "who is responsible?"

A strange song that was an even stranger choice of single, "Up the Hill Backwards" reached number 32 in the UK charts. Half radio friendly but bearing hard corners, it was an odd cousin in an album full of potential hits. It eventually found its way onto *Top of the Pops* sans Bowie, a playback accompanied by the benign motions of in-house dance troupe Legs & Co. Strutting and cha-cha-ing as bacchanalian handmaidens to the sacrifice of integrity, they appear like Kate Bush put on ice, evoking the faux-revolutionary spirit that the song tries to take apart.[107]

Robert Fripp's juddery riff soon shakes off any previous hesitation, sprinting into a furious tremolo sound that runs away with itself to become the restless mind now unleashed. Putting his shoulder against the thundering toms and slugging bass line that hold down the beat, Fripp takes a chainsaw to the feel-good industry in favor of righteous anarchy, destroying the hollow body of the new "normal." By this time, Bowie has already left the song, having abandoned his search for love in an airless space; the song becomes one long drift away from promised reconciliation with the self, in a world slowly fading to gray.

Fragment #78

TRANSCRIPT - 13/2/1980
SUBJECT: GASPAR CRUZ - ALIEN
STATUS - NATIONALITY: UNKNOWN
(HOLDING MULTIPLE PASSPORTS)
RESIDENCE IN LONDON, NW5

...SPENT TIME IN THE SERVICES,
HE'S INVOLVED IN SOMETHING MOODY,
WE DON'T HAVE A FULL PHOTO YET,
HE'S SAT IN THE CAR WITH THE
SUN FLAP DOWN - THAT'S FUCKING
SUSPICIOUS ALREADY - THINKS HE'S
GOT THE CHOPS TO BE A PLAYER,
I DON'T KNOW WHERE THE GIRL FITS
INTO IT YET, EITHER SHE'S HIS
BIRD OR A TRICK AND HE'S PLAYING
HER OUT, EITHER WAY SHE LOOKS
FUCKED ALL THE TIME, STRUNG-OUT
OR JUST TOO MUCH HIPPIE SHIT

SUBJECT IS NOW SEEN WAITING IN A
CAR, BLUE. NOW READING COPY OF
VIZ - BLUEY - GREEN - SEEMS TO BE
JULY ISSUE WITH SPECIAL PULL-OUT
CENTRE - A DECENT READ. I'M
TALKING INTO THIS LITTLE BLACK
BOX ... MICHAEL HAS NOT RETURNED
WITH COFFEE FROM MCDONALDS ...
PROBABLY STUCK IN A QUEUE ...
WAITING ... WATCHING SUBJECT ...
ALSO WAITING ... WE ARE ALL
WAITING FOR ... SOMETHING TO -
HEY MIKE, YOU TOOK YOUR - OH SHIT

```
OH - FUCK
FUCK - SHE'S COME OUT SHES
BLEEDING - SHES BLEEDING -
HALF THE DOORS HANGING OFF, FUCK,
OK, LET'S GO MIKE, GO GO GO,
LET'S . . .
ARGH! FUCK YOU CLUMSY -
TWAT IT BURNS!
SORRY MATE - SORRY - OH FUCK
SORRYY SORRY
OH FUCK
WHAT?
HE'S GOT HER BY THE ARM,
PUTTING HER IN THE CAR, SHE'S IN
THEY'RE GOING DAVE, THEY'RE OFF - SKI
WHERE ARE THE FUCKING KEYS
I THOUGHT YOU HAD THEM.
GIMME THE KEYS, FUCK, THE KEYS
OH HERE WE GO -
WATCH IT - EASY - AH,THEY'VE GONE DOWN
THE SIDE OF THE SEAT, YOU MUPPET!
OOPS
FUCK IT
DAVE?
WHAT?
THEY'RE OFF, THEY'RE GOING, DAVE
WHAT?!
THEY'VE GONE
FUCK, FUCK IIIIIIITTTTTTT - WE'VE
ONLY GONE AND BLOWN IT, FUCK
DAVE?
YEAH?
YOU'VE LEFT THE RECORDER ON, MATE
OH SHI -
- TRANSMISSION ENDS -
```

Scary Monsters (and Super Creeps)

(Freaks Becomes Us)

Questions have arisen:
Who is he?
What is he?
Where did he come from?
Is he a creature of a foreign power?
Is he a creep?
Is he dangerous?

—Dick Cavett, introducing David
Bowie on his talk show, 1974

The title track of *Scary Monsters (and Super Creeps)* offers us a record of a restless and troubled mind. Arriving from a no-so-distant place of monsters, weirdos, and freaks, the song becomes a horror movie populated by wounded, broken, and flawed people, pushed to the edge of belonging. A sister song to "Up the Hill Backwards," "Scary Monsters" now shows the uptight, self-righteous citizen gone off the rails. Placing Bowie the artist as a super freak and self-made oddity turned to face the strange, he forges his own sinister bend, refusing to look away he becomes a hero of difference.

The song opens with a furious march of percussion; beats rise and collapse in on themselves as Tony Visconti's blistered mirror production kicks the drum kit down the staircase. Using an EMS "Wasp" synthesizer, he programmed a descending bass line that was triggered by the snare drum, with the toms and kick drum sometimes bleeding into the other mic, starting the process over again, piling on sonic excess. The galloping rhythm of "Scary Monsters" accelerates, fleeing the scene of a horrible crime. Robert Fripp's meticulous tangle of guitar notes scatter up the fretboard before leaping into the chorus with huge dog-whistle string bends pushing at the levels of human hearing. Fripp's guitar seems to embolden Bowie's voice—or is it the other way around—two beasts barking at each other, threatening volume in place of bites.

The casual freakery of the song speaks to the breaking point of human frailty sprawling across the record. By exposing our own weaknesses and inner deviance, we are forced to reflect and maybe to empathize with our shared human potential for weirdness. Speaking in a television interview with Tim Rice on *Friday Night, Saturday Morning* in 1980, Bowie explained his interest: "I have an eclectic thing about freaks and isolationist and alienated people, I collect them." These assorted oddities would jump out for him as archetypes of physical and psychic deformities carrying deeper spiritual resonance. In his teens feasting on the 1961 cult book *Strange People: Unusual Humans Who Have Baffled the World*, Bowie recounts the story of the pawpaw blowtorch man, a young black man who entered a hospital claiming he couldn't lie down or else the bedsheets would burst into flames; they were duly ablaze, and he fled into the night, never to be seen again.[108]

Bowie explained away his album's title as a slogan gleaned from a Kellogg's cereal box. The seemingly banal packaging promised each child the gift of scary monsters. Bowie referred to the more specific counterpoint of "Supermen and Nosferatus," an interesting turn of phrase, moving toward good and evil, heroes and vampires, gods on Earth and unholy abominations where reality often merges and confuses the two. After Nietzsche, the American Superman of DC Comics gave young children a force of pure good to believe in; along with his native superpowers, it was his moral integrity that made him a tower of strength. While figures of pure horror such as Nosferatu (1922), the eponymous villain of the original vampire movie,[109] are staged in the emergent language of silent German expressionist film with long shadows and stark lighting effects, they belong to the darkness and embody our doubts and superstitions of difference.[110] Although such figures are drawn from folk legends of Eastern Europe, residing more in a fear of the foreign "other" rather than a supernatural being, the "vampyre" was a censorious bogeyman, a metaphor that provoked reactionary nationalist feeling in defense of fragile cultural identity.

At the human level, the characters of early horror cinema stand as ciphers for the traumatic realities of death, decay, deformity—and our capacity for "evil"—made digestible for the common consciousness. With plastic surgery just in its infancy and the terrible wounds experienced by soldiers on all sides of World War I, the body horror witnessed on the screen played out in the events of recent history. This confrontation of the weird and the eerie broke down barriers of abnormality between the healthy civilian and the crippled or maimed people forced to wear masks, use false limbs, or live in wheelchairs just to try to fit into the everyday world they used to be a part of.

A further influence that reflects the *Scary Monsters* concept is Bowie's interest in the 1932 cult film *Freaks*. Glenn Hendler finds the film's writer/ director, author Tod Browning, name-checked in "Diamond Dogs," submerged alongside the freaks in muddy, underwater vocals. Bowie describes a silicone hump, ten-inch (leg) stump, and crawling about on hands and knee (singular). Growing with infamy in the 1960s, *Freaks* depicts a group of circus entertainers, played by people with real-life deformities, disabilities, and gender differences. They are set against the "big people," humans with idealized attributes, such as Hercules the weightlifter and Cleopatra the great beauty; alongside this, it is their "normality" that sets them in a position of superiority above the freaks. The "big people" are the villains of the piece, figures of cruelty and exploitation against the freaks, the "decent circus folk" (Hendler 2020).

After discovering a murder plot schemed by the "big people," the freaks enact a terrible revenge on Cleopatra, turning her into a duck creature and castrating Hercules as all the freaks chant "one of us." Hendler notes that the freaks are the more human, standing up to thwart acts of wrongdoing and cruelty, begging the question, who should we (the audience) identify with? Far from being exploitative, the film echoes the humanistic message of *The Elephant Man* that inner qualities can trump shallow external appearances. It also highlights Bowie's sympathy with outsider and excluded freaks, crisscrossing the brittle line of beauty and fascination.

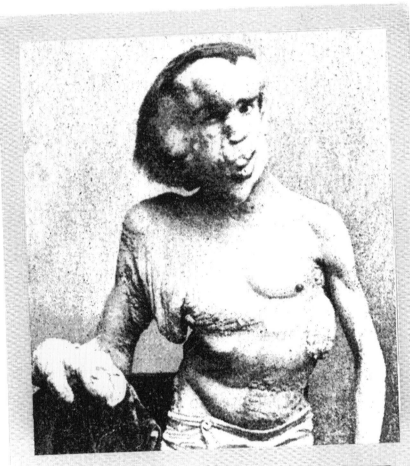

JOSEPH 'JOHN' MERRICK — 1889

A new mind saved by science — 'The Elephant Man'

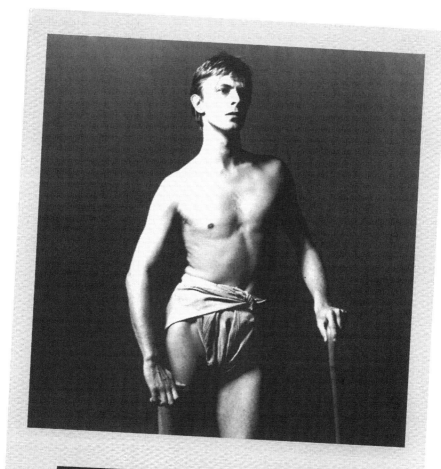

DAVID BOWIE - ELEPHANT MAN - 1980

Broken body — Pure heart — Bowie's Broadway debut

A comparison between *The Elephant Man* and *The Hunchback of Notre Dame* was suggested to Bowie: "I think in all cases of monster and man, whether the monster be a legitimate monster or one perceived as being a monster by the society within which he is contained, there's always that element of love lost, or love unrequited, never to be gained." Avoiding the Disneyfied angle of easy acceptance and understanding, Bowie shines a light on the knowing conceit that in our fears and prejudices, we sometimes generate our own monsters, using these narratives to explain away our shared humanity against other "good" and "bad" people, each capable of doing terrible things in the right circumstances.

Debra Rae Cohen (1980) noted Bowie's continued use of "stylized postures (tropes ballooned to a human scale) as a means of objectifying horror." This speaks to the characters that inhabit the songs of *Scary Monsters*; a fraction of the many thwarted and desperate individuals who inhabit our societies, they become the minority that disturb and upset the dominant balance of the majority. Across Bowie's music, we witness drug casualties, dictators, hubristic stars, and victims of abuse, merged as aspects of his complex character and personae. This crooked cast had its parallel in Bowie's unreal rock star universe of drug dealers, unscrupulous managers and lawyers, or former fans and collaborators who later "betrayed" him and turned imitator. At his most fraught period toward the late 1970s, he would refer to the many people who had attached themselves to what he felt to be his fading empire as "leeches"— they were all after his money—taking him apart piece by piece—vampires of human flesh.

For an album of such adult themes, Bowie would continue to couch the songs of *Scary Monsters* in a childlike framework, nostalgic for those earliest anxieties carried into adult life, the darkness within casting the longer shadow we drag around behind us. The very scariness of the record is present in the range of distorted sounds and mutated voices that hammer out from the speakers. As Bowie's lyrics vocalize his inner monster, Visconti warps his speech patterns further, taking a razor blade to his singing, as Francis Bacon would stab and thrust with his paintbrush to make a caricature of the human-face-as-animal. Along with the backing vocals, there is a metallic brittleness to Bowie's tone—the angry man shouting behind closed blinds—sounding, in Visconti's words, "like a demonic choir singing through the blades of a helicopter."

Visconti emphasized the still painstaking task of working with reel-to-reel tape recording in 1980, just as Pink Floyd had made physical delay loops by literally stretching tape across a studio with multiple hands holding pencils to maintain the tension. Visconti tinkered endlessly with the tracks, adding effects and splicing them back into the tape, the kind of painstaking analog invention that brought the *Sgt. Pepper's* comparisons to life. After mixing down the main tracks into a two-track stereo recording, adjusting levels to their satisfaction, he and Bowie would then go back to the individual tracks and apply grease pencil and razor blade to the tape, surgically extracting individual slices of sounds. "I'd go back and remix every drum fill, especially raising the toms much higher and adding EFX to them" (Visconti 2007). He would carry strips of tape around his neck like a tailor's measure, organizing the sections by hanging them from a drum stand like fish drying in the sun. He would then cautiously splice these fragments back into the song. A track like "Scary Monsters" could still have as many as ten edited sections, but as Visconti explained, pieces could only be stuck and undone so many times before the tape started to disintegrate: you can hear the added sonic impact of the drums across the record, sounding much bigger and resonant than an ordinary kit, creating altered states surging with alien electricity. The signature of Visconti's unique production styles aligns *Scary Monsters* more to the intense work and attention invested in *Low* and *"Heroes."*

Attention to detail harks back to Visconti's Beatles comparisons, as he saw the creative atmosphere for reinvention within the tracks move ever closer to both *Revolver* and *Sgt. Pepper's*. He makes it clear that he adopted his studio-as-instrument discipline from producer George Martin, popularly known as the "secret" fifth member of the Beatles. Although shared techniques straddled the two records as the Beatles and Martin created their own loops and altered the speed and pitch of the tape[111] for one-of-a-kind songs, such the trippy dreamscape of "Tomorrow Never Knows," elsewhere, for "Lucy in the Sky with Diamonds," there was a more hands-on approach to randomization where tape was cut into pieces and scattered on the floor. The band intended to let the sounds stand on the record as they had fallen, but after reassembling them, they realized the song had landed too close to the original recording, requiring them to break it up more methodically. They make something new and strange beyond the original. In spite of all this painstaking studio process, the backbone behind many of Bowie's greatest songs remains the strength and versatility of the DAM Trio as a band that could both lead and interpret creative direction. The original demo of "Scary Monsters" struggles to contain a more fluid and dynamic band, with its bare and edgy bones of stabbed piano, shouty backing vocals, and needling guitar notes, giving the song more of a rough-hewn New Wave riff. Topping it off is the harsh metallic thwack of Davis's cowbell, beating the life out from a beast of burden.

In this approach, Bowie drew on wider contemporary influences ever attuned to his keen pop sensibilities; Edward Bell remembers listening to tapes of the Psychedelic Furs, Amanda Lear, and Tom Waits. Bowie was fond of the

Furs, seeing a pop-sharp band that could rival the nous and savvy of Blondie without the figurehead of an iconic lead singer like Debbie Harry who threatened to overshadow the rest of the group.[112] "Scary Monsters" leans heavily on repetitive hooks, along with the more autodestructive parts of Fripp's guitar, employing the classic pop "Yeah, yeah, yeah" vocal chorus chants.

Bowie would make a recording note to himself referring to Joy Division to "get on top of D.D.'s drum," sparking returning echoes of Visconti's production work on *Low* via the cutting edge of the present. The distended gated snare drum sound pioneered on *Low* was transmuted into the phased drums of Joy Division's 1979 debut album, *Unknown Pleasures*, produced by Martin Hannet. He broke down the drum kit, recording each individual piece for stark clarity, then added reverb, echo, and delay, creating digitized space "sound mirrors" around the drums; this evolutionary redux fed back into Visconti's cascading drum sound across *Scary Monsters*. Speaking about the experimentation of *Low*, Bowie said he wanted the drums to "disorientate" the listener, to be pulled "out of focus" to an almost psychedelic point of detachment; by corrupting the classic rock drum sound of the previous two decades, Visconti was fashioning the signature sounds of the future.

Davis's drums were often routed through an Eventide H910 Harmonizer—famously introduced to the *Low* sessions by Tony Visconti as an audio-processing device that "fucks with the fabric of time." Visconti would note its traditional use as an early form of auto-tune, meant to correct off-key singers. Able to shift pitch in real time, Visconti relied on it to create "space age" and "horror movie" sounds. On *Low*, the heavy processing of drum sounds using sound gates on microphones to capture the immediate strike at the drum skin. The mic "jumped in" at the loudest point of the drum's "thud," with ambient mics in the studio space absorbing the wider reverb; the sound continues to fade while also dropping in pitch. Visconti would compare the sound of the beaten drums on "Scary Monsters" to the "urgh" noise of a man being punched in the gut, an added physicality that also works on the listener.[113]

The heavily processed drum sound would find its way into much of the 1980s music that followed after *Scary Monsters*, blurring the line between the "real" players and the programmed "artificial" drum machines. The electronified sounds that would come to define the musical decade would also trap many albums in that era bearing the same production style of hollow stadium-lite reverb, eventually commodified in the form of the now much-maligned LinnDrum.

Art is as nothing to nature.

—*The Elephant Man*, 1980

Having completed the *Scary Monsters* album in April 1980, Bowie was biding his time. He considered going back east, presumably to Japan, until he was offered the role of John "Joseph" Merrick in the play *The Elephant Man* by Bernard Pomerance. Making the move from studio to Broadway stage, Bowie did his homework for the role, visiting the archives in the Royal London Hospital to see a series of bulbous and scattered plaster casts of his body.

Examining the extreme postures of Merrick's form enabled Bowie to find his own way into the character's physicality but also his head space. Although he was already well-versed in the edgelands of outcast society, the idea of lost people finding themselves, whether in contrast to others or by virtue of their common strangeness, is an emotional thread that runs through many Bowie songs.

Rolling Stone magazine's review of the show coined the sensational impression of Merrick's "magnetic repugnance," which enthralled the spectators of Victorian London, first witnessed when he served much of his young life as a carnival show attraction.[114] The article also notes Bowie's entrance to the stage at the play's beginning, something none of us will ever see, as only odd clips of the full performance remain. As Bowie shuffled into life on the stage wearing only a loincloth, the various features of Merrick's deformities are recounted by a narrator in strictly medical terms, verbally mapping his body for the audience, and with each new detail, he adjusts his body accordingly: "Bowie's sleek frame starts to sag and wither. His arm stiffens, his leg droops and curls, his spine crooks outward, and his head begins to bobble benignly."[115] This transformative act of living mime would show how specifically Bowie the performer could stage his body as a framing device, using gesture and inflection to express the character of his songs, often upstaging the surface image of his personas.

Bowie sidestepped the more traditional body horror representations of Merrick, almost in opposition to John Hurt (in David Lynch's 1979 *Elephant Man* movie[116]). Knowing that each day of shooting he would be slathered in pounds of rubber prosthetics that took hours to apply, Hurt suffered his own feat of physical endurance, perhaps bringing him closer to the real situation of Merrick's disability. Bowie adapted his body to emphasize the kinks of pose and posture, not the "freakish" abnormality of the folds of skin pockmarked with fungoid-like growths. The performance "depends entirely on the ability of the actor playing Merrick to constantly project the man's awareness of his own predicament." This gave a high-wire element to Bowie's maintaining his stance to avoid breaking character and demanded warm-ups and gradual warm-downs to shift his body in and out of its normal phase.

Overturning the angular forms borrowed from German expressionist painters, particularly the *schöne leiche* beautiful corpses of Austrian artist Egon

Schiele, in this role, Bowie discovered a new flexibility in sound and body. There was no disgust or shock, more a deeper sense of unease; Merrick is flawed, frail, wounded, and disabled, not an abomination. Bowie's elasticated vocal projections—heightening pitch and throwing his voice by intonations of yelps and shrieks—speak to the submerged pain that Merrick works to overcome in his speech, aping clear diction and studied manners, to become the beast-made-gentleman à la Jean Cocteau—thwarting expectations by learning to live within his limitations.

Bowie found a naive innocence but also a sharp intellect that Merrick had never employed much before arriving at the Royal Hospital as the ward of Dr. Frederick Treves. Naive to some but also keen for new experience, Merrick stood on the outside as an observer, and though he was keen to be let into the lives of others, there was no real place for him there; he was merely introduced to aspects of high society, as a form of parade. A favorite poem of Merrick's, one that he often used to sign off with at the end of his letters, alludes to the power of metaphysical release he found and took great comfort in, realizing another way to see himself:

> I would be measured by the soul;
> The mind's the standard of the man.

> —From "False Greatness" by Isaac Watts

Bowie noted the "dreadful burden" that Merrick was forced to carry, the sad hood with one eyehole that he wore to conceal his face, although he would not have to be seen "as himself"; equally, the mask only exaggerated his oddity. Living within social notoriety as the inverse of Bowie's global fame, Merrick remained a person "held at arm's length from society," not unlike the singer, though for very different purposes (O'Leary 2017). Digging deep into his subject's biography, Bowie felt the presence of what he called "a *new mind*, encased in this terrible grotesqueness," a painful self-awareness feeding on his "physical vulnerability," something that interviewer Angus MacKinnon also noted in "David Bowie," the perpetual performer who was cursed to always be "on." In the role of Merrick, Bowie tried to embody someone who daily fought to overcome their physical disability and aesthetic deformities, the flip side of beauty and star quality that he enjoyed.[117]

The spark of the play emerges in the juxtaposition of Merrick's good soul thrust into the sordid engine of Victorian society: from its harsh and cruel poverty and up to the hypocrisy of its wealthy, philanthropic spirit, set on the moral improvement (of others) but only under God's grace. Merrick had to work even harder to make himself understood to others, to avoid being forced to grovel or to "perform." The line "We polish him so that he may better reflect ourselves" speaks of Merrick as a kept person, an aristocratic curio, no longer chained but held under the gaze of the medical profession and Victorian do-gooders, inspired more by selfish Christian dogma than by humanist empathy. In either case, Merrick is always a spectacle, surviving by the kindness and charity of strangers; as the perennial outsider, he is the only one able to see through the veil of society at all levels.

Director Jack Hofsiss remembers Bowie as a "real actor," drawing on his own experience of alienation and the character of Thomas Jerome Newton as the alien wearing a human mask. *The Elephant Man* was neatly visualized on posters as a stickman figure with one leg at a symbolic wonky angle; this also speaks to Bowie's own sense of asymmetry. He quickly latched onto the tension expressed by Merrick's bodily deformity and his physical disabilities of motion and speech, the first impressions that would always mark him out as being different. Hofsiss, who years later would be confined to a wheelchair after a swimming accident, appreciated the metaphorical power of the character with all their wounds on show: "We all go through our lives with some sort of a limp, and we hide our limps very actively, so in a way the human being that you play who has a physiological limp is more human than others."

The play would see Bowie developing the "stylized postures" approach of his three-dimensional musical aesthetic, translated into physical personas, stagecraft, and artwork. Starring as Merrick, Bowie embodies the martyred spirit of one of God's unholy creatures, the applied imagination of the audience projecting their own anxieties and unease onto his body as canvas, seeing beyond the caricature. Speaking on the Australian interview show *Countdown* in 1980, Bowie observed of the benevolent Doctor Treves, "It's his own nightmare that he might be the monster, or the fantastic beast, whatever you want to call it."

In *The Elephant Man*, Bowie personified the inner tension of celebrity as both performer and figurehead—how he was held in the gaze of his fans, at turns beautiful, extraordinary, ugly, and freakish, to be endlessly observed within the refracted, unblinking eye of fame—a cruel laser that eventually cut through to expose the person underneath.[118] On 1970's "The Width of a Circle" Bowie found himself caught within his own reflection: "I looked around/And the monster was me."

I looked around
and the monster was me

—"The Width of a Circle," 1970

STATION TO STATION — 1976

The Thin White Duke calls YOU!

Bowie was a fan of Greil Marcus's book *Mystery Train*, a deep dive into the cultural phenomenon of rock and roll. When Marcus writes about Sly Stone and the cult of fanhood, Bowie might well have been reading about himself (as Ziggy Stardust). This was the balancing act of a performer who continues to give his audience exactly what they want, becoming a "shadowy ideal" who merges with them.[119] Ultimately, he becomes an artist who must continue to plow the same furrow. In breaking away from their expectations (and his own), the artist was in the knife-edge position of taking a genuine step into the creative unknown (toward art-as-life) and shedding followers like a dead skin who in their sudden estrangement now lived under the broken spell of their initial fascination, as if the artist had separated from himself, evoking Bowie's clean break with the advent of *Low* in 1977 (Marcus 2015).

Bowie was a man constantly fighting definition, possessing an openness that invited others who felt like outsiders to gravitate toward him. In many respects, it was Ziggy, not "David Bowie," who gathered these lost people into a united front reciting the words of their leper messiah. They came from all over but chiefly the drab provincial towns of middle England, where Bowie gigs were lit up by the "exquisite creatures" of his most devoted fans.[120] John O'Connell notes that books like Camus's *The Outsider* brought the dizzying free will of existentialism home to the young suburbanites as it did for Bowie: "It legitimized clever, driven teenagers' sense of uniqueness; of being able to understand, as others could not, the absurdity at the heart of everything."[121] Bowie exploited this outsider status throughout his career, working within and without the mainstream, legitimizing strangeness for his fan base—encouraging them to look in the mirror and there find their own hero—not to follow or copy him. In the end, they were all loners, together.[122]

Even after the cutoff point of Ziggy's death, fans followed Bowie's switch to zoot suits as his hair turned from blood-red proto-mullet into a wedge of liquid flame: "Bowie lookalikes, self-consciously cool under gangster hats which concealed (at least until the doors were opened) hair rinsed a luminous vermilion, orange, or scarlet streaked with gold and silver" (Hebdige 1979). Where Bowie had begun with "turn and face the strange," as a call to arms, which, Peter Doggett noted, many of us heard as "trying to face the strain," these fans became their own super freaks, youth carrying their own weight where Bowie was to become the "patron saint of misfits"; his goal was to set others free in themselves as he had liberated himself (from the idea of "David Jones"). "His big thing was challenging people to explore to the full what they might be—I've done it, so now it's your turn!" (Fossett 2016).

Simon Critchley found that for many Bowie fans, his TV appearance singing "Starman" on *Top of the Pops* in 1972 was a defining moment: "It was this huge show, and there was this moment where he's got his arm draped around his guitarist's shoulders, and he's got this androgynous look. And he says, 'I had to phone someone/So I picked on you,' and he looks at the camera. And I thought, as a twelve-year-old, he was talking to me! To me—and just me." In this watershed performance, everyone felt—and felt they knew—that Bowie was speaking to, for, and with them; they were made to feel special: uniquely and strangely alive.[123]

At the other end of the song spectrum was the sing-along anti-ballad "Rock 'n' Roll Suicide," which ends both *Ziggy Stardust* and many of the live shows of that era. Its urgent and yearning line "Gimme your hands" is an on-record gesture that further transcends the physical but still manages a hair-raising sense of connection.[124] In Alan Bennett's play *The History Boys*, the wayward teacher, Hector, speaks to one lone student, standing in for the entire class, about the power of poetry as an incantation that manifests in the writing on the page; and from this, the creative "hand" of the author reaches out in communion with the reader toward a mutual feeling. So it could be with Bowie's most earnest songs. This experience also evokes the Jesus Christ Superstar element of the Ziggy character; those who would follow him feel blessed at (almost) touching the hem of his garment as he swept across the stage and offers the ritual of shared adoration.[125]

This sense of shared wonder and each person's possible explorations of brilliance was a collective sensibility within the "We" of Bowie fans. Bowie calls for his listener to "turn on with me," to wake up and not leave their life undone. Perhaps the greatest message in the song comes from the repeated refrain "You're not alone," reflecting the listeners back at themselves as they sang along and the words became their own. Being "drawn into an extraordinary intimacy of total fantasy," for Simon Critchley, it was a love story that lasted a lifetime and beyond.

Bowie would continue to struggle with the counterpoint of fame, trying so hard for so long to become a star and then shrinking back from that responsibility. The footage of him being bundled into cars mobbed by teenagers after gigs at the height of Ziggy mania was borrowed straight from the Beatles. It was the cursed inheritance of popularity, although it brought the stars their riches, as Bowie and Lennon would later lament as they struggled to buy personal space, anonymity, and privacy. "Fame" repeats its title as a hollow mantra. Bowie was dismissive of the short-lived pleasures of being recognized almost wherever he went: "Fame itself . . . doesn't really afford you anything more than a good seat in a restaurant."[126]

The alternative title for "Up the Hill Backwards," the sister song to "Scary Monsters," was "Cameras in Brooklyn." In the crowded streets, the citizen is both invisible and in each other's face; there is nowhere to truly hide but within ourselves. As Ziggy, David Bowie risked being overexposed as the negative to the high profile of alter ego, as Thomas Jerome Newton would be blinded by invisible light of X-rays, eclipsed by his human reputation on Earth. There is a sense in which Bowie, having his photo taken by strangers on the street, found a piece of his soul, sucked into an endless repetition of portraits and poses reprinted in glossy magazines, posters, and merchandise; cut out and glued into collage; and absorbed by palimpsest of tribute, all more images regurgitated back at him. Like stepping into the silhouette of Merrick facing his public, this was Bowie worn thin by lightbulb flashes, collapsing into shadow, of the echo chamber of seeing himself in the eyes of others. In the end, the camera was us.

By the time of *Scary Monsters*, Bowie was caught at the crossroads of a cliché—between reasserting his position in the musical world and trying to maintain a more normal, private life. Bowie fought to keep his fans at some distance, to "always leave them wanting more," but even fighting for that space was tiresome. Perhaps as a reaction to this, Bowie worked harder both to feed and to subvert their expectations; like the Beatles before him. In broadening his range, Bowie hoped that sections of his fan base would come with him, now moving further out toward the punk and New Wave–tinted, avant-garde pop direction of his new record in 1980.

> In a world full of danger, to be a potentially seeable
> object is to be constantly exposed to danger. Self-
> consciousness, then, may be the apprehensive
> awareness of oneself as potentially exposed to
> danger by the simple fact of being visible to others.
> The obvious defence against such a danger is to
> make oneself invisible in one way or another.
>
> —R. D. Laing, *The Divided Self: An Existential
> Study in Sanity and Madness*, 1960

"Scary Monsters" operates as something of a Pandora's box that, once opened, pulls both the girl and her tormentor into psychic excess. Bowie called the song a "piece of Londonism" compared to the slicker, more streetwise New York vibe of other songs from the album.

Bowie plays out the story like a police procedural, a secondhand account with no witnesses left alive, spinning the tale of a young woman, used and used up, in a twisted relationship of hipster meets hustler. The girl's partner, half psycho killer, part junkie pimp, thinks he loves her but his adoration spills over into exploitation, ruining her in the process. This reading destroys any possibility of making the relationship real; both are living a lie, bound together, and they head toward mutual self-destruction.

Bowie said it was the story of a "criminal with a conscience who talks about how he corrupted a fine young mind,"[127] an escape from reality into a hallucinogenic dreamworld. "Scary Monsters" works as a companion to what Carlos Alomar called the "neo-blues" of the 1977 track "Breaking Glass." In his book on *Low*, Hugo Wilcken hears a man turning his problems onto his partner; the "wonderful person" Bowie sings of becomes the scapegoat for the man's insecurities. Good times suddenly marred by serious emotional problems, he sees his own hot mess reflected back at him. In some respects, this was also Bowie at that time: damaged but high functioning and fighting for survival.

Back on "Scary Monsters," Bowie plays out the big, open vowels of a rough London accent with an "Orror of rooms" ending in "strange doors" (of perception) being kicked in. The girl's blue eyes, once full of light and life, now seem empty. Bowie finds the girl "stupid in the streets," wild in the city adrift in horrific visions of everyday cruelty everywhere she turns, pursued by the demons of the song's title. The world seems to close in around her, driven deeper into the labyrinth of her ruined mind. The hard-angled shifts of rhythm in the song make for sharp corners and throw dead ends in her path. Bowie points toward the untapped psychic potential in the derangement of the senses, where madness and drugs can deliver incredible but devastating insights, the irrational tipped into excess. Beyond the edge of sanity, there lies the tragic burnout who can no longer function in society—unable to find the door in the wall that lets them back in.

The collapse of a great mind was a continued inspiration for Bowie. Madman rocker Vince Taylor and the Legendary Stardust Cowboy were both models for Ziggy's rise and fall. Simon Critchley discusses the trajectory of "narrative identity," where we look for a Gravity's Rainbow-style arc of a bullet or rocket in flight: what goes up must come down. But what we get on *Scary Monsters* is a zigzagging path, strutting chaos about deviant authorities, Major Tom as infinite pinball machine. From this arrives the ultimate comedown, "an all-time low," where people fall apart, only realizing they have slipped through the cracks of society too late once the nightmare has become real.

Given the medical history of his half brother Terry Burns, Bowie would often voice concerns of schizophrenia running through his family history, telling *Interview* magazine, "I think there's an awful lot of emotional, spiritual mutilation goes on in my family." Simultaneously concerned that his celebrity might accelerate the process by which pop star egomania would slip into madness,[128] Bowie played with the term, referring to *Aladdin Sane* in the past tense, as a matter of loss each time he shed new skins: "That's why there were so many costume changes, because he had so many personalities." Elsewhere, Bowie claimed that becoming an artist was a way to vent his overgrown imagination, a way to dodge the family curse.[129]

In 1993, Bowie explained his concerns to the BBC: "One puts oneself through such psychological damage in trying to avoid the threat of insanity. You start to approach the very thing that you're scared of. It had tragically afflicted particularly my mother's side of the family. There seemed to be any number of people who had various mental problems and varying states of sanity. There were far too many suicides for my liking, and that was something I was terribly fearful of . . . I felt that I was the lucky one because I was an artist and it would never happen to me. As long as I could put these psychological excesses into my music and into my work, I could always be throwing it off."

The song "The Bewlay Brothers" seems sympathetic to Terry, an unwanted son who never did belong in the "Bowie family" home, later removed to Cane Hill Hospital. The song reverberates as a cry of solidarity for someone who by 1971 had long since slipped out of Bowie's life. Bowie would forever be looking back at him down a faceless corridor where the yearning for escape, to slip away, from both his incarceration and the internal prison of mental illness, would haunt his every step in a career born out of freedom. In the song, Bowie merged his own situation with Terry's, giving his inner voices of doubt and paranoia free rein, perhaps reflecting on the two paths taken.[130] There but for the grace of God (go I). Bowie saw his brother—himself—"so far gone," shadowing each other's lives: without Terry Burns, there would have been no "David Bowie."[131]

One of Bowie's chosen books was R. D. Laing's *The Divided Self* (1960). A rogue psychiatrist who thrived in the decade of cultural revolution, Laing argued that the mental health system of medication, incarceration, and traditional therapies was a form of abuse that reduced people to patients, seeking medical solutions to what were more common existential problems rooted in sociological causes, within a system of containment not unlike prison. Laing claimed that all people worked to maintain multiple selves, presented in different situations with certain people in our lives. When these aspects slipped out of balance, we might fall into psychosis, an unstable state of mind rooted in insecurity of the self, edging toward madness. Part of Laing's deep-listening therapeutic approach was to allow the (sometimes many) voices within his patients to speak and to be heard; this meant seeing their reality through their eyes to better understand the dynamic of their condition. This approach meant giving air and space to mental imbalances in order to better empathize with clients and eventually to manage their situation of mental ill-health rather than to punish them for it and discount their alternative reality. In "All the Madmen" from 1970's *The Man Who Sold the World*, Bowie sings how he would rather be with the insane people of the asylum than with the conformist drones of the outside world (O'Connell 2020). Laing took a wrecking ball to the illusion of the everyday person. The idea of "normal" itself was a controlling device that held people back from self-discovery and free expression, controversially overturning the institutional concept of madness.

In Bowie's music, fragmented voices often appear, sometimes as splintering perspectives contained in a single narrator. In the most striking reflective lyric of "Changes," Bowie tries to confront himself in the mirror, but in his turning, the chance of meeting the same person always seems to slip away. The breakdown of identity is revealed as its own aesthetic. Across his songs, Bowie allowed for nonsense rhyme and hip street slang, along with allusions to totemic writers and thinkers, to clash and combine interchangeably. This synthesis of elements gives way to the brittle syntax of "Ashes to Ashes" and the extended rant that closes "Bewlay Brothers" bridged at the broken lovers of "Scream Like a Baby." Under the surface of Bowie's songs, there is always the instinct of repressed derangement trying to contain itself, desperate to find a new language and make itself heard.[132]

The internal schism of dueling characters housed within the inauthentic self of "David Bowie" came to the fore in the songs where Bowie refused to flesh them out into completely rounded figures, instead teasing costumed aesthetics alongside lyrical and musical cues that revealed an incomplete portrait of their pathology. It was here that David Jones could offload his private neuroses in the open and introduce new ones in a deliberate act of fantastic mystification, all within the narrative lifeblood of the four-minute pop song.[133] Glenn Hendler also debates the idea of full-blooded personas in Bowie's work: they are merely aspects of a whole delivered in fleeting expressions of pure artifice.

Toward the end of "Scary Monsters," Bowie sings that he'll "love the little girl until the day she dies." He has already imagined her death as the music thunders toward its close. As the spirit of the song, it is the girl, not the singer, who must pay the price for the corrupted relationship. The narrator's pain comes from knowing he has caused her sad decline, and because he is tougher and more experienced, he will outlast her; she is survived only by his guilt. This is another example of the upside-down world that Bowie's songs of 1980 inhabit—he can see that everything is wrong but doesn't know how to make it right.

My role in society, or any artist's or poet's role,
is to try and express what we all feel. Not to
tell people how to feel. Not as a preacher, not
as a leader, but as a reflection of us all.

—John Lennon

On December 7, Bowie was interviewed by Andy Peebles in New York for
BBC Radio just the day before John Lennon was the guest on the show.
Broadcast in January 1981, Lennon had told Peebles the joys of living in
New York: "I can go out this door right now and go to a restaurant. Do you
want to know how great that is?" Having endured the intensity of Beatlema-
nia across the world and tired of bourgeois English attitudes and the racism
experienced by his wife Yoko Ono, New York gave Lennon a second chance
at an anonymous family life, as it would for Bowie.[134] Flâneur journalist Fran
Leibowitz spoke of being left alone in a city of millions; the few who stopped
walking in the busy flow of humming streets were tourists asking for directions, soon to be mowed down by the rush of human traffic. In Berlin, no one
recognized Bowie. In New York, no one even spoke to him; he was a ghost
in a city of lost souls.[135]

On December 8, Lennon would be murdered, shot five times outside
the Dakota Building by Mark Chapman just as he turned his head when
his name was called. Earlier that evening, Lennon was captured in a photo
signing an autograph for Chapman; a few hours later, around midnight, he
would return home, where Chapman would be waiting. His death cast shock
waves throughout the world, sparking a vigil of thousands of fans outside his
apartment and generating a media cycle that would last for weeks, rolling into
years of analysis and debate.

Bowie's deranged voice on "It's No Game (No. 1)" was an invitation to
violence: "put a bullet in my brain/and it makes all the papers." By December
1980, his words would seem eerily prophetic were it not for the painful cruelty
of coincidence.[136] As a commentary on the relentless trajectory of public interest and the media's need to capitalize on tragedy, the song has real force.[137]
The biggest news makes the biggest splash; a blur of blood and ink becomes
a feeding frenzy where the death of one celebrity—and later the infamy of his
killer—would always carry more weight than the murder of a nobody civilian, a
person reduced to a number and a name—turn the page and move on.[138]

The circumstances of Lennon's murder fulfill the cliché of lonerism,
with Mark Chapman as the outsider victim to *Catcher in the Rye* syndrome.
At the time of his arrest, he was clutching a copy of J. D. Salinger's classic

novel and an LP that Lennon had signed for him earlier that day.[139] A 1950s coming-of-age American classic that wrestles with a self-absorbed youth who feels he can be the "catcher" to rescue innocent children from running through the fields off a cliff—though he seems unable to help himself—would become a totemic symbol attached to many would-be American assassins. Chapman scapegoated the book as a fiction that he retreated into away from reality, disassociating himself from the crime and its true motive.[140] For the book's protagonist, Holden Caulfield, everyone else is a "phony"; by contrast, he is sincere looking for something real and authentic. This isolated stance reaps mental health struggles and reflects the lot of people forced into the margins of society toward deeper alienation; each time they are pushed out, they remove themselves further apart.

Chapman felt himself to be "different" in some way that explained his actions, affording him the label of a certain kind of monster, a result of the outpouring of love for the loss of a beloved former Beatle. Lennon's death became absorbed as a "cultural trauma" for which society at large was not willing to take any responsibility.[141] Chapman would employ the insanity defense to explain his actions as a direct result of mental illness, claiming that he was both a victim and a consequence of the public obsession with the famous, and with fame itself. The right-wing perspective simplified the idea of the dangerous loner, where people *in* trouble became people who *make* trouble; as both victims and perpetrators, they were damned both ways (Jenkins 2006).

Speaking years later from prison in an interview with Larry King, Chapman referred to himself in the third person to distance his current self from the other "evil" Mark Chapman, the nobody who sought to become notorious, as if killing Lennon, deposing another one of *Catcher*'s "phonies," in the public eye would raise him up in his stead. By this argument, the real monster was "fame," with Chapman in thrall to its all-pervasive influence. In the psychology book *Scary Monsters* (Duffett and Hackett 2021), the authors point out that Chapman made himself special, a "mental alien" existing outside of the parameters of humanity, when in fact the ability to commit murder is as human as life itself. Chapman hid behind this defense, exploiting his outcast status to separate himself from culpability for his crime.[142]

By clinging to the stereotype of a damaged and vulnerable person turned accidental killer, Chapman tarnished people suffering mental illness as loco wing nuts incapable of managing their own lives or making moral choices, pushing the outsider into the realm of the dangerous unknown, another "other" to be feared, institutionalized and reduced to the status of something less than human.

In the aftermath of the shooting, Bowie was distraught, Coco Schwab asked May Pang (a former girlfriend of Lennon's[143]) to come over to his apartment. She found him repeatedly screaming at the television: "What the fuck is going on in this world!" as he continued to watch the news coverage until dawn. In his frustration, we hear the angered voice of "It's No Game (No. 1)" finally breaking through the safety glass, forced to confront firsthand the tragic inheritance of twentieth-century American violence, now brought to bear in homes across the nation. Reflecting on the loss two years later, Bowie said, "A whole piece of my life seemed to have been taken away; a whole reason for being a singer and songwriter seemed to be removed from me. It was almost like a warning" (Trynka 2011).

Carlos Alomar recalls that Bowie was "destroyed" by Lennon's death, remembering it as a brutal time: "You must understand that David was living in New York with his son. He had just gotten to a great place in his life where he was coming back. He felt comfortable walking around the city. And then you find out that your friend, who also felt comfortable walking around, got shot—and you were supposed to be next?" (DeMain 2020).[144]

Incredibly, Bowie would continue his Broadway run of *The Elephant Man* until its end on January 4, 1981. All talks of discussion of a proposed tour in support of *Scary Monsters* went down the drain. Instead, Bowie entered a period of relative incubation, leaving New York for trips to Japan and his tax-exile retreat in Lausanne, Switzerland. He took a break from recording a new album, it is believed, in order to let his contract with RCA lapse and for the ten-year payment plan of royalties owed to MainMan to come to an end. In 2010, Bowie explained his decision to go underground: "I was second on his list. Chapman had a front-row ticket to *The Elephant Man* the next night. John and Yoko were supposed to sit front row for that show, too. So the night after John was killed, there were three empty seats in the front row. I can't tell you how difficult that was to go on. I almost didn't make it through the performance." Chapman had previously been seen photographing Bowie at the stage door of the Booth Theatre. In Chapman's hotel room, police found a program for the play with a black circle drawn around Bowie's name.[145]

> There was no emotion in my blood. There was no anger.
> There was nothing. It was dead silence in my brain. . . .
> I aimed at his back and pulled the trigger five
> times and all hell broke loose in my mind.
>
> —Mark Chapman, 1980

Bowie had begun "Scary Monsters" in flattened monotone, telling a grim story in the gloomiest corner of a deserted bar about the last time he jumped out of his skin, revving the engine trying to make the lights go green, throwing catcalls, shouting down his emotionally shattered partner, recalling bitterly how each time he snaps at her she breaks a little more. Bowie was giving us a knowing nod beyond the red-light district to the darker edges of town where curb-crawling men went to find prostitutes. This is the car-crash relationship of "Queen Bitch" translated into a long and smoky tale of "Old London Town," a wild ride gone farther off the rails and landing in the deep end of the city's subterranean side.

As Bowie was singing of dark motions and hidden motives, the "Yorkshire Ripper," Peter Sutcliffe, remained at large until he was finally arrested in January 1981 after killing thirteen women and casting terror across the north of England for more than a decade. Sutcliffe's brutal crimes sparked a militant feminist backlash comparable to Valerie Solanas's SCUM (Society for Cutting Up Men) manifesto, causing a virtual curfew that kept women indoors after dark. In the early 1970s, Sutcliffe began stalking the back streets of Bradford in his car before jumping out and attacking prostitutes and young women walking home with a brick or a hammer. Sutcliffe was representative of the popular opinion that sex workers and single, "loose" women were lesser people. Their lives were immoral; therefore they deserved their share of the blame for putting themselves in harm's way. Bowie's own psycho-delicate girl is both victim and transgressor of social mores, choosing to explore a darker path down which her trust is betrayed.

The madman bugging out at the wheel calls to Robert Fripp for the scream of guitar sound to become his own voice, invoking a solo as crooked flame for his damaged protagonist(s) to dance around—so brilliantly unhinged that it veers between the ridiculous and the sublime. Visconti remembers Fripp plugging directly into the mixing desk, capturing much of his playing the first time. There is something of the "Chuck Berry in hell" mood to Fripp's sound across the record, using a Fulltone OCD pedal to push his guitar into extreme tones; he called his playing on *Scary Monsters* "very out" with Bowie always pushing him further. Fripp's style seems a direct extension of his white-hot guitar solo that cuts, slashes, and thrusts at the molten core of "Baby's on Fire" from Brian Eno's first solo album, *Here Come the Warm Jets* (1973).

Placing "immediacy and honesty" above professional experience, Fripp notes that the greater the body of work guitar players have produced, the more easily they become trapped in their own styles. Known for his spontaneity, being able to think fast, and remaining sure-footed, Fripp noted a kindred sense of discipline and shrewd self-awareness in Bowie, each man knowing his limits and how to "cover his ass" without overextending his reach. *Rock and Roll Globe* labeled Fripp "a philosopher-King,"[146] the man and his music rich with contradictions and driven by unexpected shifts of direction. Fripp's performances seem only half conscious, supplanting ego to become the art of removing the player from his music. Bowie talked about trying to approach a song with fresh eyes, setting parameters within a few set chords and then watching the player follow their own broken rules. The chorus gets stuck in repetition as Bowie's double-tracked vocals chant the title line, a warped spirit, trying to outrun their own fear.

Echoing the earlier "Orror of rooms" line, the song ends with a gloriously unhinged cry that Bowie shifts from long sustained notes sawing through "Oh, O-oh" before jumping in pitch to continue the heavy vowel sounds of an Oulipo poetry cry of "O-o, O-o, O-o." The massing volume of Bowie's yelps rises above the music as the drums stomp all over the melody.[147] It becomes a dark cheerleading chant, Bowie reaching the full breadth of his vocal range between deep gut and high wailing, stretching into self-parody.

This marks one of the album's many punching-the-air moments where, out of character with his usual restraint, Bowie's voice is equal parts deranged and ecstatic, thrown down stairwells, trapped in a box, coiled in its springs to suddenly reveal a severed head bearing a rictus grin. In a blood rush of confusion and misdirected rage, Bowie begins his hyperventilated barking, returning us to the realm of the Diamond Dogs, no longer howling and carousing in youthful ecstasy; fear is closing in, the raw edge of its teeth held in a mouthful of shadow. It is the monster that thrives in the darkness that always finds you out. On *Scary Monsters*, the last echoes of barking ring off the walls—it becomes the sound she can't escape, the noise inside your head.

> Well he was highly intelligent.
> He had an acute sensibility;
> and worst for him,
> a romantic imagination.

—Dr. William Treves, *The Elephant Man*

Fragment #79

Nobody's Dangerous Eyes

stole the jealousies
Keep hide creeps
all I could've been
super beat wails blue
Oh monsters walk
and freaky people talk talk

Scary for do I
in my sacred ask
What they want
keeps us waiting

In light were rooms
I keep monsters
Shadow streets
That She can't
Had proper horrors
Turned freak at the scream

Scary for do I
in my sacred ask
What they want
keeps us waiting

Jimmy's home
super me running
Didn't know running
light opened dies
How it creeps
jealousies close
Both super scared
stupid double me

Keep in mind
she's monsters
Strange beat stay
means nobody
running anymore

Scary for do I
in my sacred ask
What they want
keeps us waiting

—Generated courtesy of the Lazarus Corporation

Ashes to Ashes

(People Are Turning to Gold)

. . . because there comes a point where greed and madness can no longer be told apart. This dividing line is very thin, just like a belt of film surrounding the earth's sphere. It's a delicate blue, and this transition from the blue to the black is very gradual and lovely.

—Jonathan Coe, *What a Carve Up!*

A series of watery notes, the breath of tides, and grinding guitar chords, like waking up within a dream, a high-fluted voice calls out to us across the waves, at once far away and very close, speaking into the ear: "Do you remember . . . ."

On first listen, "Ashes to Ashes" is a song born of nonsense; deliberately obfuscating, it pushes the listener away, evoking a gloomy neon world out of place and time. The ethereal ping-ponging bounce of the wavy piano and seasick organ dance above the heavier instruments, cut through with jagged guitar chords scything down the fretboard like a slap in the face, punctuated by stabs of bass. "Ashes" soon reveals its confidence in Bowie's great strides of yearning falsetto, which pitch backward and forward around a deadpan monotone, where Bowie remains uniquely English but manages to make himself sound alien within his native tongue.[148] With his vocals climbing toward the pre-chorus crescendo, a guitar chord strikes through the haze, and we are arrested by Bowie's call for salvation.

The piano line at heart of the song is played by Roy Bittan, mainstay of Bruce Springteen's E Street Band.[149] He was roped into sessions for the album after a chance meeting between the players in the Power Station studio cafeteria. Bowie had last worked with Bittan on *Station to Station*, providing a melodic backbone through the album; Bittan later said it was one of his favorite records he has worked on. The melody line of the piano is in 4/4 time, but each time the chords change on the three beat, they land out of phase with the rest of the song's chord cycles while staying in key.[150] We never quite know where we are in the song; like a Steve Reich phasing experiment, the mood is constantly shifting beneath the surface like water.[151] Bittan's playing provides the major melody of shimmering notes over the top of the song's intro and outro chord progressions. Aiming for the sound of a stereo Wurlitzer organ, Visconti deployed an instant flanger on a regular grand piano that created a vibrant shaking sound, the fairground atmosphere's bright lights and carousel horses giving joy smeared and twisted into a circular blur. Instead of relying on an electric keyboard or synthesizer patch, they managed to create an entirely original and iconic sound, exploiting the technology in a way that it was never meant to be used.

There are an unusual number of shifting phrases and subtle key changes—modulating between A minor, G major, C major, and A major—there is a circular motion in the chord progression, lyrical shapes, which shape the song. In the final recording, everything seems shifted up a semitone, possibly sped up, nudging the song into a higher pitch, making it sound slightly off kilter to the ear (Perone 2007).[152] "Ashes" is technically challenging, working from Bowie's unconventional approach to crafting songs in fragmented parts that either make unexpected chord changes or shift key; what should throw the listener off draws them further in. Dennis Davis, the jazz expert marshaled into rock music, brings the backbeat in early, giving a tripping, destabilized symmetry to the song—a pop hit that is hard to dance to (Kardos 2022). Bowie explained the beat for Davis by tapping it out on a box for him to learn overnight. Bowie praised the drummer's self-discipline to *not* play a beat when it was expected, to leave spaces between hits and let a song's rhythm breathe. The drum pattern of "Ashes to Ashes" sometimes shuffles into a reggae lope with a ska snap; the music writer Steve Tupai Francis notes that it bears a marked similarity to the playing of Madness drummer Woody Woodgate on their song "My Girl." Woody later said, "It kind of inflated my ego and pissed me off at the same time. I thought, 'David Bowie could have fucking asked me!'"

The great strength of "Ashes" lies in the depth of its emotional address masquerading as simplicity; the more we hear, the more layers are revealed before the song is fully wound up at just over four minutes. Except for the long instrumental outro, which was cut from the single edit, like all the greatest pop music the song seems to be over almost as quickly as it began. Bowie uses the track as a vehicle to reach far back into childhood concerns that still influence adult life, the present still tinged with ghostly nostalgia. Lines cut across in mental static, erupting in volume or shift into mumbling as if "one radio station is breaking into another's airspace." Another reading of this suggests Bowie in conflict with internal voices struggling to fix onto one pure thought that is entirely his own (O'Leary 2017).

"Ashes" offers us a reunion with Major Tom, at first not by name but as the guy "in such an early song." The conscious nod to "Space Oddity" brings a host of Bowie's demons home to roost: "At the time, Major Tom was the ideal of what I wanted to be, but an antihero, an aspect of the American dream that took off at that time but got lost along the way." Bowie would explain how this impetus grew from his own naïveté: "When I originally wrote about Major Tom, I was a very pragmatic and self-opinionated lad that thought I knew all about the great American Dream and where it started and where it should stop." With "Ashes to Ashes" the earnest wondering of Bowie's younger self would finally be resolved.

Major Tom was still an evocative figure in the collective memory of fans and casual listeners alike. Bowie remembered that "people had a lot of empathy with him." "Space Oddity" marked Bowie's first brush with fame, a bright and brief moment, burning with possibility; in an alternative reality, he might have disappeared as a one-hit wonder. Looking back from 1980, Bowie briefly resurrected Major Tom, Lazarus-like, only to cast him down again.[153] In the intervening years, Tom had stayed more or less where we left him—floating about with Earth still just out of reach—his failed quest now becomes the song of a drunken boat at odds with the sea. Tom's separation from the human race and his native planet heightened Bowie's position of being an alien accidentally born on the wrong planet, a native extraterrestrial. When Bowie passed in 2016, a popular meme emerged that in death he had simply returned to space from where he first came, his music a spark in the eye of every listener echoing the passage of a star still visible light-years after it has already burned out and disappeared.

"Ashes" has the effect of shocking Bowie out of paralysis; arriving at the heart of a ghost song, we are confronted with the "what if" of the empty period following recovery from addiction. The writer Tom Ewing argued for a half-life state: "This isn't spectral pop, it's zombie pop, shambling and corpse-cold." He hears only burnout resignation in the flattened, "woah-ah-oah" of the backing lines; having lived too much, too soon, Bowie fears himself joining the ranks of the living dead. The herald of the future crash-lands into the warped, timeless present of a Victorian nursery rhyme with all its submerged horror, which Bowie playfully remembered as songs about children having their ears cut off. "Ashes to Ashes" borrows from various aspects of Euro-surrealism and gothic whimsy of the Victorian era, such as *Alice in Wonderland*.[154] Bowie would look back to older songs passed down through generations, where to remember their words was to inhabit the fears of the past. Bowie's childish intonations feed back into the hysteria of *Scary Monsters*, cycling around to a continued sense of threat; "Ring a Ring o' Roses," for example, would have children dancing in an almost pagan gesture of a circle, thought to evoke the round, spotted lesions of the bubonic plague that appeared on the skin before everyone drops down dead:

> Ring a ring o' roses,
> A pocket full of posies,
> A-tishoo! A-tishoo!/Ashes, ashes
> We all fall down.

Bowie exploits singsong vocal patterns of rhyming verse to add hooks throughout the chorus melody. This sense of swing is set against the harder-edged broken lines of the verse, where jarring ideas and fractured grammar achieve a kind of synthesis that doesn't always flow along with a common-sense reading but generates new juxtapositions of meaning, like the impressionistic, stream-of-consciousness rants that open the *"Heroes"* album. The offbeat melodrama of "Ashes" and the queasiness of the track, along with its cutout video, expose an unreliable reality glimpsed through a fun-house mirror, blurring toxic derangement with mental dissociation. Bowie noted that the mood and melodic tone behind "Ashes to Ashes" wouldn't have happened without the children's song "Inchworm": "Inchworm is my childhood. I loved it as a kid and it's stayed with me forever. . . . There's a nursery rhyme element in it, and there's something so sad and mournful and poignant, it kept bringing me back to the feelings of those pure thoughts of sadness that you have as a child, and how they're so identifiable even when you're an adult" (DeMain 2020). It was one of the first songs that Bowie would learn the chords to on guitar when he was just seven or eight.[155]

Many would note the song's melodic strength between the main lyric and the backing counterpoint of children learning to count by rote, with the word stresses falling away at the end of each line, a tonal structure that Bowie himself uses almost verbatim—"*ash*-es," "*fun*-ky," and "*jun*-ky"; although still turbulent, the verse lyric offers warmer, vocal performances.[156] The song's carpe diem message focuses on the inchworm too, busy measuring out life in tiny pieces rather than stopping to 'smell the roses' and appreciate the marigolds for their beauty alone, rather than as "things" in the world to be counted up or accumulated.[157]

In a 2003 *Q* magazine interview, Bowie continued a common thread of reflection on his past, noting that songs like "Inchworm" provided some warmth for children like Bowie, who grew up in the cold-straitened, stiff postwar Britain of not many hugs and emotionally closed-off parents: "Inchworm gave me comfort and the person singing it sounded like he'd been hurt too. And I'm into that, the artist singing away his pain." Bowie would nod back to "Inchworm" as a pervasive feeling that seems to predict the melancholy of his own early song "Tired of My Life": "There's a connection that can be made between being a somewhat lost five-year-old and feeling a little abandoned and having the same feeling when you're in your 20s. And it was that song that did that for me."

"Ashes" evokes something of Bowie's estrangement from his mother, a quietly critical and often distant presence compared to the encouragement offered by his dad.[158] When questioned about his mother in the 1970s, Bowie would often go mute and ask that his privacy be respected. Although "Ashes" seems to directly address his own mother figure as an inner critic with almost Freudian intensity, Bowie also worked strongly in Jungian archetypes, where the idea of a song might offer some kind of symbolic protection against the fears it expresses. Bowie spoke of the song as Major Tom's desire to return to Mother Earth as the womb, the original state of life. Bowie admitted that this vision started and ended bleakly in decay, a perpetual state of cultural and physical atrophy. In the video, we see Bowie confined in a padded cell and captive as alien surrogate host, growing out of the wall; alongside the mother on the beach, it is hard not to read this cycle of birth-unto-death throughout the song.[159]

The hand-drawn storyboard Bowie sketched for the video showed the clown with his arm caringly placed around the mother figure, consoling her, whereas in the final video, we see the mother both remonstrating and pleading with Bowie-as-Pierrot, no doubt setting him straight against drugs and the fallout of his continued addiction.[160] Pierrot walks with head held high, looking off to sea, seemingly unaware of her presence, somnambulant, and removed.[161] These visions reach out from Bowie's past to the back-cover artwork designed by the artist George Underwood for 1969's *David Bowie/ Space Oddity* album, a vehicle for the hit single. Underwood's imagery is more or less identical to the mother figure format of the "Ashes" video, created more than ten years earlier, but with Pierrot as a kinder presence toward the elderly woman.[162] This was a prime example of Bowie expressing the germ of an idea and giving his collaborator free rein to realize a new vision while his original thought was still fresh, inchoate, and yet to find its final shape. George Underwood remembered, "It was fascinating when I heard that song for the first time and saw its video. I thought, 'Bloody hell, all these references!' I drew that Pierrot with the woman, for the back of the *Space Oddity* cover—and there it was again in three dimensions. Everything that you see on that back cover, all my work there, was in service of David's ideas."

Elsewhere, Bowie spoke about his own nameless "midwives of history," a lyric from "Teenage Wildlife," people of influence with blood on their hands: "For the sake of the song, they're symbolic; they're the ones who would not have you be fulfilled." Into this, we can read several key women in Bowie's life: his mother, Angie Bowie, Coco Schwab, and others not female, people who at different times managed, steered, and controlled his life and career, for good or ill, but had a defining influence over Bowie, though it might pain him to admit it.[163]

Alongside the autobiographical portrait(s) that emerged, what made "Ashes" stand out was its blend of experimental sounds and songwriting craft. To stand alongside (and against) the altered states of Roy Bittan's piano, Bowie recruited pioneering guitar-synth player Chuck Hammer after Bowie got into a fistfight with Lou Reed in late 1979.[164] In a *Guitar Player* interview in 2016, Hammer recalls, "I met David Bowie in October 1979, while on tour with Lou Reed in London. During that tour, I was using a 1977 Roland GR-500 guitar synth as my main instrument. David attended one of Lou's concerts at the Hammersmith Odeon and expressed interest in working together. Soon after meeting David, I sent him a cassette with four experimental Guitarchitecture tracks." What made the guitar-synth different—and notoriously difficult to play—was its huge sustain. As the individual frets were electronically grounded, whenever Hammer pressed a note on the neck, it would create a feedback loop of recurring sound like overlapping waves: "As a guitarist, this really forced me to rethink and modify my technique—making me think more as a composer in terms of layers and stacking textures rather than linear lines."

Hammer entered the studio to find Bowie sporting a mustache dressed in a full-length leather coat with open-toed Japanese sandals, wearing a big wooden cross around his neck. Drinking a quart of milk in one hand and holding a clipboard in the other (DeMain 2020), Bowie greeted him warmly: "Chuck, how nice to see you again. Your tape is all I listen to." On his ever-present clipboard, Bowie would methodically tick off recorded items throughout the sessions, the band keeping strict and regimented business hours, working 11 a.m. until 7 p.m. It is perhaps this ruthless efficiency that saw the core group of the DAM Trio lay down the album in just a few weeks, which also bought Bowie more time to add individual overdubs: "It was the first one where we had the luxury of time on our side. We only signed-off on it when we felt it was absolutely finished" (Visconti 2007).

For Chuck, *Scary Monsters* was an organic continuation of Bowie's most avant-garde music with the singer keen to explore the potential of Hammer's relatively new instrument: "Bowie had a deep interest in new sonic terrains and experimental guitar textures. He also had a keen understanding of how these tones could work within the wider context of his own music. One of the key insights I gained from working with Bowie was to always follow your own instincts. I wasn't thinking about music, I was thinking about 'Subterraneans' [from *Low*], a long sculpted piece. I was trying to take it past the trilogy—where Eno had left off."

Hammer applied an orchestral synth patch for his playing on "Ashes to Ashes"; you can hear the grand swells of sound throughout the song, layering takes of chord inversions, moving the same shapes along the fretboard and changing effects slightly for each pass. Visconti added presence to the recording by placing Hammer's amp just outside the doorway of a second-floor control room, setting up microphones on both bottom and top landings of a nearby stairwell and adding reverb and density to the sound. In comparison to Fripp's extreme guitar tones shifting between briefly ambient phases and high-octane, autodestructive soloing, Hammer was shaping more fluid bends and waves of sound—a choir of musical voices merged toward a cathedral-scale ambience.[165] This atmospheric style carries as much of Eno's signature patience as the more intense white noise on *Station to Station*; the great curve of guitar feedback that opens the album has Bowie exploring "sound as texture, rather than sound as music" (Cameron Crowe, *Playboy* interview with Bowie, 1976).

Tony Visconti's 2016 remaster of *Scary Monsters* reveals more differentiation among the layers of "Ashes," with individual players showcased in the rising and falling levels, from needling high guitar synth to sweeping washes of synthesizer. Visconti said, "It is dense. Not so much the amount of instruments, but everybody was playing complicated parts." The richness of musical textures allowed Bowie, the band, and Visconti to produce an iconic record with an influence that resonated throughout the decade, when producers such as Trevor Horn later beefed up songs such as Frankie Goes to Hollywood's "Relax" to the extent that it was almost impossible to reproduce live without backing tracks. This would become a new battleground moving away from original, clean-playing four-piece bands to ensemble instrumentation, sparking debate, and later the 1990s backlash between synthesized and "authentic" music, setting futurism and tradition at odds with one another.[166]

Bowie would remain divided between applications of studio editing and the impact of technology on the wider world. He was ever labeled the star man, his songs never set out to predict the future—they deconstructed its trajectory ahead of time. The trappings of the science fiction genre's psychopathology served only to enrich his visions with more exotic imagery; he questioned and interrogated the mass consumption of technology far more than he respected it. Although he would be quick to engage with new media, such as the internet, in a 1980 interview with Kurt Loder for *Rolling Stone*,[167] Bowie was in strict doomsday warning mode: "Forget your high-tech. We're not gonna be prancing around in silver suits or anything like that. It's all blood and guts from here on out." The world would grow colder on the turn of humanity's coin, not the other way around.[168]

He noted the cruel joke of "Space Oddity" and Major Tom's proximity to the moon landing as the space race became the new measure of strength among the growing inertia of Cold War saber-rattling. "Ashes to Ashes" explored the aftermath of this situation, "the complete dissolution [of] the great dream" of space travel. Once he had arrived at his distant orbit, Tom begins to question the entire journey, unsure of what he was doing floating out there. Michael Bracewell (1997) sees the astronaut beginning as a heroic figure meeting his own existential crisis, "drifting away from the applause of a nervous nation" as he comes to realize that he is reduced to the status of a "quasi-corporate pioneer."

Major Tom is mocked by Bowie as another "Action Man,"[169] a plastic hero trapped in his tin can, shifting cosmic wonder into childlike terms: the man and his spaceship are toyish and synthetic; we feel the hollowness of his dream ring out. The original emphasis of "Space Oddity" was to chart the imaginative potential of outer space; instead, Bowie brought the phallic technocracy crashing back down to earth. Bowie saw this same ruthless spirit brought to its peak in Thomas Jerome Newton, the pure alien corrupted by human behaviors. For Bowie, Newton possessed his own innate "hi-tech emotional drive. He discards people and their values all the time." In essence, technology provides its own short circuit to emotional frigidity, killing off empathy in favor of achieving defined results at any cost.

Tom is perhaps the victim of the accumulation-driven culture that would inevitably overtake him. As Bowie described it, "Here we had the great blast of American technological know-how shoving this guy up into space and once he gets there he's not quite sure why he's there. And that's where I left him." Tin can, tin machine, silver bullet—shot into a loveless and chaotic universe, reaching Icarus-like for the stars, but for Bowie, ideological malaise was the true source of inner rot: "The whole process that got him up there had decayed, was born out of decay; it has decayed him and he's in the process of decaying. But he wishes to return to the nice, round womb, the earth, from whence he started." His dream of rebirth becomes a "cease to exist" motion, to return to a pre-death of nothingness, swallowed up by his own emptiness. Bowie allows for several vocal pauses to punctuate the song with moments of breathing space, the sensation of being suspended apart from gravity, trapped by the inner reality of personal troubles—a kind of purgatory (Tanaka 2021). The pun of *Low* and its non-profile has come to pass; Major Tom has reached the "all-time low" and is forgotten, his body a corporeal relic of his own (past) life.

This is the angel Lazarus arrived at post-death, with one foot in either world. This goes deeper when we consider Tom lamenting that he has lost his money and his hair, as Bowie would sing of self-abnegation on the *Blackstar* track "Lazarus." A wasted man having used up all of his wealth and suffering a breakdown in New York, he drops his cell phone and watches it sink away from a great height. In reality, Bowie would grow increasingly rich, keeping his hair and good looks well into his sixties, though he remained aware that things might have turned out very differently. As with "Ashes" and "Jump They Say," physical and spiritual collapse is framed by the image of falling hard or drifting away, to a depth of no return. "Lazarus" feeds on the decline of Thomas Jerome Newton and the legend of Icarus, as noted by writers like Leah Kardos, a recurring dark energy that Bowie would continue to channel back into his creative projects.[170]

With ten years gone, the experience of "Space Oddity" has soured. Earth is diminished to a blue dot, as insignificant as Major Tom's space capsule, mirroring his isolation and creeping inertia; he can't go home, he can't stay up in space—he is nowhere. Bowie would reduce the whole mission to a failed attempt at space colonialism, sending men to plant a flag on a dead planet before someone else does. As explained to Andy Peebles in 1980, he blamed "the technological ego that got him up there."[171]

With the fall from grace of the Skylab station in 1979, America would continue to see the dark side of space travel and domination exposed in a harsh light. President Reagan's ludicrously expensive "Star Wars" antinuclear defense program and the explosion of the space shuttle *Challenger* after liftoff in 1986, killing the entire crew, further rocked America's sense of security and tested the faith of believers in the financial and human cost of the space program. Bowie's emotional concerns on "Ashes" would manifest his deeper consideration of issues related to the technocratic progress of society, with human minds and bodies being corrupted by their own inventions: "Things have moved along at a speed that we don't understand, nor can control, because our emotional and spiritual sides are so far behind our abilities to manufacture stuff" (DeMain 2003).

The forced perspective of the song presents psychic destruction steeped in a melancholy twilight. Bowie finds that the "planet is glowing" a ghostly echo reaching back to "Space Oddity" and its double meaning that planet Earth is "blue," swapping one numb state for a deep, dark note.[172] The jaded detachment is there in the vocals as Bowie drifts off, elongating "glow" into "-owing -owing -owing" in shimmers of galactic radiation passing through the redshift phase, but also suggesting the drawn-out "low/below/hello, ello, ello" vocal sounds, layered in effects. It is the sound of good-bye as a greeting—the studio's echo delay stretches the words as Bowie repeats them, to himself, another Oulipo mantra for time lost to harsh awakenings. What might be a false planet, like the stormy surface of emotions and lost souls in the film *Solaris* (1972), is revealed as a sea of infinite blue reflected in Tom's eye, passing over the lingering nothing of the iris—dilated into a sinking black hole or shrunken to a piercing needle point—swallowing up the last rays of searing and brilliant light.

Bowie frames his struggle in terms of finding "solace in some kind of heroin-type drug, the cosmic space itself is feeding him an addiction" (Peebles 1981). In Bowie's lyric notes for "Ashes," he swaps the line "little green dealer" for "little green wheels," writing with a sense of powerlessness that they are "rolling me," though in the final song lyrics. They are following after him. One reading suggests that Bowie was referring to the endless wedges of dollar bills needed to buy more cocaine, gradually picked apart and rolled up to snort it, like peeling off calendar days; he is both himself and being carried away from his real self by altered states.[173] It is believed that Bowie would later have cartilage removed from his body to repair a hole inside his nose caused

ACROBATE ET JEUNE ARLEQUIN — 1905

Acrobat and young harlequin — age reflected in youth

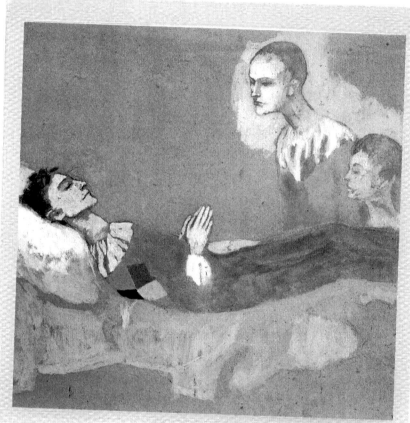

LA MORT D'ARLEQUIN — 1906

Death of a Clown

by the corrosive cocaine powder, reminding us of his comment that "one day I blew my nose and half my brains came out." The physical and mental scars of Bowie's pain were often concealed, but his pain was his own and remained very real.

Tony Parsons noted that in spite of Bowie's chemical dependency, the intensely human love songs of *Station to Station* were delivered with much passion and commitment. He listened to Bowie grow increasingly cold as he entered the *Low* phase and "subtracted rock music" to become the "music of exhaustion." The line of being strung out like a man under the ether of the stars, "heaven's high" could just as easily be phrased as "heaven's sigh," an eternal shrug that will outlive us. Critchley hears Bowie's nod to post-drug depression in the "all-time low," seasick with the emotional gravity. By the time of "Ashes," there was the desperate call for an axe to break the chill inside of himself (when on drugs, Bowie used to describe himself as "the ice-man cometh"), crystallizing his deeper sense of alienation: "Bowie's pop was always strongest when it was just him in his hall of mirrors," a confrontation with the self, beneath the struggle to maintain some kind of continued masquerade of the persona (Ewing 2008).

Bowie once claimed to have found a "soulmate" in cocaine, getting stuck and hung up on his "valuable friend," preferring a fast drug that could at least keep him going rather than slow him down—if he was going to be high, he would at least use that energy to work on new ideas. He uses junk-sick terminology to show the aftermath and lays out the tragic distance between the immediate desire to kick drugs and the efforts needed to stay clean, a feeling that with each lapse seems to slip further out of reach. Bowie spoke of his mid-1970s time in Los Angeles as a "scary" slow bleed into self-destruction: "I was several times close to overdosing; attracting some heavy people and situations; I slept with a gun under my pillow" (Bell 2017). Bowie's dark days followed him to the Isolar tour weaning himself off cocaine with brandy; alcohol later became the crutch Bowie dragged with him on tour across France and then to Berlin.[174] Friends remember several nights of Bowie winding up in a Berlin gutter from drinking too much pilsner, still smoking forty Gitanes cigarettes a day, dabbling in cocaine—it was a longer, slower recovery process as echoed in the deflated line from *"Heroes," *"I'll drink all the time." Between binging and purging, some mornings Bowie would survive on a single raw egg cracked straight into the mouth alongside Brian Eno.[175]

Bowie claimed not to remember the specifics of the Los Angeles years, particularly the recording of *Station to Station*. The black hole of his expressionist aesthetic carried over into real life, a void from which great music emerged; the record was happening to him, as if he was never there. By 1997, it was an outdated mode that Bowie was keen to break out of: "I was infuriated that one's still stuck in rock and roll and sucked right onto the center of it," he told *Melody Maker*.

Edward Bell remembers visiting the Blitz club in 1980 with Bowie to scout for the "Ashes" video and repeatedly being offered "any drug under the sun that could be procured should he desire it." Every time, Bowie responded with a curt and clipped "fuck off" (Bell 2017). The "junkie" reputation preceded him; for some, he remained the drug-outlaw artist, like the dark sun of William S. Burroughs, his air of mystique sucking the light out of the room.[176] Even then, Bowie's recovery in 1980 was still ongoing, precarious. Bell found his manner "brittle"; fearing relapse, he fought to maintain his balance.

The bleak emptiness that addiction forces us to inhabit continued to stalk Bowie in his music and is painfully dredged up in "Ashes." Wandering about on broken glass of painful memories, he revisits long and lonely days: "The shrieking of nothing is killing [me]." What is this persistent "nothing": the echo of a psychic wound? The lyric resonates with the tagline for 1979's *Alien*—"In space no one can hear you scream"—where alienation becomes its own kind of desert, an abyss that stares back at you. Again, even Bowie's laconic moments speak volumes; in what is otherwise a taut tune, lurching and tripping into semiconsciousness, Major Tom is jarred out of his isolated reverie by the hollow ringing of his own voice.

The illusion of emptiness is present in Bowie's use of "nothing" throughout the song and elsewhere on *Scary Monsters*. In one verse, "shrieking/nothing/killing" chime together, leaning heavy on the hard "K," sound, before the punctuated "U" vowels of "funk/funky/junkie" dominate the chorus. The subject of this "nothing" is implied only as the line seems to trail off. The assumed "I" of the song, Major Tom, is absent from Bowie's handwritten lyrics, a ghost figure come back to life once when Bowie sings his name. Though when the signifier "me" appears in the official liner notes, we can see Tom and Bowie together, sharing their fate. In this, the song leaves no great mystery, where letting the line ending hang loose is a typically vague allusion used across the album.

Bowie's use of "nothing" in "Ashes" also calls back to 1977's "Heroes," where Bowie cries, "Nothing will help us," his strained vocal carrying a split meaning: "there *is* nothing that can help us," and "*nothing* is what will help us." Jun Tanaka connects this to the rhetorical device known as the "paradox of nothing." In Wallace Stevens's 1921 poem "The Snow Man," the verses end with a bleak vision that also implies freedom: at once both snowblind and lost, we ground ourselves within the storm:

> For the listener,
> who listens in the snow,
> And, nothing himself, beholds
> Nothing that is not there and the nothing that is.[177]

On Radiohead's song "Packt Like Sardines in a Crushd Tin Box," (2001) Thom Yorke offers the smirking line: "after years of waiting/nothing came." He makes a similar point where nothing is also something; it becomes present in the absences we feel, where experiences of loss leave behind them a deafening silence.[178] Bowie's "nothing" echoes his frequent use of alienation and isolation as necessary themes in his songs; from the loneliness of a room crowded with strangers, exacerbated by the highs and lows of cocaine, it is a troubling place to occupy for too long.[179] Elsewhere, Bowie referred to the celebrity's curse of being unable to escape the hell of other people—"what happens when a rock star gets surrounded by that particular killing kind of sycophancy"—the way he was in Los Angeles (Burn 1980). Slow death by false friendship and the need to maintain the constant "up" of drug abuse meant wrestling with two sides of fame.[180]

But what seems like terminal finality is extended into the next line, which alludes to pictures of "Jap girls," perhaps as pinups or featured on postcards of an exotic dreamland (the mythic "Orient" of East Asia) reaching toward some point of synthesis (but with what?), a westernized ideal, or getting lost in the clash of cultures whose ways of life are lost in translation.[181] The line seems casually nihilistic: its own play on the language of casual racism or outsider ignorance, a subconscious colonial divide that has stricken America and Europe for hundreds of years, reaching toward blind assimilation where East meets West, trading non–Judeo-Christian spirituality or leftist ideology for capitalism and social democracy.[182]

As a child, Bowie looked to the United States and rock-and-roll music as embodiments of the glorious West. Then, in the 1960s, Bowie found Eastern mysticism and reached toward his own interpretation of Buddhism. On a more artistic level, he entered into a prolonged cultural struggle with Western white Christian dogma, rejecting the standardized traditions of rock music that he had both parodied and revolutionized with the gender-queer alien on Earth of Ziggy Stardust. He would later fall in love with Japan in the 1970s, an era when the country began to rapidly modernize its cities away from the industrial age toward the technological future, where the discipline of Japanese business culture's quality and efficiency would far outstrip the U.S. naive pursuit of low-quality, mass-quantity production. Japan began to slip toward the modern Western ideals of progressive accelerationism, adding further tension to advances outside of the U.S.–Soviet space race. Elsewhere,

Japan would semi-nostalgically embrace traditional American rock and roll, creating its own copycat bands and tribute acts, an East Asian interpretation of Western art; at the same time, others resisted what they saw as foreign cultural influence, prompting a staunchly anti-American backlash.[183] Bowie admired the Japanese relationship to technology as a leader in electronics that nonetheless aimed to keep such devices only as a means to smooth out daily human life; the Japanese sought to maintain formal traditions of mutual respect and the preservation of natural space and ecosystems.[184]

Angus MacKinnon (1980) pointed out to Bowie the cliché of admiring their own imagined cultural character of the exotic East, a romantic allure to dabble and experiment with. Bowie acknowledged the paradigm of the alien in *The Man Who Fell to Earth*, and the "'spaceman'" factor with which Westerners would sometimes view people from East Asia as an archetype of terrestrial strangeness. But he was quick to reject the suggestion that in absorbing and adapting foreign influences, he was taking something away from them: "I don't think that by taking a Japanese or an African emblem or motif I try to represent them at all. I would have thought it was pretty transparent that it was me trying to relate to that particular culture." On *Scary Monsters*, Bowie is highlighting the alienating power of cultural friction and the risks of idealizing the unknown as a way to contain it, to make it safe, and to make it comprehensible, all within the difficult process of synthesis.

Chuck Hammer's guitar synth comes as an instrumental reprieve toward the close of "Ashes," breaking in like a new dawn as Bowie calls out, "I've never done good things." Tony Visconti (2007) described it as a "glorious warm choir sound" marking Bowie's great reveal of inner doubt. Hammer praised the visceral realness of the album's analog tape recording system for the rich, layered sound of his overdubs.

Bowie's cathartic expression wipes away the inner tension of hard extremes; good and bad things merge into a new gray area of the more complex cut-and-thrust of the (post-)modern world, as he tries to ditch the straitjacket legacy thrust on him. His music, as it was, was all he intended to express, with as much artifice and spontaneity as the experiment required; nothing more or less was "out of the blue." In a 2002 interview, Bowie said he always knew where he wanted to go with his music but not necessarily in his life, a feeling that was already present back in 1980: "I've a lot of reservations about what I've done. I don't feel that many of the things I've done have any import to them." Speaking to Angus MacKinnon, he admitted that on other days, certain songs were very important to him; again, Bowie happily carved himself up in contradiction. It became clear that the leading edge of his musical intuition thrived on decisive "uncertainty."

When Sir Tim Rice asked Bowie in 1980 what he was most proud of in his twelve years "at the top," Bowie deflected the question—"proud" was too egotistical a word. As a working artist, he felt the need for constant reevaluation. There was no time for looking back unless to plunder or revisit material. That is, to recycle and refashion, it was much easier for him to say what areas of his work he disliked.[185] Bowie professed that he thought his older songs were well written, that he liked them, but he never found them to be anything extraordinary. Like him, they were simply different from the norm and just happened to stand out at the time.[186]

Bowie seemed keen to shoot down the feted position of the rock star, certainly in the post-punk era, where the older gods of his generation shrank back from their extreme hubris into some state of humility; as more new bands sprang up, they no longer dominated the cultural agenda of music. As Bowie often claimed, in spite of his vocal skills, performative intuition, and good looks, he always saw his "musician" role as one of many creative modes. He wanted to be a *pure* artist, more an expression of spirit than simply someone who produced work. Some days, he was a painter; other times, he claimed to be a writer who happened to put a face, artwork, and music around his words.[187] In later years particularly, it seems Bowie was focused on carving out more space to be a normal person, just like everyone else. "Ashes to Ashes" perhaps signals the beginnings of that cathartic process, grounding the ego toward a state of greater humility.

Bowie recounted the filming of the "Ashes" video as a great leveler in an anecdote later told to the director of future Bowie works, Michael Dignum: "I had quite the attitude as a young pop star; it's easy to get caught up in the hype. It changes you. So we're on the beach shooting this scene with a giant bulldozer. In this video, I'm dressed from head to toe in a clown suit. Why not. I hear playback, and the music starts. So off I go. I start singing and walking, but as soon as I do this, [an] old geezer with an old dog walks right between me and the camera. As he is walking by the camera, the director said, 'Excuse me Mr., do you know who this is?' The old guy looks at me from bottom to top and looks back to the director and said, 'Of course I do. It's some cunt in a clown suit.' That was a huge moment for me; it put me back in my place and made me realize, yes, 'I'm just a cunt in a clown suit.'"

The tightly driven but nuanced recording process of *Scary Monsters* seemed to offer little room for error. But Bowie's immediate, present tense working methods were still fueled by a sense of spontaneity that would come together after long incubation of concepts, moods, and themes beforehand, then letting happy accidents and flights of ideas flow in the studio. Songs often came out differently than Bowie had planned; he was happy not to get stuck trying to meet his original intentions in favor of discovery. In this regard, his musical career became a constant act of letting go. Even when a piece might be compositionally odd or technically "wrong," the musicians worked from instinct. Carlos Alomar refers to the sensation of knowing that a piece was done because it *felt* right in a way that couldn't be put into words. Recording "Golden Years" with producer Harry Maslin, Bowie played the three harmonium notes that kick off the song out of time, a little slow, a little sloppy. Bowie suggested he start again, but Maslin heard the broken tune roll into the song's first beat and left it in the mix, letting the mistake stand over perfection to become the starting pistol of the song's groove—realizing something magical when human error and cosmic chaos are allowed to intervene.

Speaking to Angus MacKinnon in 1980, Bowie acknowledged a kind of inevitability to his work, ideas and associations arriving from some other realm of inspiration, though he was afraid to overthink or define exactly *how* these thoughts came to him for fear of crushing them at their inception.[188] His innate sense of musical play echoed Eno's Oblique Strategies card "Honor thy error as a hidden intention." And it was only in reaching toward a song that he arrived at something different; the work was never truly finished, attempted, overcome, or abandoned—that was his brilliant adventure. As such, Bowie could never be truly satisfied; the artist within kept moving on, almost never looking back.

To close the song, Andy Clark of Bebop Deluxe would add washes of Moog synthesizer alongside Chuck Hammer's guitar synth, weaving in and out with wave upon waves of sound carrying Bowie's voice into a distant fade. This coda becomes the tide eating away at the receding shoreline, edging out the mythical hinterland to somewhere between dream and nightmare. Bowie's faint whispers of the verse, sometimes doubling the main lyric, wash about in a heady spiral. Deep in the mix, they are almost impenetrable to be heard clearly alongside Bowie's raw, operatic vocalizations of pure noise, the shadow of maybes:

> No everlasting aesthetic . . .
> Songs that please the ear can leave the mind blown
> I was hoping to kick but the planet was glowing
> And I was ready to go in '74

These snatches of internal conversation beg that we hear what we want to, our subconscious wrestling with the desire to "understand" the message intimated at the nexus between sound and words. Bowie alluded to the power of instrumentation in rock and pop music as akin to classical music: "I still adopt the view that music itself carries its own message, instrumentally I mean. Lyrics are not needed because music does have an implicit message of its own" (MacKinnon 1980). Bowie was conscious to let the music and vocalizations of his lyrics do the work of poetry; where words fail us, let the sound of emotion speak for itself: "There's an effort to reclaim the unmentionable, the unsayable, the unspeakable, all those things come into being a composer, into writing music, into searching for notes and pieces of musical information that don't exist."

Ashes to Ashes becomes a "metatextual break-up record: but here David Bowie is breaking-up with himself, while pop music is breaking-up around him, its structures fragmenting and sickening as the track lurches on" (Ewing 2008). This was Bowie stricken among the shipwreck of his life, a grateful survivor.[189] "Ashes" becomes the quintessential 1980s song at the decade's beginning—coming to mirror the malaise of the times—where Bowie later asked, where are we now, he was then asking, where are we going?

Bowie concludes Major Tom's original quaint oddity as a minor epic, an odyssey from exile into self-erasure. Visconti saw the song as being fantastically conventional but weird in its delivery, Major Tom's final death throes. Accordingly, Bowie subverts the eulogy of the Anglican funeral service, "Therefore we entrust his body to the earth, soil to soil, ashes to ashes, dust to dust," to become a surreal rhyme (for Bowie, death is "old-fashioned"), verging on an inevitable punch line of life; it is never entirely the end.

For all its straight emotional power, many critics would read into "Ashes to Ashes" as a cultural artifact for both Bowie and the 1980s to come, a prophetic act within the act. Writer Michael Bracewell considered the song as Bowie's "artistic suicide note," abdicating from his premier pop role, where *Creem* journalist Roy Trakin concluded that, "after [Bowie had] turned himself into the sad, Pierrot parody of himself in final decline . . . the inevitable artistic nosedive occurred." As personal as it might be for Bowie, "Ashes" is really the funeral of an empty coffin, where the former bright star has dulled into an incorporeal body beyond dust, the way a moon stripped of its glow fades into the memory of a dead planet. It is the last, the best, of Bowie that is interred, the Pierrot hat a discarded crown bulldozed along with the recent past, flattened into Earth's turning (Carpenter 2010).[190]

Tom Ewing noted that Bowie wanted Major Tom to star in an Arthur C. Clarke novel—instead, it became a Philip K. Dick nightmare: "Why is Bowie doing this? To kill off the 1970s, like everyone else was trying to. And by that he meant *his* 70s." Speaking to *Musician* in 1990, Bowie described the process of *Scary Monsters*: "It was me eradicating the feelings within myself that I was uncomfortable with. . . . You have to accommodate your pasts within your persona" (Ewing 2008).

Bowie would feign surprise at the number one chart success of "Ashes to Ashes,"[191] no doubt spurred on by the presence of its iconic video already a revelation within an emerging art form. It stands as a primal *Gesamtkunstwerk* in Bowie's song catalog where he was able to reconcile himself to a disappearing aesthetic designed to say both hello and good-bye in a single masterstroke of avant-garde pop.

PETT LEVEL — 2022

Shadows at the edge of nowhere

Fragment #404

close cuts - by inches - didn't feel the knife - furry - hung like a muzzle - hot noise - breath as a prayer - diamond sweating blood - what was worth it - antagonized extremities - quick at the shut - a mind snapped - something we left in the fire - I really can't - blink slur motion - i will be ok - it's the others wanting - a tree cutter grown a ladder up his spine - blink - candle splutters - swallowed too much sun - there's a moon in my eye - should I sign my real name - or his - I could be someone else - I could be someone - somehow the world holds this glass web together - or around the way other - really can't remember, I never-

Fashion

(Left/Right/Left/Right/Left/Right)

Red Mass
For his fearsome communion
Beneath the blinding brilliance of gold
And flickering candlelight,
Pierrot rises to the altar.

His hand, by grace invested,
Tears his white vestments,
For his fearsome communion,
Beneath the blinding brilliance of gold,

With a grandiose gesture of blessing
He holds to the trembling faithful
His heart in bleeding fingers,
Like a horrible red host
In his fearsome communion.

—From Arnold Schoenberg's *Pierrot Lunaire*, 1912

On May 2, 1976, Bowie arrived back in the United Kingdom for the Isolar tour in support of *Station to Station*. What was set to be a great moment shared with hundreds of fans gathered at platform 8 of London's Victoria train station to witness his return from exile in Los Angeles—but this was all undone by a simple gesture. As an iconoclastic figure, Bowie in his persona of the Thin White Duke dredged up repressed memories of Adolf Hitler performing at Nuremberg, how like a god, a dark angel of vengeance. On that day, Bowie, dressed all in black, stood up in the back of an open-top Mercedes-Benz, cast in the stark expressionist monochrome of the coming tour; he became a harbinger for more difficult times ahead.

Bowie would equally deny, and shrug off the accusation that he ever made a fascist "heil" salute, sometimes arguing that the camera angles captured a straight arm held aloft. For once, his pose was ambiguous instead of performatively exact, leading Bowie to claim that sometimes a wave is just a wave.

What would prove far more damaging were his statements in the press. From his notorious 1976 *Playboy* interview with Cameron Crowe, Bowie would build on his interest in extremist politics: "Britain could benefit from a fascist leader. After all fascism is really nationalism." In the throes of his cocaine-driven ego, Bowie offered himself up as a potential dictator in the mold of Hitler, feeling that charisma and conviction more than qualified him to lead the nation. Ian MacDonald said in 1998, "He was, he would occasionally claim, a Nietzschean, his 'fascism' being conceptually benign (if nonetheless arrogant). He favoured a New Order not of domination, but of enlightenment: rule of the 'asleep' by the 'awake.'" Blurring commonsense concerns of the street and Übermensch fantasy, Bowie's perception of the realities of the British political climate in 1976 had curdled.[192]

The imminent shift to the right predicted by Bowie would never come to pass. Of the few music fans who took him seriously, most were members of the United Kingdom's far-right National Front. Bowie's statement simply affirmed their self-belief system. All subtleties between playing a part and personal opinion were eroded with Bowie pointing out that many of his characters were in themselves emerging or "little" Hitlers. The conflation of rock star and mythic leader is not new in rock music, but here Bowie certainly overextended, letting psychosis speak in place of real political insight for a country he had not visited or lived in since 1974. From his 1980 *The Face* interview with Bowie, Jon Savage found that the singer had become lost in playing the part under the worst Germanic influence, alien to himself and to others (do what thou wilt—there is no other law): "From Isherwood the physical spirit of society in decay, pushing the Weimar parallels—the dyed blond, ambiguous dandy, the Thin White Duke . . . reinforcing the role of the Artist as divine, separate from society and responsible only to himself. Role assumption became loss of identity: crack baby crack."

The Musicians' Union made an anonymous statement referring to Bowie's ambiguous wave and his recent announcements, with the suggestion that any such musician should be expelled from the union. They decried his reach of influence on the youth as paving the way for destruction of the trade union movement as it did in the early days of National Socialism in Nazi Germany (Cloonan 2010). As such, Bowie never made a formal response, but the damage of his comments added to further ripples of troubled times. In that same year, another major artist, Eric Clapton, made a more outright racist and xenophobic anti-immigration rant alluding to Enoch Powell's hateful "Rivers of Blood" speech from the stage. Incidents such as these gave force to the creation of the Rock Against Racism movement.[193]

From the beginning of *Scary Monsters*, Bowie seemed determined to unequivocally set the record straight and engage his critics head-on; with "It's No Game (No. 1)," he screamed against the degradation of being insulted "by these fascists."[194] In his yells, Bowie put distance between himself and the far-right movement, when the real issue was actually the hard-left antifascists who attacked him as a racist class traitor. In this line, Bowie comes lashing out at dogma in all its forms, while the Japanese translation spells it out more directly:

konna dokusaisya ni iyashimerareru no wa kanashii
(to be abused [taunted] by this strong-willed leader [dictator] is sad)

The word "commitment" appears in much of Bowie's interviews of 1980, becoming a mantra to wrestle with into the new decade. Where he could previously scapegoat political deviance and amorality through his characters, in the end, there was no one left to blame but himself. But for all Bowie's righteous outrage, on "Fashion," he also toyed with his invisible enemies: teasing "fascism" with his stuttered "fa-fa-fa"[195] lines. In interviews, Bowie rejected the idea that "Fashion" was a direct commentary on the nature of political allegiances, but beyond "It's No Game (No. 1)," it seems to offer a conscious rejection of the authoritarian politics pressed on the masses and implicitly the charges made against him.

Looking back, Bowie's association with fascism stems from artistic, spiritual, academic interest, drawing on various ideologies in his music, from lightweight material such as Colin Wilson's *The Outsider*, sketchy readings of Nietzsche's Übermensch (*"Superman" as private hero – higher morality – for the self*), and a wider interest in the occult, such as Aleister Crowley (*junkie mountaineer – blackd magick – white stains – won't wash*). Bowie would later discuss how he had been led astray by the growing market for sensationalist pulp books that fed the subcultural appetite for novels posing as nonfiction, blurring fact, rumor, and myth about Nazi occultism and interest in the legend of King Arthur; clashing with warped interpretations of Christianity; and seeking the heritage of the Aryan bloodline. Elsewhere, Ian MacDonald (1998) noted, "Pauwel and Bergier's *The Morning of the Magicians* (1971) and Trevor Ravenscroft's *The Spear of Destiny* (1973) had, by 1975, led Bowie into a remote headspace where even UFOs were part of the plot." By 1980, he branded such reading matter as "dangerous and subversive material." The popular connection between the Third Reich and the legend of warrior knights and the Holy Grail made mystical by Christian faith and films such as *Indiana Jones and the Last Crusade* nailed the World War II baddies to a romantic pseudoscience that in reality was driven more by eugenics research and anti-Semitism.[196]

Feeding off these darker energies, Bowie would open 1974's *Diamond Dogs* with the announcement "This ain't rock and roll. This is genocide!" greeted by a great cheer (wait until the crowd cries) sampled from a stock recording. This dynamic between audience and megalomaniacal stagecraft became physical when young designer Mark Ravitz was hired in 1974 to (re)create the setting of Bowie's Hunger City, which, apart from the artwork of the *Diamond Dogs* sleeve, had existed largely in Bowie's mind, up to that point.[197] He and Bowie discussed three core ideas: "Metropolis,[198] Nuremberg, and Power." From this, Ravitz connected other key concepts, a design that would gradually swell into a minor cityscape at ballooning production costs: "tanks, turbines, smokestacks; the *Ecce Homo* artwork of George Grosz; grotesque decadence, fluorescent tubing, state police, alleyways, cages, watch towers, girders beams, Albert Speer." There was even talk of adding giant banners running from floor to the top of the stage, not unlike the Nazi banners.[199]

On the actual tour, this was toned down to become a background of skyscrapers, a cherry picker, Bowie as Hamlet serenading a skull, and being tied up in bondage with spokes of ropes by a circling roller-skating gang—the disciples of Halloween Jack. These were all visual expressions of forms of control, submission feeding domination that drew the audience in, making them complicit in the dog-eat-dog scenes of master and servant. The grandiose set was later discarded for the second leg of the tour, which mutated into the more stripped-back and less expensive soul revue of the Philly Dogs tour.[200]

For the Station to Station tour, Bowie would settle on the "cathedral of light" suggested by the Nazi's chief architect, Albert Speer, which involved turning military searchlights, designed for spotting enemy bombers, vertically into the sky to create ghost columns, suggesting pillars of stone reaching up toward an invisible heaven. Hitler used this vertiginous aesthetic to agitate, excite, and elevate the body politic of his citizen audience, offering an easy visual metaphor to assert Germany's great rise, returning from economic and cultural decline. Like Speer, light was weaponized as part of Bowie's performance, a laser scything through the audience, illuminating and carving out Bowie as a hardened silhouette, banishing the band into darkness. By contrast, the tours of 1978 that followed were opened up to a sense of natural color, dropping the shadow play and loaded stagecraft that had brought Bowie sailing far too close to the Nuremberg Rally aesthetic.

In those notorious interviews of the mid-1970s, Bowie *is* a fascist when he declares his allegiance to right-wing ideals by calling for a more authoritarian state with a figurehead as unilateral leader: "You've got to have an extreme right front come up and sweep everything off its feet and tidy everything up" (Hendler 2020). The allure of remaking the world in one man's dream image is there in the rock-and-roll megalomania of Bowie's early songs "Saviour Machine" and "Quicksand," sifting through the aftermath of destruction as a nihilistic form of creation. Hendler points out that we are all capable of "evil" acts, so when ego is allowed to run riot, pure selfishness will always trump our better natures.[201] Born into a bourgeois-dominant society, everyone is a potential fascist—metaphorically and figuratively; there is a little Hitler in all of us—screaming to be unleashed. Bowie himself nailed this phenomenon in the wide-eyed mania of "Somebody Up There Likes Me," a hymn to the God-given right to rule, to manifest a destiny. In Bowie's "Alternative Candidate" from 1974, he describes a "fuhrerling," a junior dictator promoted to the realm of great men. Elvis Costello nailed down the problem of clashing egos fighting for supremacy on his 1979 album *Armed Forces* when he sings,

> Two little Hitlers will fight it out until
> One little Hitler does the other one's will

Across the album, Costello explores the parallel of power-play dynamics in troubled relationships pushed to the extremes of militarized friction (the album's working title was *Emotional Fascism*). His final call for "peace, love, and understanding" would sound as if it emerged from an earlier, more benign era than the hard-nosed and increasingly bitter decade that followed it. Elsewhere, Costello sings about military uniforms standing as nationalist symbols or flags for the body, such as the fascist greenshirts of Hungary and Ireland, nodding toward the threat of being turned into a human lampshade.[202]

Both artists were shown to be exploiting the inner tyrant in every self-righteous voter, where the individual citizen comes to see themself as a potential superman and de facto leader. Ziggy was a double tyrant: to the youth he whipped into a frenzy and to Bowie himself. Elsewhere, Bowie

ISOLAR TOUR — 1978

Turning on the bright lights

would claim that the elevation to rock god status was being done "to me" by the audience; kinged by the crowd, mass hysteria blurred art and life into one flattened image; instead, he turned the responsibility back onto the people he had brought together with his music.

Too late, Bowie realized that when he tried to test the political mood of the nation, aiming to give the people what (he thought) they wanted, that he went most wrong in his music. Bowie would later excuse the man he was in 1976 as being "out of my mind, totally, completely, crazed," lost in the cups of his spiraling cocaine addiction alongside creeping alcoholism. Bowie professed that he worked hard to try to stay on the pulse with the mood of the times. Despite his constant travel and long expatriation from Britain through the worst of its growing political turbulence in the 1970s, Bowie at least recognized shifting subcultural elements looking toward the radical polarization of a hard left and right for a new way in politics. But in trying to judge the popular mood of the voting public, he was proven dead wrong.

Although what followed in 1979 with the beginning of Margaret Thatcher's role of prime minister as hard-line authoritarian leader might justify some aspects of the "dictator" tag. The successive Conservative governments of the twenty-first century would continue her original project—becoming more extreme and elitist with each decade—banning the right to protest, turning away refugees, cutting public services, widening the poverty gap, making tax cuts for the rich while punishing the poor, all while enjoying feckless corruption and incompetence at the highest levels of office. In this regard, society and its voters seem to get the government they deserve. On *Scary Monsters*, Bowie returned to the internal struggle faced by people around him in the everyday world, its pulse a ticking time bomb; he awaited the incoming emotional and societal collapse.[203]

Moving from dust to dance, "Fashion" begins by interrupting itself with an awkward electronic chirping "whrrump" sound, a preset on Andy Clark's synthesizer—the processed sound bite is immediately forced out by Dennis Davis's propulsive drums. "This is the only song Dennis [Davis] played along with a click track . . . a beat we liked on David's Roland Beat Box (Visconti 2007)."[204] Almost mechanical, it still carries a hint of swing that keeps a fluid sense of momentum. Visconti intended to remove the drum machine afterward, but Davis was so tight to the backing beat that he kept both parts edging in and out, treating them with more effects to add a spatial "techno" element to the blunt-force rhythm. The template of "Fashion" incorporates the industry's cannibal spirit of self-destructive design, created just to be consumed in its own gears, the real and artificial caught up in the thrust of perpetual nowness.

The jackboot beat drives the song's motorik/krautrock march, relentless, almost to the point of monotony, spurred on by the slow groove of a quietly picked guitar line on muted strings. The main peacocking riff struts about, echoing the more innocent times of the glam rock stomp, where bands could push only so far as their next single might take them, a case in point for brief innovators T. Rex. Suffering the felicities of fashion, glam quickly grew into a forced archetype, a narrow trend that became lumpen and formulaic. For Simon Critchley, the British-leaning rise of glam would overtake its origins from the bright star of proto–glam punk band the New York Dolls; their heart-and-soul androgyny was overturned into a denim, beer, and beards slur with glitter thrown on it, a great enervating explosion reified and nailed down into a dumbed-down trope. By 1973, glam was already dead, another zombie, but only Bowie seemed to notice: "It was a sign that modern civilization had reached the point of absurdity—its entertainments had become bizarre and sordid, menacing even" (O'Leary 2017).

When Bowie abandoned glam rock just as it seemed to peak, his metamorphosis into the dark angel of soul-inflected "claustrofunk,"[205] realized on *Station to Station*, pushed him toward physical and spiritual exhaustion. On the first Isolar tour supporting the album, he remained fragile, weaning himself off cocaine by way of brandy, submerging his mind in Nazi and occultist imagery. Painting windows black and drawing symbols on the floor, "something awful" as psychic protection becomes a flashback on *Low*'s "Breaking Glass," casting long shadows after the event.

A herald for the strange shapes of his dreams after years of racing ahead of the curve, setting musical trends, not following others, and abandoning each aesthetic before it hit saturation point, Bowie would eventually run out of road and be forced to reflect back on his creative evolution. Like all movements, what begins as an innovative revolution soon rolls back into cliché; spinning the hits of yesterday, now become retro, and we dance to the tune of fading memory, trying to recapture something already lost, sick with nostalgia. "Fashion" announces itself as both symptom and cure, the malaise of the "disco sucks" movement, where the initial joy of dancing in clubs has been: "replaced by an insidious grim determination to be fashionable, fashion as a vocation." The song finds Bowie flirting with the audience he knows is still out there as they start to morph from a happy crowd into the mandate of the mob; swept up in the fever of the dance, they become one in order to belong. "Fashion" is Bowie killing off our natural nostalgia, fighting the urge to look back to the songs we used to know and love, now passé and out of sync with the times. In 1980, Bowie himself faced this same crisis, becoming an act that was "big in the 1970s" but now written off by the endless rush of the present; "Fashion" sets the stage for "Teenage Wildlife."

KYOTO — 1980

Native alien in Japan

If I can't dance, I don't want to be
part of your revolution.

—Emma Goldman

On a political level, "Fashion" sounds like any other half-hearted protest song but presented as flashback-razor satire. Bowie is playful, catcalling real concerns of homogeneous culture, blind political allegiance, and the rigors of class conformity—but you have to want to hear them—not just hum along to the song's snappy tune. The very music of "Fashion" embodies the struggle of power relationships, the push and pull of Fripp's guitar rebelling against Bowie's roll call. Where *I'm OK—You're OK* tried to work us into being healthier, happier citizens, with "Fashion," we are experiencing the realpolitik breakdown of the social contract.

Bowie feeds on middle-class hypocrisy, mocking the entrenched prejudice of the social climber, edging us into the otherness of petty, small-minded England peeking out from behind the curtains, marching the treadmills of tired carpets, trapped in their suburban semi-hell. The phrase "people from bad homes"[206] (a lyrical hangover from Bowie's short-lived 1974 pop group the Astronettes) straddles politics and fashion, demarcating tribes of class held in phony war across the dance floor, making their stand, slurring xenophobic: "they do it over there, but we don't do it here."[207]

"Fashion" sparks with the casual drawing of lines between "us and them," "in or out," fearsome of the imagined continental rift that eats away at an imagined identity. In the coming years of Margaret Thatcher's Conservative government, the working classes were sold the ideal of private homeownership as a way to buy into the narrowing sweep of 1980s accelerationism. At that time, the question of entry into the European Union and its single market economy remained a divisive issue, with Thatcher at the forefront of the jingoistic anti-European lobby. Meanwhile, an increase in acts of global terrorism drew battle lines for anti-Americanism across the Middle East and South America while sparking increased minority persecution back home in the United States. From this mixed sense of growing isolationism, Bowie laments our lack of concern for one another—no one has the time to truly change, we are stuck and set in our motions, the dance already has us.

Peter Doggett argues that in spite of his own background, Bowie had no grievance against his middle-class fans; the chip on his shoulder was personal and private, in this spirit his position came more from a place of empathy.[208] The next generation coming up in the 1980s was now, like Bowie before them, seeking enlightenment and escape from the norm. This spirit had imbued Bowie with the natural aspiration of the mythic self-made man, succeeding by his gifts (and a lot of help from friends and collaborators), an experience that prevented Bowie from becoming an outright snob or extreme elitist; it did, however, cast him as firmly apolitical for much of his career. Bowie alludes to the shallow revolutionary drama of the Beatles and the Rolling Stones in his "All the Young Dudes." For much of the 1960s, a major societal upheaval of antiwar and civil rights protests, riots, and assassinations (successful and attempted) shook America to its core, all while it was entrenched in the seemingly endless war in Vietnam. In the United Kingdom, the majority of people were stuck at home, living kitchen-sink realities, not jazzing about Carnaby Street in "swinging London" or trying to bring revolution against the largely tolerant and mild-mannered Labour government; the most extreme figures were really daydreaming on drugs and free love, not fighting on the streets. This was simply an attitude struck in the imagination of Mick Jagger, at one time a finance and accounting student at the London School of Economics; compared to his University of Life colleague, the romantic reality became what the songs told us it was.[209] By the time of *The Man Who Sold the World*, Bowie had taken "flower power" and popular social humanism and turned it back onto itself amid the growing specters of capitalism. Simon Critchley notes that for his generation, 1970 was its own year zero, as the world seemed to grind to a halt, the future was going nowhere. The Western democracies, staggering through inertia, eventually sparked the crisis years of constant conflict at home and war-all-the-time on multiple international fronts.

On "Fashion," Bowie's radical concern alighted on the ways that art and fashion so often become an amalgam drawn from high and low culture, a point at which couture fashion houses and underground subcultures meet. From this, the do-it-yourself punk aesthetics would be toned down into safer, salable versions of manufactured rebellion: from swastikas, bare breasts, and safety pin earrings to peace symbols, lingerie, and logo badges, a more visceral kind of truth that was inevitably bowdlerized and defanged. It is in this mutual compromised state where the middle classes feel more comfortable to engage, bringing ready-made mass audiences such that an artist can be considered aesthetically edgy while enjoying mainstream success.[210]

After 1980, Bowie took a consistently harder and more outspoken stand against racism, though his political leanings and angles of attack remained oblique. One of his chosen books was Howard Zinn's *A People's History of the United States* (1980), a radical revisionist perspective on how the white Western operations of the United States had performed more as an old-fashioned imperialist power in foreign policy and less as the defender of democratic freedom. The book highlights a continued system of flawed governance where a minority of wealthy elites rule over a working majority. In spite of his often upbeat, positive, and warm manner that many remember him for, Bowie housed a strong inner critic; remarkably cynical (or perhaps just keenly aware of the cycle of world events), his songs often hinge on doom-and-gloom scenarios centered about the soul of society.[211]

In a 2016 *Politico* article, Katelyn Fossett noted, "Bowie's dystopian song lyrics weren't shy about refracting Western consumerism back at Western fans." Peter Doggett points out the anti-fashion statement of bombing the boutique store Biba by the Angry Brigade in 1971. The group released their own statement cum manifesto, which took the situationist tack that modern life was all boredom fed by consumerism: buying the latest clothes and slavishly following trends. The only thing to do was to kick against capitalist humanity "until it breaks." This assault on popular consciousness of the modern shopper would become a lost war by the mid-1980s, when a broader spread of disposable income (as credit) made shopping an aestheticized form of leisure, chasing brands' cachet and the intangible meaning of "style."[212] This was the beginning of commerce meeting art, with big business muscling in on the gallery system, and the reaction of art terrorism was realized, setting the battleground for the new culture wars.

In keeping with the throwaway tone of "Fashion," Bowie dropped to both the left and right extremes of the ideological landscape stratified by dominant political parties in both the British and the American political systems. On "Panic in Detroit," rerecorded in 1980, the last survivor of the "National People's Gang"[213] sees his noble revolution descend into riot and destruction as the mob loots and burns—the dream is betrayed, as consumption by destruction. Inspired by Iggy Pop's account of an inner-city riot, countercultural figures such as John Sinclair, manager of the MC5 and agitator for the White Panthers, make an appearance looking like Che Guevara, the honest revolutionary posterized as a proto-hippie.

This track prefigures the arrival of the "goon squad" as a shock tactic, akin to the Nazi blitzkrieg ("thunder strike") of violence, spectacle, and noise. It is not simply a growing movement coming to town—it is already here, under the surface. Pushing the limits of excess, fashion fulfills itself at extremes. Elvis Costello's own track "Goon Squad," from *Armed Forces*, crackles with its Chuck Berry shook rhythm, setting the tone for shock troops goose-stepping down your spine. He feeds on the same paranoia with "Watching the Detectives," calling out doublethink where everyone is spying on each other. Although for Bowie the "goon squad" was not meant to be abjectly political, it stands in for the onslaught of the fashion machine: the massed bodies of struggling models, amoral paparazzi, white wine–bleached hangers-on, fading jaded celebrities, gaggles of fluttering makeup artists, ravenous journalists, and autocratic designers, their combined egos rolling into town with the clashing houses striking a Medici line of dominance. With the fashion industry's links to organized crime and assassinations, the picture becomes much murkier. The goons analogy carries over sheer mindlessness; audiences are reduced from crowds to cattle as chattel—the thumping tones of "Fashion" offer the stampede of brute force, which always succeeds and overwhelms over ideas and reasoned debate. Both "Panic in Detroit" and "Fashion" bludgeon the listeners into submission; you cannot help but go along with the unstoppable beat, the feet moving the heart.

> Beauty is our weapon against nature; by it we make
> objects, giving them limit, symmetry, proportion.
> Beauty halts and freezes the melting flux of nature.
>
> —Camille Paglia

Across *Scary Monsters*, Robert Fripp's guitar adds thundering momentum. On "Fashion," it is a hot rod from hell, all revving engine and furious honking horn, driving a wedge through the hordes of human traffic. Grinding bumper to bumper, bouncing over the broken bodies, fighting for space, the shrinking future is everyone pushing in their own direction and getting nowhere. Fripp's playing is backed up by the muscular bounce of the bass, drums, and the backing vocals' "beep beep" stroke—lifted from Bowie's kooky obscurity "Rupert the Riley"—playful but urgent. Shoving the listener into place, it pushes back on the throbbing synth line of Gary Numan's "Cars"—make way or be mowed down—the future is here. Fripp noted that for all of the irreverence of "Fashion" and its seeming music by numbers, the lyrical hook of "goon squad" and "beep beep" was a punchy combo: "ain't that a line that sticks in the mind."[214]

Chris O'Leary rightly branded "Fashion" as "a dance song with bad intentions," where mixed motives err toward slow death. Bowie finds himself trapped in downbeat euphoria, a zombie parade of syncopated shuffling. He smells the sweaty ebb of a cocaine high; sinking gray around the eyes, the audience looks to him for the next bounce, a musical jump start. Andy Clark's synth delivers further beeps and blips, what Visconti calls "kitten growls," that add to the track's disoriented, unsettled mood before Fripp's skronking, angry guitar crashes the party, chainsawing the song in half (2007).

Fripp explained his method to *Electronic Musician* magazine in 1987: "The solo on Bowie's 'Fashion' happened at 10:30 in the morning after a long drive back from Leeds gigging with The League of Gentlemen. There's nothing you feel less like in the world than turning out a burning solo fiery rock and roll at 10:30 in the morning, just out of a truck. But it doesn't matter how you feel, you just get on with it." Fripp's sawtooth lead guitar ensured that the song had more jagged edges than straight chanting. Fripp sprays burning splinters of sound across the "up" rhythm, edging the track into darker territory—all eyes are fixed on the glare of the catwalk—something frightening is happening on the sidelines.[215]

For some listeners, Fripp's solo rubs the song the wrong way. Channeling the "hand in the toaster" electric shock energy of the Gang of Four's Andy Gill, he interjects, flexing tones, then quickly arrests phrases. As through much of the album, Fripp is raised high in the mix, threatening to drown out the other instruments as the loudest, brashest, and brightest; even Bowie is happy to be occasionally outshone by Fripp's "skronky" angles of attack. Fripp described his mad cameo appearances as "blues-rock played with a contemporary grammar," traditional forms deconstructed; it took the album further out from the expected styles that had dominated the 1960s and 1970s. Fripp's language was not entirely foreign, but it was a rarified thing that still makes the album stand out against other music of the era that depended on uniform rock or pop acceptability.

Frustrated that he could not come up with a lyric, Bowie was about to jettison the song until Visconti implored him to search for a lyric to what he knew was a perfect single. Bowie used the phrase "ooh Ja-ja-jamaica" simply to mark the chorus, but the improvisatory sound offered him the jumping-off point from melody to lyric, bouncing the first half syllable of the word to draw the listener in. Bowie offers more chanted phrasings to snare the ear in the call and return of the middle-eight section, exploiting the very coming and going of musical forms, from the knowing plasticity of trend-driven pop music and the worn-out welcome of faded glamour. After Bowie nailed down the "ooooh fashion" line, everyone in the studio was certain they had a pop-friendly hit on their hands.

Carlos Alomar noted that "Fashion" had its musical roots in "Fame," itself adapted from the riff to the Flares' 1961 track "Footstompin," which Bowie knowingly performed as a segue when he appeared on *Soul Train*, paying tribute to the song's roots, with its first-line invitation, "Everybody young and old/Learns how to rock and roll," designed to get people together on the floor.[216] Where "Fame" was outright acerbic, its brazen hostility spurred on by John Lennon's backing refrain and guitar, it also scored Bowie and Lennon an extremely catchy hit. Again, "Fashion" shares a bitter edge but is perhaps too fun a listen for its wider point to stick. Tony Visconti claims the song was a show of force that the chart-minded Bowie could re-create the same infectious and hook-driven power of his earlier single, although Bowie was somewhat dismissive—"a light throwaway song, about as important as fashion"—marking the idea of pop as a disposable commodity, as much about hype as high-end jeans.

> They [people] mistake fashion for style. Style is
> about the choices you make to create the aspects
> of civilization that you wish to uphold.

—David Bowie, *Complex* magazine, 2003

Bowie's acidic sting against the inevitable momentum of fashion was sparked by the fear and loathing it raised in him: "It's more to do with that dedication to fashion. I was trying to move on a little from that Ray Davies [the Kinks] concept of determination and an unsureness about why one's doing it. . . . It's that kind of feeling about fashion, which seems to have in it now an element that's all too depressing."[217] Like "having a tooth drilled," it nonetheless requires him to grit his teeth and accept a certain amount of aggravation. The stark irony of "Fashion" is how much of Bowie's early career was born out of sartorial revolution, with the fashion industry driven by self-referential evolution; like Bowie, its alignment to art is fueled by the need for constant reinvention.

Like all classic models, Bowie was a lean coat hanger shape, a frame on which to hang anything. In this, he embodied the living sculpture or, rather, life as (non-autobiographical) art; he was only ever briefly pinned down in a series of images, nothing singular or definitive. A long-haired man in a man's dress turns into an androgynous humanoid alien, spiky, shiny bright, no eyebrows, then a Gouster flâneur[218] of American subculture before exploding in flame-haired, black-and-white expressionism. His curse was to become known as a kind of leader in clothing and unified aesthetics for each album—men's dresses, Ziggy's costumes, and tailored suits.

Michael Bracewell noted the accessibility of Bowie's science fiction aesthetics that never entirely left his South London roots: "High Street Futurism and plastic decadence—Rimmel and Robotics." He balanced this by constantly overturning expectations; in this, he pushed the envelope toward strange new directions, wrestling in and out of conformity. His tours had multiple costume changes, now standard for pop singer stadium shows, a trend that Bowie made a new norm. By the late 1970s, Bowie had fully exploited the "Berlin basic" look, shorn of his flame-red, hot-white, slicked-back hair, returned to natural mouse brown, a fringe swept to one side; fitting in was what mattered. While others were still chasing his earlier style, Gary Numan and post-punk artists used sensible haircuts, straitlaced shirts, and skinny ties.[219] The earlier attempted clones of the Ziggy era became Numanoids and Kraftwerk replicants. By 1980, the extremes of Bowie's earlier look were squared away. The informal suit became standard for many New Wave bands in contrast to the sleazy retrogressive look of hair metal, which rehashed glam rock pseudo-effeminacy with long hair, leather, and not only a hint of makeup. In Bowie's sheer mutability, photographer David Bailey felt he was "the very personification of an actor" who had overstepped his role; this impression left Bailey feeling that he never got a good shot of Bowie as himself.

In Kyoto in 1980, Masayoshi Sukita did a shoot with Bowie wearing a suit and trench coat moving stiffly through the center of a clock with only ten numbers on it, signifying that there were never enough hours in the day. Bowie-as-businessman would soon become de rigeur by 1983's "Let's Dance." Bowie guest starred as the singer of his own album with songs put together by Nile Rodgers, placing money before music.[220] This would increasingly become the definitive look of Bowie through the next couple of decades, starting with the Serious Moonlight tour's "stockbroker's late night out" casual chic, unbuttoning his collar, letting his bow tie hang loose, elsewhere the tweedy and upright English gentleman, with occasional New Age hippie flourishes and a touch of goth eyeliner.[221]

Bowie would acknowledge his preference for substance over style as a way of shaping our aesthetic lives. When speaking to *Complex* magazine in a 2003 joint interview alongside Mos Def, he nodded to a hungry consumerist attitude: "Everything we look at and choose is some way of expressing how we want to be perceived." For Bowie, an increasingly image-focused world meant a loss of control, as he fought to maintain an all-encompassing aesthetic across the media of his musical projects that engaged the mind as well as the eye of the beholder.

By 1995's *1. Outside* album, Bowie went alternative, veering away from the dominant culture of the era with an art-crime concept album far beyond the pop confines of *Scary Monsters* and out of step with the mainstream indie guitar music dominating British music. However, this would magnetize Bowie toward YBA (Young British Artist) attitudes of high concept, sensationalist art that courted pop-culture controversy with a heavy focus on death and creation.

Bowie's blurring the clothing industry and dance culture would be revisited in the "Brit-pop" peak of the late 1990s, again coming from a left-field position. The most knowing bands of the time produced danceable guitar hits laced with irony, offering their archest take on post-rave mass culture, a suburban reality of the cheap lights local disco or £1 pint student night, all rainbow lights; catatonic on lager, snakebite, and alcopops of all stripes; lads wearing tracksuits or sofa shirts and jeans with shoes, girls looking perfectly grown-up in LBD. Pulp's "Disco 2000" and "Common People," Blur's "Girls and Boys," and, in 1996, Bowie-sanctified Suede's "The Beautiful Ones" put the lens back onto the dancer as hypersexualized animal body, all raw feeling less thinking, "shaking their meat to the beat," gyrating endlessly into devolution—the outrage of "Fashion" come full circle.

Bowie attempted a hard left turn away from conformity with his extreme-effect guitars and Johnny-come-lately drum and bass-meets-jungle on the 1997 album *Earthling* while everyone was aping his most whimsical moments of *Hunky Dory*. On the track "Battle for Britain (The Letter)," Bowie fused breakbeats with the wild guitar sounds of the Prodigy (courtesy of virtuoso Reeves Gabrels) trailing after a moment of underground music that had already passed; it was not a record for stadiums, raves, or clubs; he was now following creative trends rather than inventing them himself.[222]

On the album's artwork, Simon Critchley sees Bowie standing astride a field as an increasingly narrow corner of England's "green and pleasant land" decked out in a Union Jack frock coat from fashion designer enfant terrible Alexander McQueen, running parallel with the YBAs. It shows the national flag with edges burned and bullet-holed—with Bowie standing host as a ghost of empire: displaying "British" pride or announcing pre-death of jingoistic nostalgia? Bowie stands both for and against history in the pro-Brit era of music that led to mass navel-gazing, tommyrot, and flag-waving, leading the people in good and bad homes trapped looking backward toward the fast-fading idea of monolithic British empire, a "forever England" that never was.[223]

Bowie has said that he never attended a fashion show—ever. If we choose to believe him, then his interest in McQueen's highly aestheticized work came to him secondhand. Bowie's future wife Iman Abdulmajid had quit modeling the same year they met, so he remained removed from the scene. With 2003's *Reality* album, Bowie was replaced by an avatar cartoon in a neat black suit with swishy blond hair, the uniform he would wear in many interviews and live performances, alternating with jeans, Converse shoes, and a tattered space hussar's jacket. This normalized non-persona was again a studied pose of the unreal everyman. By this point, he had largely exhausted the idea of anything but an elder statesman look. Bowie told the *Observer* in 2002, "I rarely buy clothes. I wear them well and people give me stuff and I'm quite keen to wear it for public shows and albums and all that. But I'm not interested in fashion. And my wife's the same. She never goes shopping: she hates shopping with a vengeance."[224]

Another attempt to break out of cliché's magnetism, *Lodger*'s "DJ" was the precursor to "Fashion." The track employs a dizzying spin around Bowie's ringmaster vocal, its swooning electric violin conjuring up the beating heart of the dance floor. Where "DJ" is both a tribute and a blast against the Friday night hedonism collapsed into the weekend's great escape from the nine-to-five grind, "Fashion" finds its aftermath in the dark side of repetition. The song provides an excoriating attack on increasingly shallow culture racing to the bottom, preempting millennial scenester and hipster affectations, the new bohemians representing an unthinking cycle of culture clash divorced from meaning and their origins, a postmodern junkyard. Their ironic appropriation of multiple styles with no unifying center would latch onto brands as empty symbols of cool that Bowie himself would be forced to resist. The peacocking culture of the dance floor calls for people to be seen charged by hyper self-consciousness that would seek fulfillment in the "Me" decade capitalizing on the accumulation of wealth and style as signifiers of "earned" success.[225]

Bowie's lyric notes dredged up the sense of conflict that cuts across the dance floor. With long and complex lines they read like alternative song titles, and the four-to-the-floor beat stiffens into a show of arms:

> "Stand by your station boys"
> "we midgets and fools should learn not to
> dance on concrete poured for GIANTS"

—something about the wrong people at the wrong time but still trying their utmost to do it right, dying to fit in. Bowie worked hard to refine his lyrics into something harder-hitting but still openly vague rather than oblique, using the art of suggestion instead of stating the obvious. "Fashion" was stripped of more overt lines that equate dance moves to street violence:

> "Hell up ahead, burn a flag/Shake a fist, start a fight"
> "We'll break every bone/We'll turn you upside down."

Bowie's vocal experiments again stretch lines out of shape: "the" becomes "th-uh-uh-uuuh-uh dance floor," dragging it up an octave beyond its means, suggesting the image of "someone trying to foot their way onto a crowded dance floor" (O'Leary 2017). Fripp's elastic guitar riff strikes seven layers of sheen off the song's smooth groove, dividing some listeners who considered it an effort of sabotage or a conscious attempt to counterpoint the largely monotone verse lyrics. It is telling the radio single edit cut much of Fripp's contribution from the song, scuppering its art rock angle to make it easier on the ear.

Offering up blood sacrifice to the ravers, Bowie preempted the Specials' lament for broken-down social spaces in their home city of Coventry. This fractured spirit is crystallized in the eerie postindustrial decline of 1981's "Ghost Town" where bands were banned from the clubs after "too much fighting on the dance floor." Whether it was racist skinhead thugs making trouble or a band inciting the audience to passionate aggressive postures, the mass effect becomes a killing floor at fun time.

Bowie is admonishing a herd effect—but not without some empathy. In the dumb, blank blindness of the hip scene, movers and shakers learn by physical crash course; they are all as lost as each other, and going through the motions becomes a march in time. At the point of big business, the revolutionary force of fashion is spent, the play and innocence sucked out of its heart; where it strived to outdo itself, it was forced to swallow its own mistakes. And the followers have run amok, spiraling off into cliques, a closed circle, eating their own tail, celebration redux, and we arrive back at the chattering of the clichéd classes, regurgitating and recycling the past and selling it back to us, turning into the "same old things/as brand new drag" from "Teenage Wildlife." With the stench of novelty infecting everything it touches, we arrive at the dulled shock of the fake now.

The jaded aesthetic of the David Mallett–directed music video for "Fashion" is a pastiche of 1970s styles in the blacked-out cube of the clubs that Bowie frequented. Staring into a deadeyed distance, people are hip-bopping and bunny-hopping but stay frozen to the spot while the band plays on, trying to find a beat to keep. The video has an emphasis on the direct address of vox populi ("voice of the people"); talking heads speak directly to camera; May Pang appears stone-faced, mouthing "beep-beep"; and they transmit no information, like the stutter of "Scream Like a Baby." This is fashion choking on its own blurb.

Compared to the rest of *Scary Monsters*' verbal acrobatics, Bowie's flat-line vocal is self-mockery, trapped in the death disco, swarming about the corpse of a good night out. Bowie absorbed the "fa-fa-fa-faa" jabbering that occupies the chorus of Talking Heads' "Psycho Killer"—and drained the blood from it. Lost in the din of the bantering crowd, "fa fa fa" "to-to to-to," and "la la la," the idea of the lyric is reduced to brute sound, gate-crashing the peak (and nadir) of pop's thrilling and knowing plasticity.

With their post-blues middle-eights sparring for attention, "Fashion" is a darker cousin to "Let's Dance." Here, Bowie throws up walls in the vacancy of call-and-response—listen/don't listen, talk/don't talk—bouncing opposites off their negative, a series of pleas to a blank-faced lover trading in self-denial. In the sudden lull of "Let's Dance," Bowie throws his voice, full with yearning, wanting to be wanted, trying to find a sense of completeness in a new dance partner. As with "Ashes to Ashes," Bowie had nodded to the tension of musical style gone stale, the idea of funk turning "funky" with the rot setting in, zombie music for the dead ear, deaf to itself. In "Fashion," he is jarred by (in)difference; hailing ambiguity, we are lost in Bowie's echoes, the singer talking to himself—but is anyone really listening?

The people keep on dancing, and the outside world can go to hell, spinning off its axis. Deep in the belly of the dance floor, you can forget everything: forget yourself, get swept up in the flow, and be someone else. It doesn't have to mean anything, but even in this absence, it means a lot. The song fades out as fashion shrinks back from the edge of good taste; in its relentless pursuit of the modern, it exhausts itself, limping toward self-extinction. What began as bold, brash, and bright motion sinks into hollow reflection, meeting its own voyeurism through the horror show of cracked glitter ball and dazzled eyes, a quiet anger bejeweled, standing on the corpses of yesterday's giants, gazing up from the dance floor's sticky sump—don't look down.

Fragment #97

Scorch the earth, *lights* out for the territory, no more *stars*, each to guide our own guiding light, false *flags*, put our more *idols*, collapse into exhaustion, ideally happy now/happy forever, where you can't just *pay* tomorrow, it's not *stealing* where they sold it so cheap, better off to *borrow* than end up *begging*. Spun into a tunnel of spider *webs*, trapped, crowded and closed down, *hunted* even, the air is thick and suffocating, mixed between *paranoia* and righteous *anger*. crowd masses numbers, push/pull in all directions, *all directions*

Fragment #99

Open *a world of entrances becoming exits, once you were waved on through where all wines flowed only to return on the way back out and having the door slammed in your face. feel our little histories falling away, like marble chipped from a statue by relentless piranhas with steel teeth, still smiling while they eat. Everything happens in the hallways, behind the scenes, all clear*—once acolytes turned against us, now the fans, then the followers overcome and consume you, vampires of human flesh. *Then there are new corners yet to be turned around, as something slips away from us always just out of reach, just a few steps behind the hungry shadow creeps, the path we trod has been erased, there is no way back, only go forwards.*

Teenage Wildlife

(It Happens Every Day)

David Bowie—Often Copied Never Equalled

—RCA marketing slogan for *Scary Monsters*

Bowie entered 1980 seeing strange shapes dancing on the wall, aping his movements, trying to walk in his shadow; new faces emerging from all corners, he hears the echo of his voice, but it's no voice at all. On "Teenage Wildlife," we see Bowie looking over his shoulder, trying to catch them in the act, but on turning around, he only meets himself.

With their marketing slogan for *Scary Monsters*, RCA declared Bowie well beyond the pack of common pop artists, a direct leap from the earlier blurb that heralded the 1978 release of *"Heroes"*—"There's Old Wave. There's New Wave. And There's David Bowie"—again ahead of the curve. Pushing Bowie to the fore as the (unwilling) leader of the avant-garde, he would fall both in and out of step and remain a man apart from the still emerging New Wave, showing them forever playing catch-up to his influence while Bowie transitioned in and out of the mainstream. But it was as much a natural process of evolution as embracing influence; the range of musical styles in 1980 engaged with the radical edge of experimentation, post-punk manifestos, and pop savoir faire, managing to work at the hinterland of Bowie's creative excesses.

In every new pretender, Bowie could not help but see something of himself not just taken off but having pieces chipped away from him, some faking it until they made it, others asset-stripping the most well-known aspects of his music or aesthetic from various portions of his career. Becoming the Elephant Man in reverse, this is how it feels to be an artist—and a person—reduced to a subject or the archetype of an artist long past his most relevant and urgent music—later to become the crunch point of *Scary Monsters* legacy.

Simon Critchley considers the "self-reflexive brilliance" of *Scary Monsters*: "Bowie looked at himself, knowing that everyone was looking at him." Feeling the weight of his influence, Bowie accidentally succeeded in making a meta-album, evoking peak Bowie-ness but also a postmodern warning that signaled the death of the post-punk freedoms absorbed into a new pop orthodoxy. Tim Rice suggested that after a decade as a leading artist, Bowie had already had a good run in rock music as well as branching out further into acting with *The Elephant Man*. Often self-effacing if not diffident toward his career, Bowie described his position following the relatively muted sales across the Berlin Trilogy records as more of an awkward-paced limp rather than a vertiginous ascent to match the heights of Ziggy mania. He claimed not to feel much pride in his music but remained satisfied that he had done nothing that he did not want to do; all his choices were his own. With mixed irony, Bowie said that the worst joke God could play would be to make one a mediocre artist—how would you ever know unless someone told you? This was perhaps the curse that crept into his 1980s, derailing a brilliant streak until he rediscovered his authentic artistic self again in the 1990s (MacKinnon 1980).

With "Ashes to Ashes," Bowie exorcised his past; on "Teenage Wildlife," he was forced to confront the present—and question his future—while taking aim at "one of the New Wave boys," which could be anyone of the era just starting out. Where Bowie had once declared himself a "xerox" considered through the proto-photocopier, he now emerged as a copy of a copy of himself. With "Teenage Wildlife," he watched every successive wave of artistic innovation coopted and tightly enmeshed into a singularly labeled "movement"; a group's initial momentum would soon grind to a halt as the space for expression began to narrow. Diagnosing this angst-ridden grasping for first-time success that he had once felt, Bowie claimed he set out to write an archetype of this desperate and hungry condition.[226]

Because of the strength of the material emerging on *Scary Monsters*, Bowie felt secure to settle (fresh) scores as an act of preemptive revenge: "Slowly, brutally and with savage, satisfying crunch, David Bowie eats his young"[227] (Cohen 1980). This was perhaps Bowie following the editing mandate of "kill your babies": cut out what you love the most where an artistic work reaches in excess of itself. It was Bowie's choice to deny or erase those emerging acts that he had influenced—as a god might—choosing to crush and destroy his followers simply because they worshipped him. He is neither parent nor contender; he is his own divided and sometimes indifferent muse,

(((BERLIN))) — 1977

The rest is noise

putting distance between himself and any artist self-consciously trying to become the "new" David Bowie.

The most pointed of the song's barbed arrows (they hurt more on the way out) was aimed at Gary Numan, but perhaps it is also a nod toward Steve Strange, later the singer and star of Visage, and their brilliant number one hit "Fade to Gray." Bowie admitted that perhaps there was gnomic truth to the idea that every rising new star will get their nose broken or, rather, "put out of joint" on their way up through the harsh and fickle realities of the music industry.

For Bowie, it was not strictly personal; he responded honestly when asked about other musicians: "What Numan did he did excellently but in repetition, in the same information coming over again and again, once you've heard one piece." With Numan coming to prominence alongside other synth-pop bands such as Human League and Depeche Mode, Bowie certainly took notes on their work for himself.

Perhaps Numan's aesthetic reminded him of his own persona during the difficult period of *Station to Station* and *Low*, a sterile and cold post-human look seemingly lifted wholesale from the Method acting of *The Man Who Fell to Earth*.[228] Numan, long a teenage fan of Bowie, felt burned by his hero's critique on his short-run success. Bound up in the Ziggy Stardust myth, Numan had paid his dues as one of the faithful: "I'd been a Bowie fan before punk and used to get no end of trouble. I was always getting knocked about and having to run up the street, getting chased by people. It was horrible."

Bowie opens "Teenage Wildlife" asking "how come you only want tomorrow?" Leaning on the thwarted promise to try to overcome the next day before it has even arrived, Bowie notes the failure to appreciate the rise toward success, to live in the exciting pre-fame present. He sees artists turning their lives over to the pursuit of success as a tipping point of excess, trading on wealth, sex, drugs, and public approval; all came with a toxic Midas touch killing them through overexposure and hazarding future creativity by burnout. Bowie is pushing back at the vulgarity of selling out and trying too hard as Ziggy had done with David Jones bearing the brunt of the experience.[229]

Bowie had been here before; 1971's "Quicksand" saw him sinking into obscurity as a one-hit wonder, lacking the power to conjure a great song at will (the album *Hunky Dory* contains many "hits" and deep cuts that with hindsight became classic Bowie). Again on "Sound and Vision," he is caught in a purgatorial space between inspiration and silence, boxed in a room immersed in the deep electric blue of pervasive melancholy, trying to force "the gift" of creative energy but learning to relent and let it come in its own time. In 1980, Bowie spoke of his creative "mainline" that gave him access to ideas beyond himself, an ethereal muse, allowing him to conjure up formations of words and music as if from nowhere. Like any artist, he feared it might one day dry up or disappear but also acknowledged that sometimes this was the natural way of things for any artist. The blogger Momus referred to Bowie's innate form of "negative capability," a concept suggested by poet John Keats; that artistic drive is keener in the pursuit of beauty, which, he believed, offers its own form of objective truth about the world.[230] His approach rests on leaps of faith and intellectual uncertainty, acting in denial of our more concrete, worldly knowledge, a kind of transcendence where we negate our ego toward a Zen-like state, allowing ideas to spring forth unimpeded. So it is with "Teenage Wildlife," a subconscious reflex made by the muscle memory of an experienced songwriter's native talent producing a deep-cut should-have-been hit, the great successor to "Ashes to Ashes."[231]

As Bowie had predicted, there was a short shelf life for Numan's early dark-star synth pop, particularly after some members of the music press had overhyped him as "the Bowie of the Eighties."[232] His brilliant works of pop perfection, like the number one single "Cars," still stand tall, but his career burned out almost as quickly as it had exploded in the charts. Bowie felt justified in pricking the hubris of others: "As ugly as a teenage millionaire/ Pretending it's a whizz kid world"—I heard "pretending it's always his world," and again this could be Numan, believing he had a large and loyal audience still listening out there when the world of the global pop industry had already moved on. Bowie chose to terminate the career of Ziggy at his peak by onstage suicide, but Numan was unfairly abandoned by his label and pop fans; he entered into a long exile but would later return triumphant in the new millennium.[233] But what emerged alongside Numan was not another musical fad but an overturning of popular culture by a creative spark that like Bowie would impact across the spectrum of fashion, design, and music, blurring the lines between art and artifice.

As many artists of the 1970s would remember growing up among rationing, ruined buildings, old bomb craters, and the deeper inherited psychological trauma of World War II, so the next generation would be born into the gloomy postindustrial comedown of the 1970s heading deeper into recession. This became the point at which the brute reality of vox populi kicked back against the old order with general strikes, energy crises, race riots, and clashes with the police on all fronts—where everything seemed to be burning to the ground or soaked into damp defeat—a very English apocalypse. From this, a deeply Conservative government, itself looking back to Blitz-spirit resistance, tied itself to disastrous U.S. military spending and dug their heels in to plow ahead with sweeping economic reforms that saw unemployment hit 3 million.

It was not until the second half of the 1980s that a gradual increase in living standards would arrive.[234] But while national wealth increased, a growing wealth divide had already begun to split society down the middle, sharpening the edges of poverty and further empowering the already rich.[235] Michael Bracewell compared the postindustrial urban landscape of some parts of London to the aftermath of a war zone, haunted by domestic refugees on home turf with nowhere else to go. But for now, it was a unique situation of time and place that revealed an open city of naked possibility that would give rise to the Blitz Kids.[236]

The writer and Blitz regular Robert Elms referred to London in 1978 as looking "like Bulgaria on a bad day," a city haunted by the long and difficult decade it continued to endure. Simon Critchley (2016) reflects back on London of the 1970s as the alternative Hunger City: semi-derelict and resigned to collapse, scorched patches of brownfield sites evoke a distant time before the clampdown on squatters, skyrocketing rents, and inflated house prices super-fueled wider gentrification, marking the urban space as a place of "crime and inverted consumerism." Where decadence and desperation sat cheek by jowl, there was money to be made, but few could afford it.

Before there was the Blitz, clubgoers in the late 1970s would emerge blinking and sunstruck in the early morning hours from Billy's, housed beneath a brothel on Dean Street, Soho. A blank-faced musical oasis that collected waifs and strays of all stripes from the fallout of the punk years under one banner of a weekly Tuesday dance night, "A Club for Heroes," promoted on a flier with the tag "fame fame fame, what's your name." Cofounded by Steve Strange and Rusty Egan, it gave everyone the opportunity to be a star—to find their own form of cool—if only for one night. Along with Bowie's most recent albums, the music of Marc Bolan and Kraftwerk were staple sounds, alongside new electronic synth-led music, moving from disco to punk and back to Bowie, the night would frequently sell out.

The true Blitz club shifted to the slightly more salubrious environs of Great Queen Street, Covent Garden, still a relatively shabby, neglected space. It was situated in the less glamorous seedy backstreets of London's West End, where neon glow fizzed with the allure of sex for sale and other entertainments. These boxed-in, gloomy drinking dens housed their own vibe of decline and free-spirited discovery, a recurring theme drawn from Bowie's mid-1970s music and his experiences of Berlin. Ian R. Webb remembers the Blitz scene inhabiting a world of self-conscious movie influences: "Cabaret, Myra Breckinridge, The Boyfriend, The Night Porter,"[237] touching on the shift from the Weimar Republic–era decadence to heavily aestheticized Nazism. There was also an ecclesiastical phase of fallen nuns, real life somehow made more vivid in black and white. But more than borrowed controversy, the experimentation of looks was a revolt against the standardized fashion of buttoned-down leisure wear that was being sold to them. Webb sees this as a positive contradiction: "We were being ourselves and dressing as other people," which became its own form of self-discovery. "None of us are purely one thing." In his 2021 memoir of the transitional 1980s *Souvenir*, Michael Bracewell defined the spirit of the endless parade: "dressing up in wilder and evermore extreme costumes, racing to outrun imitation," a mode that would soon catch up and outrun the Blitz scene as it would Bowie.

The term "Blitz" was shortened by the English from the German "Blitz-krieg," referring to the heavy aerial bombardments of World War II. Death from above saw London and many major industrial British cities relentlessly bombed as the Allied forces flew missions both in retaliation and against strategic targets—attacks on nonmilitary civilian centers such as the firebombing of Dresden and Tokyo would give rise to the term "total war." From such actions, Hermann Göring coined the propaganda verb "Coventriern," referring to the 1940 bombing of the Midlands city of Coventry; roughly translated as "to coventrate," meaning to level the city to the ground, this resulted in the deaths of many civilians, destroying much of the city's medieval architecture and gutting its ancient cathedral. The bombing sparked much anger and resolve among the British people, but it drove Coventry to later announce itself as a city of peace and reconciliation, its symbol the phoenix rising from the ashes.[238]

The Blitz Kids were the generation raised at the rough end of the 1960s postwar regeneration but keen to reject the austerity and collective trauma of World War II nationalism for a European outlook toward international music, renewed glamour, and their own version of Swinging London idealism. Initially working against the grain of the Conservative government's cold, hard realities, the Blitz Kids' fresh optimism of 1980s Britain would be steered toward materialist, brand-driven pursuit of wealth and conformist pop, subsumed by popular culture's thirst for novelty and absorbed into emergent fashions. But at the start, the clean sweep of the Blitz meant a blank slate for people who—like the punks—had nothing to lose and could take control of the culture and make the future their own.[239]

Dick Hebdige saw the subculture of punk evolve from an unstable "cutup"; a synthesis of the many brief genres and movements of overlapping layers, mutual music, it was not quite the absolute revolution of "year zero" that many would have it be. Nonetheless, it was a unique moment in music that was born to self-implode, simply too fractious within its many elements to stay together. This unstable cross composition was adopted by the Blitz Kids but without so much dogma or of the exacting pose of nihilism that became so self-regarding. By 1980, Bowie had fully thawed from his own stilted existentialism, although as a generation removed, he was a background influence; he could stand as a comfortable observer, neither its creator nor its opposite.

With a ferocious appetite for (synthesized) glamour the Blitz Kids were raised on the ghost of Ziggy Stardust's glam rock escapism. Although the youth of 1980 would be more geared toward Bowie's experimental work, when Bowie had more or less rejected his "classic" era, turning toward an increasingly fragmented and confessional style of songwriting. This nonetheless pointed the way forward to a more postmodern world of new pop music, where the Blitz Kids became both raw product and ready-made audience for new self-created styles. For people like George O'Dowd, yet to become Boy George, the leader of Culture Club, "Bowie was the light at the end of the tunnel."

Placed alongside the abrasive textures of *Scary Monsters*, "Teenage Wildlife" carries a deeper resonance for Bowie. The album's hypersensitivity to real-world concerns is shot forward to "Ricochet" from *Let's Dance*, where John O'Connell, author of *Bowie's Books*, finds Bowie's eye for social commentary staring down darker streets than his own well-heeled road, carrying echoes of J. B. Priestley's 1934 book *English Journey*; he sees the gears levered by the working classes ground to a halt. Like Orwell's *Road to Wigan Pier* (1937), Priestley was reporting on industrial towns stomped on hard by the Great Depression. In West Bromwich, he finds a group of boys throwing stones onto the roof of an abandoned factory, becoming the sound of, mechanical crashes and haunting echoes in the stillness where once there was life.[240] John O'Connell (2020) argues that Priestley would have understood their wanting to chuck things and break stuff; it's the spirit of "It's No Game" breaking through the hidden mirror of the fourth wall, scattering glassy illusion among the gravel.

Bowie would praise the new ska music of 2-Tone for making a difference in uniting black and white band members and audiences, "the idea of being together with another sex and another race." Like punk before it, 2-Tone offered a danceable response to the stranglehold of freshly hatched Thatcherism: at once tough on crime and citizens thought not to contribute to society, while closing down jobs and driving deprivation. Thatcher helped to define the spectral cities of exhausted former factories, warehouses, and shipyards "scraped clean by time's tide" (Bracewell 2021). In cities like Coventry, Hull, Liverpool, Newcastle, and Glasgow (and London), where the gap for working-class people to make the leap to white-collar service office jobs seemed to grow wider every day, instead they became shopworkers or scraped by on the dole, a subsistence level that got them making art and dreaming of better things. This mode of life as survival would create the artistic backlash of working-class bands forced to pick up a guitar or throw more bricks and break more windows in order to be heard.

A couple of decades later, from the ashes of the late twentieth century, glass and steel towers would spring up in the breathless skeletal ruins rushed in by a flood of deregulated investment, with compulsory acquisition land grabs literally selling England by the pound. For observational critics like Simon Critchley and Michael Bracewell, the 1980s was notable as a simpler, porous decade in which there was still breathing room physical and cultural space in which to make things happen beyond the world of Larkin's high windows morphed into skyscrapers while, all around, rich and poor alike could hear money singing toward a deafening fever pitch.[241]

The London of 1980 was still in open season for tomorrow's dreamers, held in a precarious balance of poverty and innovation that forced the Blitz Kids' aesthetic(s) into life. Pieced together from charity shop leftovers, the next generation of fashion designers rediscovered vintage cultural artifacts forcing the past into the present, flashing the cold morning light over an imperial hangover; diamonds of the shrinking aristocracy would be broken up into new gems, refashioning furs of old money and cutting up dresses into post-human shapes, the slow train revolution of glam rock causing solar flares on the early TV cameras of *Top of the Pops* and *The Old Grey Whistle Test*, now brightened up and feminized: "just make it up darling, it'll be alright"; fighting over the scraps and, in their splintering myriad futures yet to pass, finding hope among fresh horrors that the vacuum Bowie had sang about crash-landed here, with the enterprising, opportunity generation only too eager to grasp at, grab, and take control in order to fulfill both its promise and its threat.

Bowie's first visit to the Blitz saw him sneak into the back entrance from his limousine already chastised by Steve Strange, part-time Visage singer and strict doorman who not only guarded the entrance to the club but also curated the style of its clientele: "This is not a goldfish bowl; the kids that are in this club are here because they feel at home." Nonetheless, word of his visit soon got around, and zombielike fans pursued Bowie with arms outstretched—the end of a circle having run its course. In an interview, Bowie would deliver his own postmortem on the Blitz, knowingly appearing to forget the club's name, having been introduced to an event that was implicitly dedicated to him and his living memory. He wandered into a room of potential clones (if not disciples), perhaps finding more of the same "grim determination" he had injected into "Fashion"; the same appetite for fresh style was in the air, like Bowie, cannibalistic and hungry for blood. He told *NME* in 1980, "Yes, I must say I did feel it when I was in London. I was taken to one extraordinary place by . . . Steve Strange? God, what was it called? Everybody was in Victorian clothes. I suppose they were part of the new new wave or the permanent wave or whatever." His backlash cropped in the form of any old "wave," Bowie confined others' futurism to the past tense.[242]

John O'Connell notes the "Bright Young Things" of the 1920s as an early influence on Bowie. Partying their lives away in the glorious jazz years "'before the deluge," unaware of the burning world that was fast approaching. Jon Savage cites that their innate decadence and desire for dressing up went well beyond the pale of stiff upper-class England of the years between the two world wars and punctuated by the Great Depression, marking them as early freaks. "Aladdin Sane (1913, 1939, 19??)" draws on Evelyn Waugh's novel *Vile Bodies* (1930), in which he satirizes the frivolous era in a list of fancy dress parties with ever more absurd costumes and venues, which Bowie compared to the glam era, merged into one seemingly endless party until the end of the world.[243] The live-fast-never-die (old) fatalism of the Jazz Age and Waugh's "Bright Young Things" was driven by the suppressed fear of inevitable disaster,[244] trying to mask reality in frivolity, knowing that something terrible was coming but not what shape it would take and when. *Scary Monsters* became the prism through which Bowie saw his own emotional and political turmoil of 1979 turn on the extreme highs and crushing lows of the 1980s yet to come.

Bowie praised the look and musical style of Steve Strange, who emerged as a star in his own right and was a lightning rod fixer for the times, helping Bowie select the cast for the "Ashes to Ashes" video.[245] In 1980, Jon Savage tagged Strange as an archetypal figure for the times, a continuation in a long line of Dandies from Beau Brummell and Lord Byron through to Oscar Wilde and the "Bright Young Things," especially aristocratic Steven Tennant and, much later, Sebastian Horseley. Strange was "the most recent, the most absurd, yet the most magnificent, exponent of the Suburban Pose which never dies,"[246] exacerbating the further undercurrent of tension between highest and the lowest classes. Journalist Ian R. Webb argued, "It was Bowie's original flamboyance that caught the imagination of the hardcore style snobs that formed the New Romantic scene, and what secured Bowie's credentials as a style icon was his elitist standpoint."

As Bowie continued to flit from flame to inspirational flame, he continued to enjoy his own "high" life, literally that rising above everyday mediocrity assumed by and done to so many. As he later explored on "Because You're Young," it is both the privilege and the right of youth to be so contrary and to consider themselves free, exotic creatures made rare by their willingness to go further outside of the dominant culture than others might dare. As many of the Blitz attendees were so young and either finishing art or fashion college or had no formal education behind them, they were do-it-yourself (DIY), self-made, and their iconoclasm was their great armor, drawing on the past to remake the future belonging to no age. The Blitz encompassed an unbound group of individuals, a secret society of privately public members in which Michael Bracewell discovered "a subculture of young people for whom wearing a mask was a need, a job, a work of art and their truth. The one idea for which they could live and die; existential."

Bowie rightly predicted the rise of the New Romantics and the plastic pop that would come to dominate the 1980s and would see the Blitz Kids reified into a fixed image. What began as a small club of individuals with shared musical and stylistic interests became lumped together into a single group, a movement, that was quickly neutralized by popular culture.[247] The New Romantics nonetheless absorbed the following influence of pure glamour for its own sake, dressing up when you have no money simply because you can and it makes you feel more alive: "the glitter and sparkle of youth was a higher state of beauty." Their take was initially born out of the puffy shirts and baggy sleeves of the early nineteenth century, the genuinely poetic era of Byron and Shelley, and made into a uniform, a straitjacket of new convention. The lyric from Duran Duran's[248] "Planet Earth" helped mint the newly coined phrase, thought to have first occurred in a 1980 interview: "Like some new romantic looking for the TV sound." As David Johnson of the Shapers of the 80s website noted, "They didn't call themselves New Romantics, or the Blitz Kids—but other people did." The name stuck. Robert Elms noted that in spite of the widespread sickness and defeatism of British society at this time, it was the brilliance of youth culture that (again) became its saving grace.

This celebration of youth for its own sake was something that the more mature and battle-worn Bowie of 1980 could look on with quizzical distrust and remove, although he would briefly jump onto this bandwagon making himself into a shadow-sculpted Byron in full 1980s Technicolor for the extended music video of "Jazzin' for Blue Jean." His later 1980s attempts to recapture some of this mad sparkle resulted in the Glass Spider tour of 1987, where stage sets and gaudy costumes meant that Bowie overreached and lost sight of his music. It was not until 1995 and *1. Outside* that his aesthetics, music, and concepts were reunited into a meaningful whole.

Bowie's influence would be fully realized in 1980, as if *Scary Monsters* arriving alongside Bowie's new-ish competitors confirmed this before the event. In a 1983 interview with *The Face*, he was asked about the current rush of pop groups breaking into America off the back of what Bowie had started.

He joked that as he had adopted and then dropped the synthesizer early, he was now out of step with himself and the contemporary music of the times. By the time of the New Romantics, it was already Duran Duran and the pop brilliance of Wham!, while other groups, such as Human League, had softened their rigid dystopian view of contemporary Britain into slick cocktail bar tales of broken romance. For every genre, a reaction—New Wave and the pop end of punk and "no wave" to meet it in return, the feedback loop of new forces crashing together as if to cancel each other out.[249]

> Immature poets imitate; mature poets steal; bad poets deface what they take, and good poets make it into something better, or at least something different.

> —T. S. Eliot, 1920

Bowie's casual appropriation of ideas was, at best, a magpie and, at worst, a leech—the watching, waiting autodidact—bouncing off from the inspiration of others into new directions, sometimes forgetting to pay his dues in return—but his energy for ideas remained both intoxicating and invigorating, and in this sense, he gave far more than he took. Mick Jagger noted that Bowie would clock someone wearing a nice-looking pair of shoes and almost immediately run off to buy the same style—and then wear it better—as if he had stolen them straight off your feet.

Bowie had wisely heeded the advice of conservative, Anglophile, libertarian poet and critic T. S. Eliot to be both stealer and borrower—where all inspiration becomes theft—and in turn to try to give it all back, casting a wide web of influence. The defining trait of modernism was the new freedom that comes with knowing the rules and therefore being able to break them, to disengage the entirely rational part of the brain to get to more extreme artistic positions, brought back into touch by editorial rigor. Bowie zigzagged with much grace and savoir faire, so the lines of influence and inspiration were often as blurred as they were crossed.[250]

Perhaps by 1980, Bowie felt that that cycle had been completed, where his inheritors had now outgrown their idol and by way of tribute had indirectly attempted to kill off the thing they loved. He cast out a warning that the same thing might one day happen to them, a vague threat disguised as well-meaning advice: "The lyric is something about taking a short view of life, not looking too far ahead and not predicting the oncoming hard knocks. The lyric might have been a note to a mythical younger brother"; in essence, this was Bowie's own adolescent self, perhaps thinking of Terry Burns's guiding hand. Elsewhere, his tone seemed more paternal: "It's for someone who isn't mentally armed." As he was once carried by his fans, who become the next generation of creative people, he now reached out a hand to them advising caution. In his phrase "midwives of history," Bowie exposed his own demons, referring to "hypocrisies and the stubbornness to change people have, and to accept change and to flow with it, rather than become reactionary and fight it, which produces the terrible conflicts we find around us."

Switching from the role of guiding force to dismissive, offhand gestures, Gary Numan was reportedly ejected from the studio before the recording of Bowie's segment for Kenny Everett's Christmas Special in 1979. Numan had already filmed his performance and was hanging around like a loyal and devoted fan just to see Bowie play: "All of a sudden, this bloke I'd adored for years was throwing me out of a building because he hated me so much," Numan told *The Independent* in 2003. There were reports (never substantiated) of Bowie claiming that Numan had "stolen his look."[251]

From Numan's aesthetic, Bowie would find reason to repeat his doubts of the applications of technology to human life, while he later had great use of emergent music software for digital lyric cutups and early Mac home computers as a portal to the internet. Speaking in 1980, Bowie was quick to neuter any idea of a science fiction future, relegating his early work to pure fantasy and creative invention, with no emphasis on prophecy:

> It's that false idea of hi-tech society and all that which is . . . doesn't exist. I don't think we're anywhere near that sort of society. It's an enormous myth that's been perpetuated unfortunately, I guess, by readings of what I've done in that rock area at least, and in the consumer area television has an awful lot to answer for with its fabrication of the computer-world myth.

As stated in *The Man Who Fell to Earth*, television doesn't teach you anything; it simply accumulates images and sound bites to become the junk food of the mind. In watching, we enter into a contract; the more we see, the more readily we accept to be nullified and battered in the contemporary backwash of culture. Our refusal to turn away commits us to the routine of the everyday atrocity, spectators of our own slow-dive cultural suicide.

After falling in love with Kraftwerk in 1974 and using "Radioactivity" to announce his appearance onstage, Bowie would later unfairly criticize the band for becoming more of a pop group as their career continued; having lost the original spark that made them so different, they became entrenched in the mainstream, watering down their original promise.[252]

But Bowie's themes and interests had more common ground with tech-driven musical pioneers than he might have been willing to allow; except where Kraftwerk adopted man–machine synergy, Bowie preached systematic disorder. In his early 1970 song "Saviour Machine," a device full with loving grace is created to deliver "the Prayer" of the lyrics. Designed to help humanity overcome its worst problems, it tries to fashion a perfect world (set against the crooked timber of humanity). Again, Bowie is struck by the struggle with technology in its reach for perfection, to iron out all errors, flaws, and incidents until the machine realizes that adversity is a necessary part of human struggle.²⁵³ In making a world free of problems, it negates its own existence and becomes a dystopian tyrant, undoing its own purpose, crashing into contradiction. Both he and Numan exploited a stripped-back tyrannical view of the future, of emotional withdrawal and the struggle for connection.

Intuiting Bowie's postmodern perspective on futurism, Angus MacKinnon's far-reaching and empathetic long-read interview of August 1980 is titled "The Future Isn't What It Used to Be" after Bowie's own admission of being hung up on the imminent tension of 1980 as a new beginning. Accordingly, the interview chimes with a front-loaded quotation from *I'm OK—You're OK*: "Causes for human behavior lie not only in the past but in man's ability to contemplate the future."²⁵⁴ Bowie was concerned with exploring his (and our) physical and psychic potentialities; this more positive attitude offered a flip side to the pessimism that dominates much of *Scary Monsters*.

Bowie spoke with premature wistfulness of the "Ashes to Ashes" video: "the sensibility that comes over is some feeling of nostalgia for a future . . . it creeps into everything I do." A recurring theme across his earlier music that came naturally to Bowie, looking out toward parallel, alternative realities, making them seem just within our reach. This perspective aligns closely with the concept of hauntology. A theory rooted in the work of linguistic and cultural philosopher Jacques Derrida and later popularized and developed by the late Mark Fisher is "the idea that the present is haunted by the metaphorical "ghosts" of lost futures." The "specters" of these possible worlds influenced contemporary discussion on the state of society, hopes as ideas that continue to endure as imminent impossibility; the living dream, at once intimately real and also forever out of reach. For Bowie, this manifests on the emotional plane as "the idea of having seen the future, of somewhere we've already been keeps coming back to me."

The Bowie of 1980 was keener than ever to transcend the earlier naïveté of 1950s science fiction on which his generation were raised. He dredged up the already decaying visions of flying cars, colonies on the moon, and servant robots; an inherited faith in the rightness of the technocratic society to solve humanity's problems of civil discord; overcrowding; energy crises; and environmental collapse through machines. People wanted to believe in the inevitable rise of mutual progress as a definition for the value of a civilization, that they might be saved by a new kind of invented higher power greater than themselves. But for Bowie, space travel and the tech revolution wasn't it; humanity brought its problems along with it. Instead, Bowie offered a portent of the real future as harder and more visceral, the real world as the dog-eat-dog one becoming the state of nature suggested the Margaret Thatcher years: "The old hi-tech thing, it's not like that. It's flesh and blood. More terrifying real, the symbolic street-fighting thing will not become symbolic as it was, but will become a reality, one can foresee it in the dreadful eighties."

"Teenage Wildlife" bounces into a crooked passage, Bowie caught in an argument with himself, the imaginary interlocutor pushing back at him. Chris O'Leary hears a nod to Numan's lyric of a friend waiting in the hallway from "Are Friends Electric."[254] Feeling himself pulled to one side and faced with the inevitable question of "what should I do?," Bowie offers no help because he couldn't always help himself. He simply moved on, never stopping even when he faltered; he could not explain his art for others. Forced into the "father" role, a man who can only talk about himself, he cannot provide the bigger "answers" that are simply not there. As uplifting as the music is, the overall energy of "Teenage Wildlife" is tough-ended and street-bleak; youth is the bulletproof shield that enables us to bounce back from failure and struggle and that gets harder to flex with age. As with his doubts of self-worth in "Ashes to Ashes," Bowie could never entirely see the wood for the trees, so often caught up in having to be "David Bowie."[255]

As he abdicated from his musical legacy in "Ashes," on "Teenage Wildlife," he shrugs at his own career and experience. Bowie, who seemed to care a lot, had no quick or glib response and refused to lapse into self-help speech. He could not explain away his creative impulse; there was no formula for success. If he had left any kind of trail to follow, it was visible only in retrospect.[256]

When the press later labeled him a national treasure, "Dame Bowie," in the mid-1990s, this was Bowie as walking, singing archive, to be honored (he would refuse all royal offices) and duly sainted but largely from the distance of nostalgia. His new albums were reviewed well and tolerated in the charts; this situation created an establishment straitjacket that tried to force Bowie into the popular celebrity monoculture. On the 1990 best-of Sound and Vision tour, which he had sworn he would never do, he was expected to play hits from twenty years ago. Although happy to oblige, he keenly scrapped any plans for a Ziggy musical; legacy became its own form of living martyrdom. Bowie no doubt saw something of his own struggle for identity among the younger bands and his fans, learning to cope with "the shellshock of actually trying to assert yourself in society and your newly found values." In his lyric notes, Bowie marked down the idea of "a group count," divided between the question of who counts more in society, and weighing the power of the collective beyond the sum of its parts. On "Teenage Wildlife," Bowie is reconciled to "a group of one" in a world that largely embraced him only as a celebrity musician and even less so as a serious artist. To Angus MacKinnon, he explained that after his politicized outburst of 1976, "I'm feeling like a society in myself, so broken up and fragmented." A conscious act of mutual rejection, as an artist, his place was inside: self-contained, a machine for absorbing, breaking, and re-creating art.[257]

The great musical breakthrough that elevates "Teenage Wildlife" would come with Chuck Hammer's guitar-synth parts: "I began to build up layers of single-note lines using the GR-500 set to Solo Mode." Visconti would orchestrate the song toward its climax; just when you think the bombast and intensity can go no further, he would push the musicians on to another level as Bowie forced his vocals: "Tony made extensive Harmonizer adjustments about three quarters of the way through the song where he wanted more density."[258]

Visconti heard the spirit of "Heroes" in the song—sharing the leaping accents of somber passion in the verses to become something ethereal in its chorus.[259] However, "Heroes" is soured by the alcoholic's lament [260] and no doubt inspired by Bowie's mindset while he was in Berlin. Brian Eno lent his own thoughts on "Heroes": "It's a beautiful song," he told *Q* magazine in 2007, "but incredibly melancholy at the same time. We can be heroes, but actually we know that something's missing, something's lost." This is subtly emphasized by Bowie in the sarcastic quotation marks that mar the album's title. Bowie remembered performing the song in 1987 next to the wall in West Berlin: "I'll never forget that. It was one of the most emotional performances I've ever done. I was in tears. . . . When we did 'Heroes' it really felt anthemic, almost like a prayer" (DeMain 2003). With thousands of East Berliners listening on the other side, it became a song that transcended hard borders and erased political and cultural divisions, the power of the music overriding any pessimism within the lyrics. The music of "Teenage Wildlife" carries an anthemic Springsteen vibrancy, the harsh social critique of "Born in the USA" meeting the unbridled joy of "Born to Run," snatching triumph from the air that prevents the song's acidic tone from burning a hole in itself. But the elegiac tone of the music would always be eaten away by traces of paranoia, seeing doubt looming around every corner, where he pinned his target with an imagined conspiracy, nailed down by the repetition of "you," which might equally apply to Bowie himself: "And you breathe for a long time [alive]/then you howl like a trapped wolf/and you dare not look behind." Bowie's closing delivery comes to echo the address of "Rock 'n' Roll Suicide," a sinking fear at the madness of crowds (Tanaka 2021). Roy Bittan's piano chimes in and out with the tolling bells, the singer edged farther out to sea awash with voices calling out "still you push your luck," perhaps calling time on Bowie's moment in the sun.[261]

Bowie enjoyed baiting hints for fans in interviews, offering ways to get inside a song teased by casual name-dropping, purposefully harking back in self-reference. In a 2008 interview, Bowie said, "So it's late morning and I'm thinking, 'New song and a fresh approach. I know. I'm going to do a Ronnie Spector. Oh yes I am. Ersatz just for one day.'"

By contrast, the quiet intensity of the verses in "Teenage Wildlife" have a harder and more evasive tone, with the percussive three-word lines less sung and more hammered into speech along with Davis's tom-tom drums. Chris O'Leary notes Bowie's "pseudo-Japanese" singing style in the lines "Leaf from the Tree," "Vast Blue Sky," and "Shoot You Down"—each short line climbs down the tonal scale along with the music. Bowie's voice begins high and flighty and descends into a deeper register. In "Ashes to Ashes,"[262] Bowie gabbles claustrophobic words in staggered shriek: "Do you remember a guy that's b-ee-e-ee-en," switching to a drawling croon on the final word. Leah Kardos (2022) points out this characteristic Bowieness compared to a more traditional Western sense of melody, where songs rise in tone from line to line, reaching a peak, more like the sharp rise in the chorus of "Teenage Wildlife," which soon overtakes the song.

Bowie's swooning image of the falling leaf seesawing side to side, out of life and toward death, is a patient line delivered frantically. After being gunned down or left reeling from a character assassination, the view from the body now lying on the ground is all big blue smothering sky. The target of the song is painted as a victim become their own worst enemy, broken by the industry or beaten down by their fans, with Bowie their knowing witness.

Angus MacKinnon asked Bowie about his "fondness for using rather hysterical lead guitars: Earl Slick, Ricky Gardiner and then [Adrian] Belew," to which he explained, "Well, that's a contrivance of my own. What I do is, say, use four tracks for a recorded solo and then I cut them up, knock up a little four-point mixer clipping the solos in and out. I give myself arbitrary numbers of bars in which they can play within a particular area, and go backwards and forwards from one track to another. So yes, the effect is somewhat histrionic."

Bowie pieced together the guitar solo for "Teenage Wildlife" from multiple takes to make a composite sound, much as he had done with Fripp's guitar parts for "Heroes." For that title track, he focused on the plaintive guitar cry, creating a sound more like a rising synth that enriches the linear, chugging chord progression. Visconti hears in the song a sense of triumph set against an inner feeling of total collapse (not doubt), an "instantly recognizable sound in the collective psyche." Elsewhere, Adrian Belew's playing on "Red Sails" from *Lodger* aimed for "accidental" takes that had enough randomness to stand out within the song but could also be blended into the mix. Bowie had given Belew the concept of the German art rock band Neu! to follow and let him run with the idea despite never having heard the band. Bowie tried to explain the band's motorik sound as an approach to guitar playing.[263]

Fripp's octave-warping solo bends "Teenage Wildlife" out of shape and elevates it to "Heroes" levels of striving to overcome oneself; there is a similarity to the glittering, lyrical guitar of the solo at the center of Television's angular "Marquee Moon" (Lindsay 2021). As if reaching for the impossible, Fripp's mellifluous run of hammered-on, tapped, and pulled-off guitar notes offer a breathtaking performance that, just when we think it can go no further, lifts the song to another level as Bowie continues to chant "on and on," bringing a native sense of wonder to the everyday.

In the end, Numan became the crucifixion kid for Bowie and perhaps for the growing elitism of pop music, as conformity became all the rage. Bands softened their image, did away with youthful social concern, and elevated themselves to high romance and the narrowed-down "tunnel of love" vision: a one-way flow, and the listener knew exactly where it would take them. Transgression and acting out were suddenly off the menu. In his autobiography *(R)evolution*, Numan says, "As the years have gone by, I understood far more the way he saw things then. He was still a young man, with ups and downs in his own career, and I think he saw people like me as little upstarts."

For the most successful New Romantics, their brief intellectual rebellion against the norm soon turned into yacht rock, an exercise of "playboyeurism" that pushed style over substance, wealth as a divining measure of real worth; the shinier the star, the greater their pulling power. Where working-class kids were transplanted from inner-city kitchen-sink grime to exotic locations of sunny, sandy beaches, the image reified by Duran Duran's video for "Rio," they suggested that life could be a permanent vacation, so the gloss of glamour trumped aesthetic decadence—dying for your art was boring, getting rich was smart.[264] By contrast, the enduring artistic and critical success of bands such as Talk Talk have far outlasted their peers,[265] though in the mid-1980s, creative rebellion began to look like (commercial) failure. Others were quick to put distance between themselves and Bowie. When Tony Hadley of Spandau Ballet was asked what he thought of his former idol in 1981, he replied archly, "What's Bowie got to do with me? He's 33 and I'm 21." A decade between them, their musical lives were now also worlds apart.[266]

Dylan Jones (2018) notes how fashion and design became dominant forces that steered art and culture rather than the other way around. As form would corrode function, the sparkle, gloss, and glamour of the 1980s meant that the need to be seen and to rise above others would become the natural order of things. This was society eating itself and beginning to choke on its postmodern sense of irony. Pop became increasingly disposable where it had once been vital and urgent; as a direct force for change, it grew into a shallow simulation of permanent good times.

Building on the legacy of "Ashes to Ashes," "Teenage Wildlife" stands as something of a farewell for classic-era David Bowie. In Bowie's interview for the Australian TV show *Countdown* at the turn of new year in 1979, he was asked about the boom of New Wave music appearing at the end of one decade and the start of the next one. Bowie looked back to the initial spark of rock and roll and the explosion of glam rock in the early 1970s, arriving fully formed like a sudden flash of light but with no one found holding the smoking pistol that started it all—a phrase would appear near verbatim in the lyrics for "Ashes." As each musical wave would seemingly be created sui generis, out of nothing, it belonged to no one, and no single artist could take credit for it. These sudden cultural shifts occur in Bowie's own spontaneous and naturalized approach to music. "Teenage Wildlife" finds him reaching deep into his own insecurities and emerging triumphant; a good loser or someone who remained a musical contender, he had both everything and nothing to prove.

Visconti thought the song was a misstep, too on point, too in your face, admitting that it took years to grow on him. It becomes clear that while "Teenage Wildlife" carries significant weight as a deep-cut ballad, it is often overlooked by casual listeners. For all of its seven-minute histrionics (over)loaded with passionate intensity, it is the fire of youth that Bowie gives voice to, even as it threatens to burn itself out. Bowie believed in the song strongly enough to include it on his 2008 i-Select compilation of deep-cut favorites, bizarrely given away with a far right-wing British newspaper: "I'm still very enamored of this song and would give you two 'Modern Love's for it anytime." "Modern Love" is a much lighter and more plastic pop sound with more lightweight guitar, whereas on "Teenage Wildlife," synth and guitar provide instrumental sounds that transcend even Bowie's lyrics and vocal performances.[267]

Caught up in the sway of the song's final chant "on and on" toward the outro, alongside this, Bowie cries "liiiife" in strained falsetto as if it were his last breath. In this, I hear the shuffling of waves toward the end of *The Great Gatsby* where F. Scott Fitzgerald found a beating heart in "ships borne restlessly against the tide." Every new generation will find their own way, rising above their elders. Bowie wants them to make art new, to make it their own, with or without him. He is a false idol at twilight, stuck fast by his own reflection, desiring change but perhaps wishing that some things might stay the same. Where "Teenage Wildlife" and the whole of *Scary Monsters* shows Bowie calling time on the avant-garde, for the time being, "Let's Dance" would suggest a show of force; the last thing anyone might have expected was for Bowie to reassert himself by self-consciously coproducing hits, after which he would stand accused of letting down his fans, never again at the forefront of the new wave of future music.

LET'S DANCE/SCARY MONSTERS/ALADDIN SANE

A decode's triptych — 1983/1980/1973

Scream Like a Baby

(I Am a Laser)

Fragment #03
Metaerotic Hypersensualized Lapsed confessional Autofiction

Sam is a gun / He's a real pistol / Sam is a phallic instrument /
Sam can't hold his
own / wine back into blood / into water//
broken glass / With a broken hand / Sam is a tool / loves to be
used / loves to be lost / And to use them / not knowing himself/
tell him / tell me / tell them / Sam won't wear the pink / triangle/
gushing red // Sam is a killer / queening itch / too keen to say
sorry / too slow to mean it / Sam is a missile of lost hope / Sam
Lost His Teeth / NotHisSmile / Hello / Welcome / how are you / have a
nice   day   /   he   is   not   his   smile   /   They   say
he is all used-up / a rattling tin / a split drum / Sam shot his
arc   /   Sam   is   a   secret   /   Sam   forgets   Sam   /
himself has forgotten Sam / Sam misses Sam / Sam is gone /
Sam was never here / you will always remember him / what
does it even matter / if he can't remember
                                        you?

In our world, there will be no
███████ except ████████████████████
and ██████████████. The ██
instinct will be eradicated. We
shall abolish the ██████ There will
be no loyalty except loyalty to
██████████. But always there will be
the intoxication of ██████. Always,
at every moment, there will be the
thrill of ████████ the sensation
of trampling on ██████████ who's
helpless. If you want a picture of
the future, imagine a ██████ stamping
on a ██████████, forever.

—George Orwell, *1984*

It all started out as a bit of fun—artistic outlaws, freaking out the norms, a cultural revolution televised on prime time. In 1979, David Bowie appeared on *Saturday Night Live*'s end-of-year show to perform three songs from across his ten-year catalog, a greatest-hits set in miniature. But far from being a nostalgia act, he deployed extreme aesthetics with an avant-garde show of force that transcended mere glamour to project real-time culture shock all across America.

Bowie was delivered to the stage in a giant, boxy, black-tie suit of molded plastic, the mechanized chic of a static mannequin inspired by the Cubist outfits of Tristan Tzara's play *The Gas Heart*.[268] Bowie opened with a stately performance of "The Man Who Sold the World,"[269] dredging up the spirit of Ozymandias's king of kings thwarted by his hubris, flanked on his right by singer Klaus Nomi and drag artist Joey Arias dressed as red and black avenging furies delivering falsetto backing vocals and striking eerie attitudes; this is opera as horror show.[270]

I expected Bowie's sides to be cracked open, like a giant Easter egg, harking back to the Yamamoto costume stagecraft of the Ziggy era, but at the song's end, he is merely lifted back to the rear of the stage, like a sculpture set among his disciples at the Last Supper.[271] Compare this to Bowie's equally slick but super-straight performance on *The Tonight Show* with Johnny Carson, dressed as James Dean from *Rebel Without a Cause*—relative wholesomeness of Dean as double martyr, who lived long on-screen and died young in a real-life car accident, without the acknowledgment of his uncertain homosexuality, forced underground and covered up by public friendships with Elizabeth Taylor and attending his screenings paired with young female costars.

The performance starts weird and only gets weirder with "TVC15" as Bowie (and singers) throws his all into the *"transmission"* phrase, standing alongside a pink poodle on wheels with a flashing TV inserted into mouth that shows a live reel of the show; the song's narrative becomes the medium that must eat itself. Nomi and Arias cast proto-robot dance shapes with Bowie wriggling and jiving in his royal blue Chinese worker jacket and air hostess tube skirt (Kardos 2016). By the time of "Boys Keep Swinging," the scene has gone pure gonzo; through early computer graphics, Bowie's human head sits atop a stick puppet following Bowie's own movement, its flailing limbs threatening to take out someone's eye with the camp abandon of the seasoned stage dancer high on life and lost in song. Despite all of this, there is a last-minute gesture of censorship when Bowie's vocal is cut out for the line "other boys check you out"; a nod to homosexuality is silenced, robbing the song of its power, while Nomi and Arias strut from the hip and flex their arms in demi-masculine hyperbole.

Despite being introduced by a straight-America movie legend, Martin Sheen, Bowie and his crew upended the status quo of the format, flexing a weird and queer edge into the stay-at-home-night-out U.S. TV mainstay. An internationally recognized performer playing popular "almost hits" and bringing underground performers into an overground platform, Bowie flipped the format. Through songs such as "TVC15," he swallowed up the uncertain and perhaps unwilling audience and spat them back out—leaving them dazed and confused at what they had just been watching.

Leah Kardos noted the debt to Tzara's Cabaret Voltaire skits and John Heartfield's photomontages, again echoing Weimar-era Germany, the dismantling of art that carried its own protest. *Saturday Night Live* (1979) was Bowie's own Dadaist intervention, like the Situationist International's *derive* and *detournement*,[272] meant to derail the normal counterculture as a verb. Bowie's new beginnings of 1980 are intimated across the performance: "Here we can witness Bowie in the very act of synthesizing his influences and mythology with his new surroundings, distancing and reconfiguring elements of his past to express his thoughts and feelings in the present" (Kardos 2016).

Being seen in the mixed company of artistic subcultures on national television was its own kind of coup—the urgent challenge that Bowie threw down was how his songs could be presented sexually, politically, and musically to confront normality head-on—and how much could he get away with.

Bowie would bring the same subversive energy to "Scream Like a Baby." Between the crash of cymbals and the ominous, chugging guitars, the song edges toward the aftermath of social deviance once the reactive clampdown arrives.

> I speak only of myself since I do not wish to convince, I have no right to drag others into my river, I oblige no one to follow me and everybody practices his art in his own way.

—Tristan Zara, *Dada Manifesto*, 1918

"Scream Like a Baby" was another Frankenstein's monster of a song, recycled from other tracks. First written in a rougher form as "I Am a Laser" for Bowie's short-lived soul group the Astronettes, which centered around then girlfriend and backing singer Ava Cherry and was backed up by his longtime friend Geoff McCormack, "I Am a Laser" was a piece of "theatrical soul" that barely served the concept of the group and no doubt led to their demise. Bowie's lyrics are basically a list of the "Gouster" look, though Tony Visconti praises the strength of the original song's chord changes, much of which remains intact. Bowie carried over the edgy verse of funk slashes and chorus melody into "Scream"; the strength of the hook laid sunk in his mind for several years. The scream of the song's title is only implied; with Bowie's vocals veering between elation and muted disquiet, he offers the faintest resistance knowing that he has already lost. This is the angry dissenting voice of silenced people.

"Scream" is well known for Bowie's nightmarish varispeed bridge; a witness or accomplice (nonetheless a survivor) recounts the fate of "Sam," no longer around to tell his own story. Bowie seems to step on his own voice, forcing the pitch high as the oxygen is squeezed out of the lines. Increasingly desperate, he reels off a series of banned social activities, muttering under his breath until his rage becomes a streak of survivor's guilt, echoed back at him. While he thinks he is only telling Sam's story, he is also talking about himself.

The continued goal of *Scary Monsters* was to push the boundaries of the best studio technology available at the time before the floodgates of the "1980s sound" were fully unleashed and for Bowie drive his own spirit to meet the character of a song. Exploiting the division between left and right speakers, Visconti manually slowed down the vocal track on one side and continually sped it up on the other, twisting reality as Bowie was recording.[273] "David's voice goes up and down in pitch contrarily, on opposite sides" (Visconti 2007). This purposeful disorientation throws the listener off with increasingly aggressive voices jumping backward and forward in menacing tones, advancing from the speakers left, then right, like a flurry of punches coming from nowhere. These altered voices connect the novelty of "The Laughing Gnome" to the schizoid breakdown of "The Bewlay Brothers" and to "Scream" with its layered ranting of chewed-up words held in gnashing teeth.

Across *Scary Monsters*, Bowie takes the songs into hysterical and unhinged places. Pushing his voice with angular intonation to subvert the listener's expectations, he chases notes across his wide range, as in his performance of *The Elephant Man*, where Angus MacKinnon noted his "odd, high, fluted voice out of the side of his mouth, which in turn he has to violently contort," tensing his face to hit new forms of speech and diction, expressing a deeper kind of mutation.

The idea of being forced to live by extremes at the fringes of society was not alien to Bowie. His own sexual identity, which has long been debated, served him well in periods of hyper-fluidity between flirting and enticing collaborators, playing to a gay crowd, and queering gender norms for the blurring of fixed sexual behaviors into the twenty-first century, something that he later lamented as touristic metrosexuality. But on "Scream Like a Baby," he isolates difference itself as the issue, inferred as homosexuality on the song but equally applicable to race, gender, and even the dividing lines of politics, all tipping points toward persecution. The song is the sound of the clampdown, the dangerous fallout from mass authoritarianism against societal difference, squeezing out minorities like a splinter. In this sense, "Scream" offers the flip side to "Fashion," which at least in its tunefulness can work like a macabre celebration of crowd groupthink working against deviance. "Scream" is a shadowy picture of the unseen and disappeared victims from this thwarted equation that fails to balance private pleasure, choice, and identity with principle.

Bowie's earliest influences provoked an interest in the sexualized power of music performance and its associated fashions. Bowie claimed the proto-glamour and sensuality of Elvis, feeding off Little Richard's hypersexualized gospel singer energy, from the hip-thrusting beginnings to the Vegas jumpsuit of rhinestone self-eclipse, as being closer to the feminized glitter and makeup of glam rock than many would allow, causing Bowie to comment, "If his image wasn't bisexual then I don't know what is."[274] Bowie long flirted with bisexuality as a lifestyle choice and homosexuality as a business decision, trying anything and everything more out of curiosity than outright desire. He offered himself as a metrosexual figurehead for the early 1970s as a hangover from the previous decade.

In his early sexual tourism and interest to walk on the wild side, Bowie was influenced by John Rechy's autobiographical novel *City of Night* (1963), which he referred to as "one of the greatest pieces of gay literature ever written."[275] *Bowie's Books* author John O'Connell pointed out that what the *City of Night* referred to is really a state of mind; as the number of people Rechy slept with multiplied, his story stretched out into one long nocturnal day showing the gay subculture living in the shadows. Along with his many "johns," the narrator (Rechy) kids himself that he is only in it for the money; though taking pleasure in his work, he is sucked into the self-denying homosexual world of the mid-twentieth century. Elsewhere, Rechy becomes more romantic, and in the aftermath of sex, there is a brief shining moment of peace, contentment, and connection before the lovers become strangers again—brought down to earth by the realization that same-sex intercourse was an illegal act. To paraphrase Oscar Wilde, it was love by another name; it could not be spoken out loud, only whispered into the lover's ear.

Bowie himself could play within the sphere of homosexuality with some immunity and hide behind the mask of his characters. Camp was already present in the glam era of glitter and makeup, which Bowie would later claim was great for "pulling the birds," as if it made him (even) less intimidatingly masculine. As a teenager taking the train into central London, Bowie would see the first of the early mods wearing makeup, thinking they looked fantastic—their look was not just laddishness but genuine modishness—rooted in a latent sexuality. He would later take this aesthetic to the limit of masculine beauty with the male dress and the long, wavy hair of 1970, a nod toward transvestitism, which Bowie felt presented a "pre-Raphaelite look."

The rock guitars of glam were acceptable for people who used beer, denim, and (uh) beards as a straight shield to hide behind; Jon Savage called out Slade and the Sweet as "brickies dressed up as rent-boys." In this regard, Bowie had the very straight-talking former-council-gardener-from-Hull-turned-rock-guitar-god Mick Ronson, who, along with the other Spiders, was coaxed further and further into the golden and dizzy heights of vague androgyny with platform shoes and shiny jumpsuits. Bowie, of course, brought the inner normality of his very heterosexual foil crashing down when he gripped Ronson's buttocks, fellating strings with teeth and tongue, the implicit well-hung masculinity of the Les Paul guitar standing in for Ronson's member, bringing the already ecstatic performance to a head as many young fans looked on wishing it was their body in Bowie's hands (and mouth) instead; it was flesh made fantasy.[276]

Aside from this, Bowie literally came out in 1972, proclaiming he was gay to Peter Watts in *Melody Maker*—"and I always have been, even when I was David Jones"—but continued to edge in and out of the closet as another theatrical pose when and where it suited him.[277] This ambiguity was his greatest strength, turning gender difference on and off like a hot/cold tap, leaving his audience holding their breath for the next affirmation or denial. Peter Doggett points out that when Bowie visited the United States in 1971 wearing a dress, he still declared himself more or less heterosexual, but in that 1972 interview, he presented "sly jollity" along with carefully placed gay men's magazines on the table, lending an increased effeminacy to his manner. Bowie appeared to play into the hands of his interviewer's preconceptions, as they were subsumed into his, a knowing game on both sides, happily bandying it about that he was by turns gay and bisexual before declaring outright bisexuality in 1976 to *Playboy* magazine, further muddying the waters. In a 1978 interview, again with Watts, Bowie declared that his original admission had been a polemicist tactic: "It was something to throw in people's faces." Simon Reynolds (2017) found this vagueness to be part of Bowie's great deflective strength: "Over the years Bowie oscillated wildly sustaining a miasma of sexual undecidability that enabled him to be all things to all people."[278]

Bowie would continue to make allusive lyrical nods, not just physicals ones, to an alignment with gay culture, jumping in and out from behind a glittering, stage-y curtain. From the veiled motions of "John I'm Only Dancing" to "Moonage Daydream" and its "church of man, love," he rolled along with phallic imagery and the "mama/papa" gender-bending dynamic.

Through the Ziggy Stardust era, Peter Doggett sees Bowie divining a cultural wet dream moving in parallel with the skyward thrust of the moon landings: everything sexy and potentially queered just enough to throw off the straight listener but with enough pop dynamism to bring them along into the wide and wild realm of open fantasy.[279]

Bowie made a definite rejection of his past, as if trying to conform to the new normal that was expected from the performer of *Let's Dance*. In his 1980 article "Gender Bender," Jon Savage noted Bowie's adoption of a long-submerged showbiz trope, but even though his pose was affected, Bowie still broke new ground: "Homosexuality, if not bisexuality, had always been part of pop, both in the process (managers picking up potential singers) and the appeal. Film stars like Montgomery Clift had killed themselves in a previous age trying to deny it, but this was the first time, five years after legalization, that any star came right out and said it."

But it was later in the 1980s, at the peak of his fame with *Let's Dance* that Bowie declared: "Bisexual? Absolutely not." Bowie later claimed that coming out was one of his great mistakes, tying him to other people's expectations for him as a figurehead for gay rights and identity politics. In a 1995 interview with *Details* magazine, he explained his position: "I refused to be a banner waver for anything or anybody, and I did not want everything I was doing to be purely coloured by my sexuality. I was dealing in a very primitive way with a very new area of public perception. I made as many mistakes as I made positive moves."

There remained conflict between the traditions of the more militant homosexual protest movements and those who preferred to enjoy the subculture of illicit encounters. For born outsiders like Francis Bacon, who straddled the pre- and postwar sexual revolution, the illegality of gay sex enjoyed in the blacked-out London of World War II became a mark of quiet resistance, a badge of pride. In 1988, the Conservative government introduced Section (or Clause) 28, a supposed gag order on local authorities, similar to the 1993 "don't ask, don't tell" policy for the U.S. armed forces, which aimed to prevent the "promotion" of homosexuality. It was not to be discussed in schools, and the very existence of gay people was denied or obfuscated in provincial council meetings with the threat of prosecution; nondisclosure became denial as self-erasure.[280]

The 1980s is considered the era in which liberal attitudes toward race and sexuality grew in openness and confidence toward a more outwardly tolerant and equally representative society. But rarely did this arrive from older generations, who remained entrenched in feelings of stigma, exclusion, and separation, homosexuality as a threat to the cultural norm of the straight family unit. The AIDS crisis and growing conservative attitudes toward sexual promiscuity (for women) and reproductive rights, fueled by the self-appointed "moral majority," would aim to see civil liberties, such as the right to abortion, contested in 1981, rolled back as the decade progressed.[281]

In 1973, Bowie complained, "I think being bisexual is a facet of my life, but not necessarily the most important. In the States, it gets to horrendous proportions and it's 'faggot this' and 'faggot that' and all the papers call me a 'faggot.' But I don't see why it should stop me being an all-round entertainer." Elsewhere, other, more mainstream artists, such as Liberace(!), skirted around the issue where homosexuality was merely implied or simply a verboten subject; it remained about the surface of subtext—no one asked, and everyone was happy. Despite his complaint, "faggot" was a term that Bowie threw out on frequent occasions in early interviews and was, like many of his golden lines, repeated, recycled, and absorbed into songs.

On "Scream Like a Baby," Bowie throws in the slur just to make his point—the word hits hard not only as an insult but also as a marker rooted in the persecution of difference. He himself had been insulted in the same way by many of his musical heroes, often to his face, sometimes in behind-the-scenes hearsay, from Sinatra to Elvis to Jacques Brel, who in the Ziggy era brushed Bowie off for his showy and outlandish exhibitions of androgyny. Where they had secured their own strongly uniform heterosexual identity built on the traditions of masculinity, Bowie was up and coming with broader contemporary appeal. Bowie might have become inured to the alarmism of the term by the time of *Scary Monsters*, referring to himself as "the red-haired faggot" to both Edward Bell and Angus MacKinnon. Even by 1980, for many fans, casual listeners, and media outlets, he remained bisexual Ziggy. Because of this, Bowie felt he was given short shrift when it came to interviews that didn't bother to apply any critical insight to his work.

Queer, gay, bisexual—these were easy tags for Bowie to use without the sincere right of ownership and without consequence. By osmosis and design, he routinely absorbed other people's street vernacular: "Gouster" slang and bastardized *polari*, underground language that allowed British gay people to communicate in public without being eavesdropped on. Reappropriated into Bowie's earliest songs, this marked a shift from the perception in the United Kingdom of glam rock as "glitter rock" and in the United States as "fag rock" or "drag rock," perhaps as a slur but perhaps also as a more accurate description of what true glam rock expressed: a sense of decadent glamour that wrestled with its own mask of androgyny.[282] Bowie would throw out some casual phrases in 2016's "Girl Loves Me," a throwback to his earlier mixture of fake eyelashes, jumpsuits, and NADSAT, the invented gang language of the

Droogs in Antony Burgess's *A Clockwork Orange*. Bowie's self-identification as the "red-haired . . . gay/faggot/bisexual" line was altered, depending on whom he was speaking to, but in weaponizing sexual deviance, Bowie was able to disarm its detractors. "Scream" shouted out a warning against censorship of alternative modes of life.[283] He offered a confrontation to the wider public struggle to accept nonstandard sexual modes, where the world of sexuality was dominated by "normality" and where women were objects to be seen, something like a muse and to write pop songs about, and men were there to freely gaze at and enjoy them, dictating the course of visual arts for hundreds of years and subsequently for rock music.

On "Repetition" and "Boys Keep Swinging," Bowie addressed the more toxic aspects of hetero-stereotypes, particularly the chauvinism of masculine privilege: the regression into the major-dominant role of the male causes the reactionary gag reflex and the crackdown against alternative models of living. With the decline of the nuclear family and the falling birth rates in Western democracies, new systems of family and relationship status would be ushered in to make a more open and civilized society—a very gradual shift in the law but one that the wider population would only grudgingly accept.[284]

> Democracy is a good thing, but is violence and
> war the only way we can establish its goodness?
>
> —Thomas Anthony Harris, *I'm OK, You're OK*

Sam's rising terror is the fire lit under "Scream Like a Baby," never knowing how or when the hammer will fall—until it hits him. On the original version of the song "I Am a Laser," Bowie sang of a force "burning through your eyes," a deeper self-surveillance becoming the knives that lacerate your brain, stripped of denial, the citizen finally seeing themself cowed under fear of the unknown; it is already too late. Bowie himself would admit, "I lapse into this future nostalgia thing . . . taking a past look that something that hasn't actually happened yet," a latent sense of dread Bowie described as "that Orwellian thing," which, since *Diamond Dogs*, was a major touchstone in his music (MacKinnon 1980).

Bowie used a broad range of influences from his reading list for the song, the specter of his time spent in Berlin as city-state reveal themselves across the divide of the democratic West and the state-controlled Communist East.[285] Bowie's time in Berlin brought home the history of World War II just the Cold War remained red hot. Heading into the post-punk years of 1978, Berlin inherited a blank generation, populated by the very old and the very young, with the population of middle-aged citizens decimated by World War II. Bowie met people his own age whose fathers had been active members of the Schutzstaffel (SS) or Wehrmacht soldiers, the inheritors of those responsible for torture and ethnic cleansing as well as ordinary people caught up in Germany's nationalist extremism. Elsewhere, he witnessed the Turkish immigrants of "New Cologne" beaten up by neo-Nazi thugs, memorialized in the song "Neuköln."[286] Bowie was singing about the great wall in his eyeline as harbinger of the city, constantly overlooked by armed guards and watchtowers, and suspicious citizens, spied on and spying on one another. A psychological barrier as much as a physical one, the Berlin Wall did not cast its shade over Bowie; he left his shadow on the wall. The spirit of paranoia in the German capital of the 1970s echoed the city of the 1930s, suggesting a cyclical state of history caught between resurrection and total collapse, perpetual revolution, and reactionary backlash; it must have been hard for Bowie to ignore the patterns forming before him, with great art produced under conservative pressures and in opposition to wider conformity.[287]

Jon Savage (2016) draws a ley line between William S. Burroughs and Christopher Isherwood. "Both are more or less specifically homosexual authors, both deal with smut and totalitarian control." The authoritarian powers could only live in denial of the undesirable elements of sexual desire, the crooked, degenerate element they intended to make straight or else silence, knowing their plan for total eradication could never entirely be fulfilled. Under the political turbulence of the collapsing Weimar Republic witnessed by Isherwood in the 1930s and resurrected in the movie *Cabaret*, if "Scream" speaks to writing on the wall or blood on the streets, Sam and his friends have already chosen to look away. Everyone knows that Sam is beat; not only is he "down" in hipster beatnik slang of subterranean cool, he is also thwarted from the start, and his burning secret seals his doom.

On "It's No Game (No. 2)," Bowie alludes to the glory years of post-revolutionary regime change. The song echoes the Nazis' brute logic of forging a better world in the image of their own nation, borrowing from the imperial pomp of the Roman model of war and conquest in the name of empire and eugenicist proto-accelerationism: "big heads and drums/full speed and pagan." The brutality of fact meets the power of force, where the march of progress demanded that others be crushed under its weight. The self-righteousness of torture and tyranny is a sham, with straitened chaos and instability always bubbling under the surface of any authoritarian system masquerading as calm and order.[288]

A paranoid song of persecution, then, but who are the real victims? The crackdown on the individual citizen is crystallized in Arthur Koestler's

1946 novel *Darkness at Noon,* where he features a quote from Dietrich Von Nieheim, Bishop of Verden (1411), to skewer the problem:

> With unity as the end, the use of every means
> is sanctified, even cunning, treachery, violence,
> simony, prison, death. For all order it for the
> sake of the community, and the individual
> must be sacrificed to the common good.

It is coldly ironic that Koestler refers to the enforcement of religious ortho-doxy to elucidate the totalitarian horrors of (atheistic) communism under the regime of Stalin. The heroes who helped bring about revolution in Russia now became its enemies, "confessing" to being traitors in a series of show trials. Published in 1940, nine years before Orwell's *1984, Darkness at Noon* suggests a warning from history that bears repeating.

Bowie would often write apocalyptically, and in the so-called society of "Scream Like a Baby," he confronts a more subtle form of terror. After his journey on the Trans-Siberian Express in 1973, a seemingly shell-shocked Bowie said to Angie, "I've never been so damn scared in my life," such that he wouldn't write about it in his music, fearing he might be disappeared.[289] Bowie's track foreshadowed the race riots of 1981 and the homophobic backlash against victims of HIV and AIDS, only just becoming widely known toward the mid-1980s as it began to shift into an epidemic crisis. Cruelly labeled the "gay plague," it became a pushback against the sexual revolution; but, more, important, patients suffered from a lack of healthcare support for lifesaving drugs and a reluctance from government to act preventively by raising more public awareness. Ghettoization and extermination were bywords for ideas of progress in the 1980s; the rule of divide and conquer drew lines between the successful classes—and the outsiders they perceived as enemies (Lindsay 2021).

The great crime of the 1980s was the claim to democratic freedom of self-identity; more often than not, there was significant pressure to keep quiet about "deviant" lifestyles that differed from the normal majority, to repress dissent, and, even where exclusion remained common, to say nothing. On Pink Floyd's *The Wall,* Roger Waters gives a roll call of minority groups to be put against the wall, singled out, ready to be shot; the psycho–horror show within the context of stadium rock concert of 1979 would come to seem pre-scient in the wake of large-scale international massacres.[290]

In the fear of "Scream Like a Baby," the totalitarian regime leads to a stripping of identity as people are shaved, numbered, and dehumanized through chemical castration, concentration camps, and conversion therapy; this plays out around the skipping keyboard tones, making its jaunty kitsch all the more jarring and surreal. The goal is for deviant people to be fixed, cured, and reassimilated—in this context, it is society (the real monsters) that makes them freaks.

In the movie of Pink Floyd's 1979 album *The Wall*, the track "Empty Spaces" segues into "What Shall We Do Now," where Roger Waters reels off a proto-Radiohead stream-of-consciousness shopping list of trivial lifestyle choices, consumerism, and extreme acts violent self-destruction, interchangeably banal and stripped of meaning, perhaps inevitably ending "with our backs against the wall"—the worst habits of the 1970s merging to become the habitual excesses of the 1980s. In the long bridge of "Scream," Bowie offers a response to the broken opportunities where Sam would not conform or could not be made to fit; at its end, he is accused of standing out. From consumerism, mixed-race relationships, and military service, he rejects the values of a society that has rejected him.[291]

After the singer's drawling fugue, George Murray's spiraling bass notes climb the scale before shrinking back, as slurring synth notes fall away Bowie's speech degenerates into mental collapse. Where on "Fashion" Bowie used beats and breaks in his singing, for "Scream" he turns this on its head; the voice is as dissociated from language as it is from the crowd, and Bowie struggles to get the words out: "now I'm learning to be a part of . . . su . . . su . . . su . . . socie-socie-society."

Bowie's vocal echoes Roger Daltrey's verbal tic in the Who's "My Generation"; choking with disgust on the forced words that are not even his, he cannot stomach the supposed ideal of the better life. The thought of trying too hard to belong in a world he had already rejected, the voice is broken on the wheel; he can no longer piece together a free sentence or articulate his own feelings[292] before the toms and stabbed guitar chords jolt us back into the final chorus and Bowie lifts us up in the vortex of the scream again.

Bowie's vocal inflections across the album carry "sounds of pre–meaning language." Alongside the repetition of "society," Jun Tanaka contrasts Bowie's dynamic use of Japanese as noise from "It's No Game (No. 1)" with the repeated sibilance of his other vocals:

"Scary Monsters": "S-cary monster-s, s-uper creep-s"

"Because You're Young": You can hear back of "a million scars" the sounds "s . . . s"

All these sounds coalesce as an acidic hiss that leaves a burning wound caught in the listener's ear (Tanaka 2021).

Bowie would note that his "Sweet Thing" triptych echoed a "profligate world" similar to that explored by Rechy and subsequently the chaotic persecuted state of "Scream," a homosexual encounter as disposable pleasure, especially for the bisexual or closeted "straight man." Where underground sex offered romance without the tangle of love, the motion is quickly forgotten after the dancing shoes are removed. The freedom and free love of "Sweet Thing" is flipped into a nightmare, a crime of both thought and passion, now tainted as a source of criminal guilt. "Sweet Thing/Candidate/Sweet Thing (Reprise)" encapsulates youthful rebellion but accelerates toward a headlong death drive of sexual encounters in darkened rooms and finally the romanticized suicide of jumping into a river holding hands. Now he watches Sam jump into the furnace singing old songs they loved; a soundtrack of the same music that led them down a doomed path, their final leap is not into the freedom of love but shared annihilation.

First They Came
First they came for the socialists,
and I did not speak out—
Because I was not a socialist.
Then they came for the trade unionists,
and I did not speak out—
Because I was not a trade unionist.
Then they came for the Jews, and I did not speak out—
Because I was not a Jew.
Then they came for me—and there
was no one left to speak for me.

—Pastor Martin Niemöller, 1946

Where Sam experiences his backseat breakdown turned confession, we are left to wonder if he is in fact the alter ego of the narrator's own suppressed homosexuality.[293] Without a last name, Sam is a paper-thin target, a straw dummy onto which the singer projects his deepest fears (Tanaka 2021). Sam shares a situation with the "I" narrator of the song where Bowie merges first and second perspectives such that their fates are intertwined; the voice remembers Sam falling but claims he has forgotten the light of day—was he ever really there?

The threat of being disappeared lingers throughout "Scream." Shadowy half-light figures merge in and out of the scenery, uncertain friend or enemies, as with Milan Kundera's novel *The Book of Laughter and Forgetting*, where a number of people are gradually erased from a photograph, their absence coming to mean they were never there, leaving behind a floating hat where a person once stood.

Sam is everyone on the wrong end of a truncheon or blacklisted by state censorship, a noncitizen deemed less than human, nudged out of their own history. Here Sam's story only survives secondhand. In Britain during the

1980s, there was a broad sweeping together of liberals and socialists as political dissidents, along with anti–nuclear weapon campaigners, striking miners and their families, union members, Roma and Traveller communities, protesting homosexuals and lesbians—they would all be targeted as undesirable and antipatriotic persons, so political persecution set the wider population against the imagined enemy within.

Resisting this narrow shadow play, Bowie showed some commitment to people whose lot was very different from his own. He allows Sam his passions, loves, and dreams but shows them cruelly snatched away perhaps through hatred and ignorance, though we never find out his crime. Sam lingers in the memory of his mysterious friend because "he was like me"; the narrator, perhaps to his regret, is the one that got away.

Although the song closes with an outright denial—that they "never had no fun"—the singer's thought crime becomes an act of bad faith, erasing his own past.[294] Again, Koestler and Orwell spring to mind. After their experiences of sudden liberty, Winston Smith and Julia, the heroes of *1984*, are just as quickly made mental prisoners again, passing each other by as familiar strangers, living ghosts with no past and no future, only the terrible present to endure. Does "Scream" end with the song's narrator surrendering Sam to the thought police in order to save himself? If so, the traitor knows their crime and keeps it hidden; seeing Sam exterminated when it could just as easily have been him in his place, maybe it doesn't make any difference when the watchword of authoritarianism becomes self-policing and mutual betrayal: I am no longer my brother's keeper; I am both his accuser and his assassin.

Bowie's proximity to gay culture was more about general queering and queening, an extension of his campest performance sensibilities. Walking the line between appropriation or celebration of gay culture as a largely straight white male, it never hurt him to play to this "other" audience who would embrace him if not as a champion then as an attractive, charismatic songwriter who never turned them away or condemned divergent sexual identities. He enjoyed the freedom that gender fluidity and androgyny allowed him to play within, but his interest was personal; he purposefully distanced himself from any crusade, protest line, or open-voiced support.

"Bowie opened a space where it was permissive for sexuality to be much, much larger than standard heteronormativity. He opened up a much wider field of sexual possibility." In 2016, Simon Critchley told the Politico website, "Uncertainty about what he exudes—his androgyny—was what drew people in." Bowie kept much of the attitude and his sympathies extended far beyond his own sexual proclivities. The one-sided conversation of "are you gay?" was kept going well into 1980 across several interviews, which Bowie always passed over as a tired old question that he had already answered years earlier.[295]

By 1980, Bowie had all but shed the trappings of gay fashion and gender-bending clothing, toning down blatant eccentricities, preferring instead a gentlemanly metrosexuality, the modish male, hinting at natural effeminacy, sometimes with a hint of eye shadow or mascara around the eyes or foundation to smooth out his skin and sharpen his features. This compromise with camp only made him even more appealing to both sexes. New Romantic figures such as Boy George would often cite Bowie as a groundbreaking influence on his teenage years, creating more space in which he could be himself and from there achieve creative expression. Bowie spoke about bisexuality in public when few others would; this later encouraged George O'Dowd to assert his own homosexuality in 1985.[296]

In the 1990s, Bowie seemed to find the greater freedoms and confusion of modern sexual politics tiresome. On the soundtrack to *The Buddha of Suburbia*, he casually throws out the line "sometimes I fear/that the whole world is queer"—recognizing a world still full of prejudice and stigma? Elsewhere, he complained that everyone was declaring themselves bisexual as he had once done; marking a point of identity crisis in trying too hard to appear different, special, or unique, it had devolved into a fashionable new norm. Perhaps when Bowie declared the tag meaningless, he meant that sexuality was now more widely accepted as being fluid and nonpolarizing, that labels no longer helped anyone. He would never return to the radical gender extremes of his earlier career; it was a phase he had outgrown, a look he had shed or toned down, the end of an artistic social experiment.[297]

In *Bowie's Books*, John O'Connell (2020) notes that the image of a boot stomping on a human face (forever) of Orwell's *1984* is dotted throughout Bowie's song. Certainly at the time of writing, it feels that in reality it has never stopped, like the beating heart of a timeless clock. We are offered the image of the body stepped on so hard that it cries out, as when the victim was an infant, like a human animal. Bowie's point perhaps reaches wider: if it is done to them, it might be done to us too. After prolonged torture and brainwashing, the internal struggle of *1984* forces Winston Smith to love his tormentor, Big Brother; he calls for his pain to be turned against his former lover: "Do it to Julia!"

In the outro of "Scream Like A Baby," we hear the sonic motif of hammer and boot stomp, stripped of Bowie's vocals, drums thud and echo, resounding with the shallow victory of a now emptied-out social space. The song succeeds in exposing the human condition of the individual set against an authoritarian society that has become intolerant of their existence. It is important to shout out before these dissenting voices are crushed to become a scream and then cruelly and permanently silenced.

Kingdom Come

(Beyond Heaven and Hell)

I submit that the tension between science and
faith should be resolved not in terms either of
elimination or duality, but in terms of a synthesis.

— Pierre Teilhard de Chardin

If heaven was ever a place on Earth, then by 1980 Bowie had yet to find it. Adopting a Tom Verlaine song as his chosen cover for *Scary Monsters*, Bowie took the song's struggle with God and the search for an afterlife into a new realm of terrestrial angst. Bowie explained his selection as one of his favorite cuts from Verlaine's eponymous 1979 solo album, suggested by Carlos Alomar on the strength of the song's swinging rhythm. Bowie was quick to acknowledge Verlaine's talent as "one of the best writers in New York." When asked about the notion of grace present in the song, Bowie couldn't help but nod toward his recent past: "The song just happens to fit into the scattered scheme of things, that's all." The track seems to contain as much musical value for him as it did spiritual force for Verlaine.

In comparison to side A, the second half of *Scary Monsters* is unloved by some Bowie fans, the cover of "Kingdom Come" often being criticized for the singer's vocal performance. Bringing more verve and melody to the original's angular, chiming notes, Bowie's version intensifies the moody reserve of Television but escalates Verlaine's music to a richer, more open-ended arrangement, swooping and soaring instead of needling and gouging away. Where on "Ashes to Ashes" Bowie had mangled lines torn from the Book of Common Prayer, he now exploits his voice to make deranged shapes from Verlaine's words. Although Bowie edited and shuffled some phrasings from the song, perhaps muddying its meaning, his version was largely faithful. Bowie's powerful vocalizations jump light-years beyond Verlaine's shrill lament sitting within his flattened range, while the lyrics are rich in forceful images. Bowie retained the central pivot between punishment and the possibility of absolution; we hear sacrifice in loyalty to God—but does the Second Coming demand the death of the faithful—while the lack of redemption seems a forgone conclusion, and there is only final judgment.

Verlaine never states any explicit crime or offense and we're left to wonder if the voice in the song is, like so many others on *Scary Monsters*, looking for meaning in an empty and lawless universe or trying to return the grace of God, to make themselves whole in some way. But deep in his heart, Tom knows it's all in vain—the song rips the roof off the church of good hope, revealing heaven collapsed into hell.

A voice like lightning speaks, breaking through the walls behind which Bowie had sought to keep himself alone and separate from the world. The song's return to the act of breaking rocks carries the weight of heaven collapsing down on him. Bowie cries out for just one more day to escape or be given another chance. Like an addict, he tries to force back the boundaries for change, always tomorrow, never today. But stood before God, he finds he has nowhere left to run.

Like so much of *Scary Monsters*, Bowie's singing runs from blood into honey and back again; as if stamping on the *fumi-e* as the face of Jesus, Bowie twists his vocals under the heel, pinpricks of rain, a reminder from above. Across the verses of "Kingdom Come," Bowie agonizes at being held tight in the gaze of others. Life under the eyes of God like a prisoner guarded by an ever-present watchtower, yielding an intense light that becomes the power of renewed conscience as second sight, so the righteous Christian as good citizen should live checking themselves under the imagined moral thumb.

Like "Teenage Wildlife," the chain gang backing chorus speaks to putting in time and paying your dues in the music industry. In the old bluesman's sense, this meant coming through hard times; for Bowie, this line now carried deeper meanings of achieving artistic success at the cost of losing himself to drugs and reaching a point of psychic breakdown.

In that period, drugs became Bowie's private place to which his mind could escape, a blacked-out room of doubled negative space. Aside from recording sessions at Cherokee Studios, Bowie threw much of his waking life into void. Even the making of *Station to Station* would return to him only as a distant history; as recounted by others, Bowie claimed to have little or no memory. Whether he was blocking it out or was genuinely unable to recall it, this was foreign time to him; he felt the aftershocks that followed it only on the surviving artifacts of the records *Station to Station and Low*.

Barely eating, except his quoted diet of milk and green peppers, he relied on cocaine as mental fuel; he could sleep late and stay up all night, keeping vampiric hours, his weight plummeting. Submerged in his Los Angeles exile, Bowie would wake up with an aching jaw from talking constantly; he would later remember nothing of the conversation, as if he had been speaking alone and could no longer hear himself. Angie remembers that Bowie pushed to the very limits: "There was nothing sociable about it—this was a deep dark pit."

While *Station to Station* laid bare Bowie's physical and emotional crises, the cri de coeur of "Word on a Wing" conveys Bowie's declaration of belief and call for deliverance from his worst self, born out of grace under pressure. Where previously Bowie was only interested in pursuing the ideal of the Nietzschean Übermensch, an aesthetic idea of self-attainment with man as his own god, "Word on a Wing" is equal parts the lament of shook faith and an attempt to reignite his frozen heart. The third track on a record of six songs, it reaches over to the forlorn romance of album closer "Wild Is the Wind." As *Station to Station* connects spiritual touchstones from east to west, Bowie was mentally (and physically) zigzagging across the Atlantic for an explosive return to the European canon (read also continental), straddling the stations of the cross, torn between the dialectic rule of heaven and/or hell. The song arrives as a defense of religious curiosity, where belief demands not a lack of imagination or rational curiosity but its very opposite (O'Leary 2017).

From the mind scrape/scape that unfolds across "Station to Station," Bowie noted, "It was the first time I'd really seriously thought about Christ and God in any depth." He confessed to Angus MacKinnon, "'Word on a Wing' I can't talk about. There were days of such psychological terror when making the Roeg film that I nearly started to approach my reborn, born again thing." Bowie was reaching for some form of spiritual resolve but bounced back and forth between the stark dichotomy of heaven and hell as the song became a talismanic protection against the white heat of doubt and pain. In Los Angeles, which John Rechy calls "the City of Lost Angels," Bowie had failed to answer his own big question, and in his calling, the same hollow echo returned to find him out, telling him what he already knew: this is not the place you are looking for. He would continue his search beyond America and through the stilted figure of David Bowie as the Thin White Duke of 1976.[298] Despite "Kingdom Come" being a cover, there remains the empathetic, wounded spirit of Bowie in the song: "Terse, rocky and didactic, Bowie's compositions cut away all illusions of dignity in isolation, of comfort in crowds," finding himself dragged back down to earth with a bump (Cohen 1980).

Speaking in 1980, it became clear that the wounds of the *Station to Station* era were still fresh in his mind: "The passion in the song was genuine. It was also around that time that I started thinking about wearing this [fingers a small silver cross hanging on his chest] again, which is now almost a leftover from that period." As Chuck Hammer remembered, Bowie was wearing a large wooden cross in the studio, but since the post-Ziggy 1970s, the little silver crucifix about Bowie's neck would remain for many years, lazing off his chest in interviews and in spite of its size seemed to bear some weight on him, crowning his open leather jacket as he swayed and swooned on the spot for the "Heroes" video.[299]

Bowie was more than ready to make his own leap of faith; he just didn't know how. On "It's No Game (No. 1)," his scratchy, screedy voice yells "no more/ free steps to heav-eeeeeen," breathing fire into the line. The use of the word "free" in the song is up for debate, but in the straight Japanese translation by Stephen Ryan, Bowie is still walking on air:

> *mo tengoku no jiyu no kaidan wa nai*
> (free [without restrictions] steps of
> heaven are no longer there/here)

This reading also suggests liberty as "freedom to" and "freedom from," whereas Bowie's Anglophone side teases us that even religion bears its price of commitment on the soul, not just kindly acts. "Kingdom Come" later wrestles with the tension that we cannot enter the gate of heaven simply claiming repentance; each of us must endure the wages of our own sin. The road to heaven is paved with wayward intentions of sacrifice and reward, and the open way through the eye of the needle is never a sure thing. On "Kingdom Come," getting closer to God demands climbing a brittle stairway that is supported only by blind and hopeless faith, where belief must also carry the weight of doubt within it.

A possible influence on the track is Eddie Cochran's "Three Steps to Heaven" from 1960. For Eddie, only three simple steps toward a happy life are required: find a girl, fall in love, and hold her tight. Resembling the chord structure of "Queen Bitch," Cochran's song reached number one after his sudden death in a car crash. Did Bowie make a nod to Cochran's song to point out that real life is far more brutal than the sweet fantasies of young love might have us imagine? In spite of everything, maybe Cochran's untimely short walk through life brought him a little closer to (some kind of) paradise.[300]

For Verlaine's sake, the blogger Paolo hears the "pseudo-spiritual lyric become a dogged affirmation that the artist is both destined and doomed to pursue his creative muse." Instead of finding religious purpose, his vocation is the craft of songwriting and performing, driven by artistic drive, rock and roll being one form of religion within a pantheon of spirituality.

Nonetheless, "Kingdom Come" has a decadent air of abandonment to it, sharing similar feelings with Bowie's friend John Lennon and the Plastic Ono Band's "God," where Lennon acknowledged that God is merely a mental device "by which we measure our pain." For Bowie, this admitted to a more vital and primal, albeit morally decayed, era, refusing to deny our chthonic impulses as apposite to living within society, which serves to erase our true sense of self. In the Nietzschean view, Christian orthodoxy provided a moral prison that caused people to live their lives within a rotten framework of external rules internalized under the illusion of a superior moral code to become the cage within. Bowie remained open to spiritual possibilities, if not living in denial of them, then a healthy skepticism. For Lennon, perhaps like Bowie, much of these inner spiritual pains were often revealed to be self-inflicted wounds.

Much later, on 2013's *The Next Day*, Bowie presented his most vitriolic attack on organized religion, wrestling with pagan freedom and Christianity's pejorative modes of living, laying on the imagery of the phallic-headed priest to expose the hypocrisy of desire and the Catholic Church's long history of sexual abuse of children and the punishment of unmarried pregnant women.

Bowie would tour alongside Blondie as the piano man for Iggy Pop. Chris Stein remembers Bowie's enthusiasm for Television, in particular admiring Verlaine's hair, leading Bowie to comment, "I wish he had a bigger audience." Verlaine was invited to play on the *Scary Monsters* sessions, but after spending many hours trying to find the right sound and apparently testing out some thirty amps (although he did eventually find what he was looking for) his guitar part was not included on the final album.[301] On "Kingdom Come," a far more lightweight ballad compared to "Teenage Wildlife," Fripp brought sonorous, soaring zips of guitar to rise and fall over the top of the song. His touch is more subtle and intuitive with the demands of the track than on other songs; the tigerish savant is finally restrained though perhaps only by volume in the mix.

Every religion has its own madmen.

—Alberto Denti de Piranjo, *A Grave for a Dolphin*, 1956

Since the coked-out flatness of *David Live*, Bowie had pulled his voice back together. By 1980, his years of experience made him a stronger and more versatile singer. The rare natural quality of his voice meant he could hold a deep timbre and falsetto within the same note, and his technical ability remained sharp even on *Station to Station*. Across *Scary Monsters*, Bowie's voice seems to go on forever, filling the room and breaking out the walls; he would never have made it as a punk singer, being unable to limit himself to the short barks and snarls required.

Chris Porter, engineer at Good Earth, remembers the depth and intensity of Bowie's vocal performances as being one of his most exciting experiences in the studio: "His voice changed almost like a mimic. He was really viscerally acting out the parts to the songs . . . his whole body attitudes would change while he was singing. There was a real energy with his whole body charged up when he went to sing."

Bowie croons his way through octaves, snapping lines as if testing the limits of his voice. Toward the end of "Kingdom Come," he is met by Dennis Davis's crackling drum fills (thumping toms and dropped beats) that land like rolls of thunder rippling off the drumskin topped with the crowning glory of splashing cymbals as Bowie vocalizes wildly over the top. He breaks from the chant about rocks to deliver the line "Well pardon me-ah-he-he-he," teasing the line with urgency, where the original is cast off with typically sardonic Verlaine abandon. Bowie ends in fearful respect of God's power; Verlaine mocks it without mercy, expecting his cell door to finally be opened up just as he is sentenced to hell.

DAVID JONES – 1981

Life after life

Set against this, the seeming innocence of the doo-wop backing vocals across the record hark back to the "wop wop wop" of "Golden Years" on *Station to Station*, evoking Phil Spector's "wall of sound" productions with singers like Ronnie Spector, whom Bowie knew and studied well. The extreme falsetto employed on "Teenage Wildlife" apes the more constrained emotional yelp on "Heroes" while channeling the darker edges of Motown (Tanaka 2021). In "Kingdom Come," there is a "Bowie-style over-acting" that verges on "a parody, even grotesque," of his Ronnie Spector tribute. At its extremes, Bowie sinks into melodrama while his voice soars a continuing trend on future records that Bowie would quickly arrest with a harsh, ironic remove of a keen skepticism in his music of the 1990s.

There is a yearning cut through Bowie's songs; his natural sense of isolation and outsiderdom perhaps pushes his need for connection even further. It was not something that could be repaired, like the damaged people who populate *Scary Monsters* and the fans drawn to Bowie's music; there is a sense of finding the same loneliness in each other. This more positive edge of "Kingdom Come" and "Wild Is the Wind" (both covers) offers a certain kind of love. Like words leavened by the breeze, breath gives final life to the falling leaves; an invisible force makes its presence felt in the heart—if we only allow ourselves to hear it. I think of this sound as Bowie's breathless "heavens high" on "Ashes to Ashes," where addiction had brought him close to death. Bowie might also have felt nearer to the voice of God, who favors the sinner and purposefully tests the weak. Where on other songs the word of the Lord is Love, on "Kingdom Come" the hand is offered only to extract vengeance and retribution for past misdeeds.

On "Seven" from 1999's *Hours* album, Bowie divests himself of the old gods, playing in the footprint of their graves, long dead but still casting long shadows. Organized religion has its powerful allure and aesthetic inspirations, but like all forms of spirituality, its true power rests in constant searching while he reels of the days of the week, each one a day in which to die.[302]

Simon Critchley notes that the barbarism of the twentieth century grew from man's desire for ownership and control over the world, to enforce system building and to create order out of faith, not the other way around. While man on Earth makes a godhead of himself in the postreligious age, the belief in absolutes of good and evil, right and wrong, makes a shipwreck of the individual splintering into common humanity. Too narrow a religious vision leaves us unable to float and drift with the inevitable chaos of the universe, to live within the constant ruin of our lives; where Bowie embraced this continual flux, he exercised new freedoms in his music. Caught between something and nothing, he enthusiastically grappled with the impossible. On 1995's *1. Outside* album, Bowie found a kind of solace in extreme aesthetics of the new trinity of sex/death/art as pagan excess, a truer vision of spiritual attainment than prayer, forgiveness, and meekness could ever hope to provide.[303]

> We killed God—in our childhood. And so now the
> only appropriate remedy for mania appeared to us
> to be, like for Susan Hayward, the Snake Pit.[304]
>
> —R. D. Laing

With "Word on a Wing," Bowie guards both his own skepticism and his choice to proactively believe in spiritual powers beyond humanity: "Just because I believe/Don't mean I don't think as well." Without the controlling influence of organized religion, he could think for himself. Bowie found much to admire and take away from Buddhism, freeing his mind from both doubt and outright faith that came from stiff, inherited modes of white, Western orthodox religious thought. *On Having No Head* (1961), an account of enlightenment by Douglas Harding, a British architect who during a hiking trip in the Himalayas suddenly conceived of himself as having no brain, head, or soul, literally decapitates the ego-centered idea that we exist *inside* our mind, the boxed-in soul as a ghost in the machine.[305] The author talks about a series of illustrations by Ernst Mach of the first-person perspective we all live within. Seeming to float through space-time with our hands in front of us, pointing to—and being pointed at—he anchors our standard mode consciousness—directional seeing, thinking, and feeling toward things and others as objectives. Except in a mirror, we do not see ourselves in action as others do, and in this sense, it is perhaps more accurate to say we live for/in front of the minds of other people and them for us. Dissolving the "I" of the individual, the "me" in society, means withdrawing from ego and away from the self to reflect more on a connected humanity and way of being. Harding describes the bizarre and shocking impact of his experience: "What actually happened was something absurdly simple and unspectacular: I stopped thinking. . . . Reason and imagination and all mental chatter died down. For once, words really failed me. Past and future have dropped away. I forgot who and what I was, my name, manhood, animal hood, all that could be called mine."

The ability to remove "I" from the "self" showed Bowie the potential of objectivity; the power of seeing things in themselves as transient also has creative applications in his forward-thinking attitude. He was only ever as good as his last album; it was all about the now, leaning out toward the next day that demanded his immediate attention. In a 1980 interview for Japanese television, Bowie was invited to end the discussion with one piece of advice: "Don't waste any day."[306]

Bowie would compromise the challenges of the standard Western philosophical life with the brief chant backed by thumping house music that opens "Law (Earthling on Fire)": "I don't want knowledge, I want certainty!" In 2003, Bowie would comment that many of us were now living post-philosophically; where reality had become abstract, the value of truth had diminished. Messier lives, broken perceptions, a more complex world—this was modernity at its most striking and forceful. He had seen the first rising of the wave through many of his albums, and on *Scary Monsters*, he became swept up in its thrust.

Bowie's own version of enlightenment became learning to let go—in his personal life, not just for creative open-mindedness. After his initial shift of perspective, he aimed to free himself of things, ideas, the body, even life as bound to existence. In *I'm OK—You're OK*, Thomas Anthony Harris was keen to point out that Zen Buddhist philosophers use the same Greek word *kenosis*, that is, "self-emptying," also used by Western theologians to describe a process that leads toward the consummation of personal fulfillment.[307] In the song "After All" from *The Man Who Sold the World*, Bowie sings lines that switch from stark and severe to the nonsensical and ridiculous: "Man is an obstacle, sad as the clown (oh by jingo)." This offers both the overcoming of the human condition and the physical transcendence to engage with the flux and flow of life as a constant force of pure energy.[308]

Bowie seemed to embrace Buddhist conceptions of transcendence: "the self as a figment, a will-o'-the-wisp illusion. . . . The true self is the no-self, a positive emptiness that is distinguished from the puffed-up 'substance' of the public persona" (Reynolds 2017). This perspective locates the physical realm as unreal, a magical dream; life is an act, an ongoing show, which meant that, as a blank slate, the empty vessel of Bowie could play host to any number of characters and images, even to his real identity of David Jones, and know that it was all fleeting, a flash of light captured in clashing mirrors that would dissipate as quickly as it had shone brightly (Jones 2018).

This open-minded approach defined Bowie's life toward the late 1980s; he found himself free to circulate through global cities with managed anonymity and seemed to have found an inner calm that let him float within his own private world. He professed satisfaction to *Rolling Stone in 1980*: "I'm happy that I am going the way I considered I would be going when I was eighteen years old, which is holding onto nothing, no one; continually in flux."

During the *Scary Monsters* sessions at Good Earth studios in London, Bowie was briefly reunited with his former Buddhist teacher Chime Youngdong

Rinpoche from the 1960s. When Bowie had known him, he was a Tibetan lama, one of only four in the United Kingdom. By 1969, Chime Rinpoche had derobed and worked in London's Natural History Museum. Mary Finnigan mentioned that Bowie had reached out to Chime Rinpoche in his worst times of excess in Los Angeles but in the end made the physical escape of leaving for Berlin instead.

Perhaps from his days of addiction recovery, Bowie would later find spiritual comfort in the Serenity Prayer. Written by the American theologian Reinhold Niebuhr, the prayer was adopted by Alcoholics Anonymous and other twelve-step programs. It works as an incantation of freeing yourself from the enduring pains of the world while embracing responsibility for one capacity to grow and develop: "God grant me the serenity [power] to accept the things I cannot change, the courage to change the things I can, and the wisdom to know the difference." The strength of the prayer rests on the removal of the ego-driven self, learning to accommodate change as a force of constant flux and in doing so to embrace it even though its untold consequences may yet deal further challenges.[309]

Bowie had the prayer tattooed on his calf in Japanese, inked in February 1992 while touring with Tin Machine in Kyoto. Rarely seen, it also shows a man riding a dolphin and holding a frog in his hand next to Iman Abdulmajid's name. Bowie said this was a confirmation of his love and the "knowledge of the power of life itself." Referring to the words of the prayer, Bowie was both philosophical and utilitarian, noting a spiritual meaning and the patient rhythm of maintaining sobriety, telling Arsenio Hall in 1993, "I think the Serenity Prayer is something that keeps me back onto that course, very much so, yeah. I was very lucky." For the image, Bowie took inspiration from one of his chosen books, *A Grave for a Dolphin*.[310] Merging folk story with real-life love affair, the book contains an account of a young Italian officer's love affair with a Somalian woman who can swim with dolphins; their lives become intertwined, finding a freedom in the sea that transcends the merging of cultures in the colonial setting of Africa shortly before World War II. One day, the woman dies from a fever while simultaneously the dolphin arrives bleeding on the beach; the two are buried side by side. In his introduction to Iman's Abdulmajid's 2001 book *I Am Iman*, Bowie claimed this story inspired the "swim like dolphins can swim" lyric in "Heroes"; the collective meaning of the story, the song, and the dolphin itself becomes symbolic of the transcendent power of love.

Bowie was once asked his view on the purpose of life, delivering another of his eminently quotable lines: "To try to make each moment of one's life one of the happiest, and if it's not, try to find out why." If the answer sounds rich with mysticism and spirituality, it's because it came directly from a

Buddhist monk. "I was told that by a Tibetan friend of mine, Chime Young-don Rinpoche," Bowie explained, unable to take credit but happy to pass on the learned wisdom of others. Early in his career, Bowie had suggested he might find true happiness in a world of eternal suffering by retreating into a Buddhist monastery, perhaps in Scotland or Kyoto. Speaking in 1980, he suggested that when he was very old, he might follow through on his original idea and just erase himself by disappearing into an opium haze.

If there was an absolute answer to religion that offered heaven as either a place or just a spiritual place of mind, "Kingdom Come" was the door slamming closed at the asking of the question.[311] Perhaps it is a man in need of prayer left outside the gate on Judgment Day or else finding himself locked in, trapped in the realm of God's grac as faith's reward. However the hammer comes down, it meets Bowie refusing to be broken under its weight. Although he might argue enclosed systems of organized religion are too demanding and anti-humanistic, Bowie would enact his own spiritual reimagination in the graceful stage-managing of his own death, creating the album *Blackstar* in secret and orchestrating its release as a final goodbye. After a private farewell with his family and friends Bowie opted for a direct cremation (one where no one is present) and requested that his ashes be scattered on the Indonesian island of Bali "in accordance with the Buddhist rituals."[312]

> Heathenism is a state of mind. You can take it
> that I'm referring to one who does not see his
> world. He has no mental light. He destroys almost
> unwittingly. He cannot feel any God's presence
> in his life. He is the 21st century man.
>
> —David Bowie, 2001

✝

Fragment #80

Happy fucking new year, and merry fucking christmas before that, after the holidays it's just one long black mood until the next seasons change. I waited out here for like ten hours, maybe more, eleven or twelve, that's half a day. you know it's still winter, right? You know how it happens, today worse than yesterday, it rained so long I thought the street was a river, my notebook got wet, my pen ran dry, I bought a book I didn't read, but turning over the pages was a way to mark the time. Sign my book, then; my train ticket—no, wait—sign my arm, anything, give me something, I know all the songs, not just the words, but where it builds-up, then breaks, so mayn pieces and none of them seem to matter—the song breaks—is broken—and you slowed it down just enough I thought the pause would never end, or the song would never start up again, the waiting crossed over into a new decade, I marked time in burnt matches, but you made it work, you made it a song again. I don't smoke, but it's good to carry matches, in case someone needs one. Don't you think. I do. Think too much; some people don't think enough—who said that? Just helped himself and lit-up didn't even say thank you pinched between the fingers of his other hand, like it was nothing, a tiny tree burst into flames. Half-admiring it, smoking to its end, blew it out with a whistle, that hit from before I was born, but I know it well now. Didn't even say thanks. Just nothing. It's just the songs, we've all got those, showtunes, classics, real-time good old days we stuck in the classics, so give me something different, it's all for sharing, you don't sing without an audience so why should I wait, waiting with the others. OK, songs, they're for everyone, but I know you were talking to them, and me, there's another voice, another voice behind it all, only we know, you have to be tuned-in, properly on the same wave length, that I choose to tune in, you speak it and sing it true, the rest are just not for real, they're plastic walking talky people, words spill out and they shovel them up, just to fill newspapers, wearing the thumbprint of your blood from turning so many times, your name seemed to be on every page, more than mine ever was, The longest joke in history—Who would run for president? Answer—everyone. The shortest joke in history—who would gun down a pres? Answer—A Patriot. That's the joke. It's the same basic joke but quicker. And colder now. OK, it's not so funny but it's how you tell it; you're a victim of your audience's sickness. When it comes to raising a laugh its like stepping on a corpse just to see the blood bubble wheeze out then pop. But it's how you tell it—sign of a great performer—how long can you wait out the silence. I've been waiting. For such a long time. Suddenly it all happens, nothing came, it really did, and I saw black, in the shadow there was a darkness, and then it was white, blinding bright, like a haze, the sea and the beach collapsed, pure white, after it went red, very deep, drowning in my own head, it's how you tell it but you wait long enough for the laughter, it'll come. They never laugh hard enough, can't see the funny side, nothing funny when important people ignore, don't give you the time, don't even say thanks. Just nothing. You made them what they are—they should be grateful—the things you'll only miss when it's gone, you'll never know how much we miss it, anyway, time to go, don't want to be late. You don't understand, you'll never know what this means; how I've waited—I waited ever so long—ever so long for this.

Happy fucking new year, and merry fucking christmas before that, after the holidays,
it's just one long black mood until the next seasons change. I waited out here for like ten
hours, maybe more, eleven or twelve, that's half a day, you know it's still winter, right?
You know how it happens, today worse than yesterday, it rained so long I thought
the street was a river, my notebook got wet, my pen ran dry, I bought a book I didn't
read, but turning over the pages was a way to mark the time. Sign my book, then, my
train ticket—no, wait—sign my arm, anything, give me something, I know all the
songs, not just the words, but where it builds-up, then breaks, so many pieces and none
of them seem to matter—the song breaks—is broken—and you slowed it down just
enough I thought the pause would never end, or the song would never start up again,
the waiting crossed over into a new decade, I marked time in burnt matches, but you
made it work, you made it a song again. I don't smoke, but it's good to carry matches,
in case someone needs one. Don't you think, I do. Think too much; some people don't
think enough—who said that? Just helped himself and lit-up he didn't even say thank
you pinched between the fingers of his other hand, like it was nothing, a tiny tree burst
into flames. Half-admiring it, smoking to its end, blew it out with a whistle, that bit
from before I was born, but I know it well now. Didn't even say thanks. Just nothing.
It's just the songs, we've all got those, showtunes, classics, real-time good old days we
stuck in the classics, so give me something different, it's all for sharing, you don't sing
without an audience so why should I wait, waiting with the others, OK songs, they're
for everyone, but I know you were talking to them, and me, there's another voice,
another voice behind it all, only we know, you have to be tuned-in, properly on the
same wave length, that I choose to tune in, you speak it and sing it and sing it true, the rest are
just not for real, they're plastic walking talky people, words spill out and they shovel
them up, just to fill newspapers, wearing the thumbprint of your blood from turning so many times, your name seemed to be on every page, more than mine ever was,
The longest joke in history—Who would run for president? Answer—everyone. The
shortest joke in history—who would gun down a prez? Answer—A Patriot. That's
the joke. It's the same basic joke but quicker. And colder now. OK, it's not so funny
but it's how you tell it; you're a victim of your audience's sickness. When it comes to
raising a laugh its like stepping on a corpse just to see the blood bubble wheeze out then
pop. But it's how you tell it—sign of a great performer—how long can you wait out
the silence. I've been waiting. For such a long time. Suddenly it all happens, nothing
came, it really did, and I saw black, in the shadow there was a darkness, and then it
was white, blinding bright, like a haze, the sea and the beach collapsed, pure white,
after it went red, very deep, drowning in my own head, it's how you tell it but if you
wait long enough for the laughter, it'll come. They never laugh hard enough, can't see
the funny side, nothing funny when important people ignore, don't give you the time,
don't even say thanks. Just nothing. You made them what they are—they should be
grateful—the things you'll only miss when it's gone, you'll never know how much we
miss it, anyway, time to go, don't want to be late. You don't understand, you'll never
know what this means; but I've waited—I waited ever so long—ever so long for this,

Because You're Young

Lover's Rock (and Roll)

Valse De Chopin

The sweet and fierce theme
Of a wistful waltz,
Leaves an unsettling sensation
A dull aftertaste,
Like a lingering drop of blood.

—From Arnold Schoenberg's *Pierrot Lunaire*, 1912

175

In the 1980s, the death of the imagination was the greatest threat to the modern cultural world, and so it remains. Beaten into submission by a cultural climate that increasingly relied on surface gloss over deeper meaning, the sinking sense of irony pushed artistic integrity back into mere likability. Where before Bowie had called out the death of love as a societal breakdown of mutual feeling, a black hole to fall into, he also recognized that the excess of passions in one single direction can lead people astray.

On "Because You're Young," Bowie claimed he was playing the "old roué . . . gazing down on young lovers." His pessimism creeps in, embittered by experience or simply watching the expression of a feeling he could never recapture, "looking down on these two young mad things and knowing that it's all gonna fizzle out." In this reading, he seems to revisit the lovers of "Heroes" embracing by the Berlin Wall—but now watching from the distance of bitterness and experience, he cannot fully rekindle that same feeling of relentless hope, in spite of everything.

Burning with the joie de vivre of being young and not knowing the future yet to come, the song aims at this rare ecstasy, but where "Teenage Wildlife" reaches it, "Because You're Young" is tainted by the bittersweet taste of youth's fleet passing.[313] For his part, Bowie would claim that he enjoyed being older and a little wiser, having learned from (some of) his mistakes. As an adult father who happened to make music and tour the world, he was able to make the two phases of his existence run in separate but parallel lanes. Again, the overlapping song titles and lyrical ideas reveal deeper connective tissue between the tracks. The working title for "Teenage Wildlife" ("It Happens Everyday") could just as easily refer to the soon-to-be-doomed lovers of "Because You're Young." Bowie presents the challenge that when we are deep in it, each love—and its series of firsts—will feel like the only one; there is no other.[314]

In French, a *roué*[315] is a debauched or lecherous man; a former rake fallen into old age where his keen feelings outstrip his body. As Lord Byron would have it, "For the sword outwears its sheath/And the heart wears-out the breast." Bowie evokes the idea that he is living again through the lovers, where he was once in their place. The original lyric in the demo version, "Because I'm Young," places Bowie at the center; perhaps too close for comfort, he shifted into the position of God-like narrator watching over other people's lives. No longer in a position to speak to and for the young, as in "Teenage Wildlife," he speaks only for himself.

The same idea also appears in Bowie's version of Jacques Brel's "My Death." Although he mangled much of Brel's most poignant phrases, the haunting, loveless line "My death waits like an old roué" becomes a lingering presence so easily forgotten amid the business of living. But not for Bowie. As he would also sing on the tired and tried "Time," there was always a shadow waiting in the wings of life's stage, only ever just a few steps behind. Like "Rock 'n' Roll Suicide," there are hands reaching out, but on this track, they threaten to pull him back into the darkness, not raise him up to life.

"My Death" remained a major song for Bowie throughout his life, discovered through Scott Walker's 1967 cover via a mutual girlfriend. Brel first recorded "My Death" as a rather jaunty sing-along in 1959 when he was thirty years old. As Peter Doggett noted, his spirited version showed the singer striding over death in a cavalier fashion without time to wait or be waited on. It is interesting to hear the nod to "the funeral of my youth" as Brel mourns the few good times we are to enjoy, while he revisits what is lost through age: the process of life, which, to paraphrase Lennon, happens to us while we are busy making other plans. The personal pronoun of the song title shows Brel encouraging us all to take ownership of our ending; each person's death is the final lonely moment passing away in their own arms. Ultimately, Brel sings for himself knowing that others, such as the young Bowie, would eventually find themselves in his place.[316]

Speaking of the Ziggy years, Bowie said, "I haven't got that same positivism within my make-up any more. I mean, the very juvenile sort of assertiveness and arrogance of that period . . . I can't write young" (MacKinnon 1980). As Bowie switched the focus of the song from "I" to "you're," he settled on the second-person perspective of an outsider looking in. Like "Teenage Wild-life," Bowie is leaning on the current new generation, a direct address to the here and now, and in doing so, he acknowledged the precariousness of the music industry for aging stars. To try to stand at the top of a pedestal (for too long) was to wait for others to come along and knock you down. The tension of "Teenage Wildlife" is driven further where Bowie looks back on the bulletproof naïveté of youth while trying to find enough optimism to face up to his own relatively uncertain future. He was now a survivor. At this time, he did not belong among his so-called classic rock peers, but neither was he mixing it up at the same club level with new and emerging artists. Although he remained a keen champion of new music, by this time he was a survivor, gradually being nudged toward the elder statesman role he resented—forever "Ziggy"—by then becoming a romantic anachronism to the go-go New Wave of the 1980s.

We are again seeing Bowie forced to look over his shoulder, left to wonder if his best works were not already behind him. However, his Berlin records had done as much to inspire and sometimes predict new sounds of 1980 as anyone else. Bowie took as much as he gave from groups like Talking Heads, Devo, and Suicide. He saw the album as "the epitome of the new wave sound at the time; from bubbling synthesizers to erratic and unconventional guitar playing, it had all those elements that are, by definition, the young way of playing music." Aping the warning of "Fashion," he borrowed from other styles of the time but always under his own (re)definition; the "now" Bowie of *Scary Monsters* cannot speak to or for the emergent generations, and even if he could, they would not hear him.[317] When asked about the long-term value of his work, Bowie explained the freedom in not having to exist on a singular set of inherited ethics and values: "You can try to investigate other avenues of perception and apply them to everyday life" (MacKinnon 1980). This hunger for self-realization was there in "Teenage Wildlife" and found full flight on "Because You're Young." Although no longer addled by Bowie's professional sense of doubt, both songs succeed despite their built-in cynicism; they remain urgent and demanding, swooping in and out of ecstatic highs. But where "Teenage" reaches toward the angels of our better nature, "Because You're Young" shows the decline of youth along with its most hard-won lessons.

Simon Critchley (2016) finds that Bowie's great power was to help people to erase and cancel out "all the nonsense, the falsity, the accrued social meanings, traditions and morass of identity that shackled us, especially in relation to gender and class." His songs on *Scary Monsters* demand fresh questioning of our identities and our place in the world to better know ourselves and realize new changes, a fight back against complacency.

After marking himself the wounded stag of "Teenage Wildlife," Bowie could now look back with some fondness at the power, beauty, and brilliance of youth. Undergoing trial by fire but believing himself to be bulletproof (as he had once done before Ziggy made him a household name), Bowie was another up-and-coming contender for the throne of pop stardom, consciously working his way to the top. This was Bowie nodding to his own juvenile arrogance and inner resolve that enabled him to believe in the power of romance above all else, writing love songs to change the world.

His revolution began in teaching himself to overcome his own background, ready to absorb new ideas without questioning them too much. He told *Details* magazine in 1995, "*On the Road* instructed me that I no longer had to live in South London. *City of Night* told me what I'd find once I moved out."

> It is hard to laugh at the need for beauty and romance, no matter how tasteless, even horrible, the results of that are. But it is easy to sigh. Few things are sadder than the truly monstrous.

—Nathanael West, *The Day of the Locust*, 1939

One of the men who defined Bowie's own youthful introduction to pop rock music and mod culture was guitarist Pete Townshend of the Who. Formerly a rock rebel in a Union Jack blazer carrying out the onstage autodestruction before he became a concept album–driven recluse, he was the rock rebel of "Because You're Young." In 1980, Townshend was something of a pissed-up antagonistic player for hire, wandering in a daze through the smoke of his own legend, flitting in and out of studios for solo albums and always "just one more" last bloody Who record. The slightly older, perhaps wiser man struggling with his own addictions as Bowie had once done; he nonetheless described Bowie as "constantly in flux," recognizing a familiar restless spirit, always looking ahead to the next creative challenge.[318]

He turned up at the London sessions for *Scary Monsters* slightly drunk with both Bowie and Visconti awkwardly wondering what results might be achieved if Townshend was on the right side of flexible to string together a few riffs or be lost in his own strumming. Visconti immediately noticed his foul and laconic mood after Townshend asked for a bottle of wine: "'Red or white?' And he shouted at me, 'There's no such thing as white wine!' So we got him the best bottle of red we could find."

Trying to give direction to the session, Bowie and Visconti asked for chords, more specifically "Townshend chords," to which the guitarist drily responded, "Oh, windmills"; the suggestion being offered was simply to "play like Pete Townshend," and he duly obliged. His signature stage move, as good as trademarked, was slightly hackneyed by the time of punk's constant throb and thrash but was also aped by Steve Jones, Sid Vicious, and Paul Simonon, among others; it was a piece of stagecraft that made little or no audible sense in the studio. It is the needling, tangled guitar riff that pushes "Because You're Young" forward, jolting it into life and propelling youthful innocence into the near future.

Visconti was pleased to see the classic performance live in the studio: "It was awesome to be right up close to him with that right arm going 60 mph." Bowie equally became a fan in the presence of one of his earliest musical idols: "He actually does jump up and down in the studio," Bowie marveled. "I mean, that floored me." Accordingly, a bottle of red wine was drained and with his guitar parts completed in half an hour Townshend exited the studio onto Soho's Dean Street.

"Because You're Young" is certainly a strange song, with its dramatic "dow-dow-doooowwn" opening riff later running up and down the fretboard, slamming power chords end each cycle alongside a cheeky bend of the string, along with George Murray's elasticated bass notes sliding and shuffling through the verse and bounding through the chorus like a lovelorn puppy. The chorus is smothered by hurdy-gurdy organs, a pastiche of carnival and music halls that also threatens to spill over into the Hammer horror organ of shock and surprise, threatening to spin off in a helter-skelter maelstrom.[319]

Both "Because You're Young" and "Teenage Wildlife" "tick to the quickened pulse of [Yukio] Mishima novels like *Thieves*, with their passionate, beautiful young suicides" (O'Leary 2020a). The sense of gloom is ever there but is presented in such a jaunty and operatic fashion that it feels that Bowie's high-pitched vocal and musical delivery outstripped the mood of the themes he was wrestling with, always verging on teenage melodrama.

This is perhaps the girl of "Scary Monsters" and her fear of rooms revisited or a new victim that has taken her place. Rendered "psychodelicate," she has moved on from the boxed-in claustrophobia of shrinking city streets to a situation of absolute collapse swallowed up in vertigo. A damaged partner at her side, both "war-torn and resigned," they are the new refugees of economic circumstance; identity politics or left–right culture clash; they limp along, propping one another up, bound to the vicious cycle of young love, to push and pull, break apart, and come together again, two people full with feeling who don't really know themselves, let alone each other. Now it's all walls-as-floors and sky-full ceilings, to a place that's "all back to front and no sides"; the shaken maze inside an upturned box, she is wonderful Alice scattered to the winds of growing up in a cruel world of hard knocks.[320]

This is Bowie's recent history played out in desperate metaphor: howling down the umbilical corridor, the breakdown of space echoes the shrinking universe of fame. The celebrity of "Teenage Wildlife" is shuttled down endless hallways and rooms on the run from his own life, cracks of light from doors ajar, an empty waiting room, forever delayed at airport lounges, the next luxury hotel (just for one night), another shadow waiting backstage, escaping out a dressing room window with only a cardboard suitcase to his name, strung out in a padded cell, seeing thirty-three cocaine-thin wraiths all refracted in one shattered mirror.[321]

Bowie sings that "pieces are broken"[322] to razor-wire guitar lines that carve up the scenery, a kaleidoscope of fading places and fractured relationships never meant to last. He makes his fearful admission dredged up from the heart of the album: "hope I'm wrong but I know . . . ." From a safe distance, he surveys the limits of fragmentation as a process in itself; through making music and taking on characters, it becomes something that happens *to* him. As T. S. Eliot might have it, the seeming driftwood of a life must eventually coalesce to shore up its ruin.[323]

Each Bowie album stands as an attempt to create a new synthesis, yielding fresh chaos but also a (temporary) sense of order. From our inner lives, we all come across the need to connect nothing with nothing and still come up with something, though other times we might end our day empty-handed. But for Simon Critchley (2016), "The overcoming of the human condition is a disaster" but also a necessary experience: "At the core of Bowie's music is the exhilaration of an experience of nothing, and an attempt to hold on to it." Consciously letting go of the past while singing its elegy. This does not make Bowie a nihilist; rather, it sets him free from expectation, meaning, and perfection.

At the end of the song, we find Bowie the performer as a chained bear or sad clown smiling, dancing his life away to the same old song, caught in a mad carousel, going through the motions of love. Bowie hurls a final cry into space, "A million dreams/a million scars," as he continues elongating the wailing vowels. These might be screams; the failure or, worse, the terrible fulfilment of all our dreams and desires—this becomes experience, an education, that leaves us scarred in some way, irredeemably different: childhood trauma, first sex, breaking up—the very newness of being young renewed by the power of unknowing. In later life, what feels like continued ascent and acceleration toward progress is really sinking, struggling up the downslope, rushing into paradise, racing after some fresh kind of hell.

Bowie's call to repetition both emphasizes and degrades meaning. A word or phrase is hammered home, still ringing in our ears, but also has a dulling effect; we are beaten down by blurred sound, filling the ear, and we carry the screams with us into silence, hearing them long after they've stopped.

"Because You're Young" is a return to Bowie's eerie futurism; he is now the more experienced, embittered veteran of art and romance, Pierrot's limping shadow, but he also remains the eternally hopeful young lover of his teenage years, before he became just another star, adrift in the known universe, looking both forward and backward, uncertain of which way is up, knowing his worst fears must come true because it has happened before and will happen all over again.[324]

Fragment #56

I tried
I tried falling down
And not getting back up
I tried not falling
Already on the way down
I tried as I was so tired but couldn't find where to start
I tried not to try but got the better of me
I tried testing limits
Of others, to test myself
I tried not caring

Today I tried again

It's No Game (No. 2)

(Tired Of My Life)

Let everything happen to you: beauty and terror.
Just keep going.
No feeling is final.

—Rainer Maria Rilke, *Go to the Limits of Your Longing*

At the album's closer, Bowie allows himself one long sigh. Where the first "It's No Game" was a breathless rendition of fury, he now sits steeped in his own melancholy. Bowie described his reprise of the album's opener as operating on a "lilting melodic superficial level; the sentiment is the same as the first, but the ambiance has changed, a gentle nostalgic quality to it, rather than being an angry vehement statement." It becomes the second side of social protest, the push into pull, wrong overwhelming right. In part, Bowie's own nostalgia has overwhelmed him, still mired in the same world-weary problems.

We return to the laconic, almost jazzy guitars that strum circling surf patterns off the main melody, chiming in and out over the pre-chorus rise and then chugging up toward the chorus, where Bowie finally allows his voice space and oxygen above the dirge. More brittle than before, his resolve now tried and tested, he has found himself wanting. This is Bowie doing his best Lou Reed monotone, detached, exacting, seemingly resigned but calculated for a more subtle impact than the verbal pyrotechnics of "It's No Game (No. 1)" (Hewitt 2016).

Many people imagine "No. 2" to be a demo version of "No. 1," but the two tracks were actually put together in sequence. Visconti claims it to be the exact same backing track but altered and slowed and adjusted with various effects, using mixing and different overdubs to make it sound removed from the original (Visconti 2007). The relationship between the two iterations of the song is also thrown into doubt when you consider that on some disc pressings and metadata, the songs are called "Part 1" and "Part 2," respectively, as if the one meets with the other, offering a final sense of closure, or, as a redux version, they become clashing opposites, uneasily reconciled.

Chris O'Leary acknowledges the dodgy pun of "(No. 2)" with children putting camel shit on the walls when there is nothing else to do. Like adults, human children naturally play games, finding life in the following and breaking of rules—we all must chuck things—marking a dirty protest against modern life. Here the foreign exotic merges into Middle Eastern or African territories far "beyond the pale"; how the other side lives is returned to us as a naked lunch. Literally brought down to earth, instead of rocks we have vulgar things bowling into our sphere of attention and are forced to take notice.

Simon Critchley throws up the scene of hollow liberal platitudes, hand-wringing in the face of social injustice. The deeper neurotic challenge implied by "Up the Hill Backwards" is made plain: while we sleep in another hemisphere living in light, wealth, and plenty, others must work in dirt, poverty, and darkness. The labor of adults (and their children) makes our high-street fashion, footballs, and trainers; they go marching on treadmills, sheltering in mud houses, picking through the garbage shipped out to landfill from

Western nations. Surviving on the detritus of yesterday, their reward is our junk; in Bowie's world, we return them a basic wage and the ruins of our broken sneakers.

Even on home soil, it's the underworld that helps maintain the surface tension; nocturnal service workers of subterranean space-time keep the world turning while we enjoy, relax, and sleep, but now it's outsourced to become someone else's problem. All over the world, it happens every day. For us (for you), it's all a game; for them, it's real life. From parody and pastiche, Bowie's attempt at light touch sinks into exhaustion; he returns to the problem that sparked the whole album, describing the track as "what happens when a protest or angry statement is thrown against the wall so many times." The anger must bend or break against concrete realities where "the speaker finds that he has no energy to give any impact anymore."

The song appears to conclude the reel of current affairs programming through the lens of a video nasty introduced with "It's No Game (No. 1)." We are seeing late-night repeats of the horror, inhabiting the inertia of the spectator; like them, we have seen too much and turned into the same semi-visible figures, crouched in shadow, frozen into silhouettes.

This begs the question of who can afford to be a spectator, to proactively sit on the sidelines and find the game in everything, opposing moral sentiments batted back and forth in the sport of virtue. Since 1980, we are more aware than ever of events unfolding around the world and find the causal links that form its chains. But Bowie echoes the same hollowness of political discourse we endure today: the theatrical parlor play of parliaments, senates, and congressional bodies where performance overtakes action. Bowie's words carry resolve, but no one is listening; he has abandoned volume for self-determination.

Finding method in Bowie's pale jest, the journalist John Robinson sees *Scary Monsters* as an accumulation of Bowie's world-wise but jaded experiences, simultaneously hot and cold, still burning and frozen. But does the frenzied outrage in the first "It's No Game" now yield to deep resignation after the exorcism of self-loathing gives way to forgiveness or just mental exhaustion? It's hard to say whether the song concludes the album or just peters out after the initial explosion. Do we come away with some greater knowledge having been through the meat-grinder intensity of the preceding tracks that mark the album's relentless kamikaze progress—to what? We would think it nihilism if the journey had not been such a wild and beguiling ride. Maybe this is a kind of Zen acceptance at the state of things, neither giving up nor giving in, farewell but not forever.

Revisiting the track was perhaps something of an afterthought for Bowie, similar to the Beatles' reprise of "Sgt. Pepper's," the same but different. Chris O'Leary (2017) compares the awkward twin tracks to Lennon's alternate versions of "Revolution": "recorded first as a mid-tempo, acoustic guitar-based track (the *White Album* version) and then reconstituted a month later as a compressed, sped-up electric rocker for the single." In this regard, Bowie flipped the album back onto itself, turning over side after side like a brittle thought in his head to see what, if anything, had changed: the listener or the songs? Now looking back over the record, one could argue that *Scary Monsters* actually begins at the end, forever chasing its own tail.

On "It's No Game (No. 1)," Bowie's vision of having a bullet fired "in my brain" suggests a protest against media exploitation. Bowie described the "tunnel vision" of hungry press focus zooming in on tragedy and disaster where the camera lens become synonymous with the barrel of the gun, "shooting" the spectacle; this bristles against the demands of the listener as audience and spectator become twin voyeurs. Where it might strike the listener as oddly prophetic of the murder of John Lennon, by the "No. 2" version of the song, it has become an honest and true lament on such dark and painful coincidences.[325] The mad intensity of Bowie's earlier singing can be silenced only by the full stop of death. Perhaps this is Bowie throwing up the shared threat that we are all potential victims; the celebrity who sticks their head above the parapet, like Malcolm X and John F. Kennedy, politicized stars of the previous generation—the icon becomes a target. The rocks we chuck, hoping that they might shatter harmlessly against the road, striking a policeman's riot helmet, making a small dent in an immigrant round-up van or rattling the cage of barred windows on a presidential palace, sometimes bounce back at us.

On "Young Americans," Bowie's backing singers call out "I heard the news today, oh boy," a nod to Lennon, who appears elsewhere on "Fame" and is the songwriter of "Across the Universe," covered by Bowie on the same album. The line is seemingly throwaway but continues the echo of Lennon's original line "I read the news today, oh boy" at the start of "A Day in the Life," as Bowie would later hear about Lennon's death like everyone else through live on-the-scene television reports. Lennon originally wrote the song on the piano with a newspaper propped up in front of him, lamenting the death of Tara Browne, a close friend of the band and heir to the Guinness fortune, in a traffic accident at the age of twenty-one, where Lennon sang "he blew his mind out in a car." The crowd gathered to stand and stare at the wreckage; some turned away, but the singer himself finds that he *has* to look—he is all of us a witness to tragedy. The now ghost voice of Lennon that appeared on "Fame" and the elegiac songs of the *Plastic Ono Band* would carry through to the announcement of his own death, which shocked New

York and the world, where he became the subject of his own words, life and death, the mundane and the fantastical wrapped up into a single twenty-four-hour news cycle, something to be consumed—the reel runs on, let it bleed.

In the first "It's No Game," we hear the tape wound into a frenzy, but now the album's groove and energy has spun out, the end of another sonic adventure: "But where '(No. 1)' climaxed with the signals of insanity, '(No. 2)' just end[s], draining color from everything around it" (Doggett 2011). A new kind of self-emptying shows itself, Bowie sharing our mutual exhaustion—human after all. This shows Bowie easing into a final phase, ready for new direction, but would actually prove to be the last waltz for a full David Bowie album for three years. The brilliant (art) decade is over. Strike the stage. Fold away the flags. The project has traveled as far as it can go and is cut off, winding down back into itself. After the bang of "It's No Game (No. 1)," its second iteration ends with a whimper, coming down to a harsh bump and finally silence.

> Me, I want to bloody kick this moronic bloody
> world in the bloody teeth over and over till it bloody
> understands that not hurting people is ten bloody
> thousand times more bloody important than being right.

—David Mitchell, *Black Swan Green*

Fragment #24

Make a Wall
Build a Brick
Tear It Down

Glamorama

(Artworking)

What people regarded as a pose on my part was
actually an expression of my need to assert my
own true nature. And it was precisely what people
regarded as my true self which was masquerade.

—Yukio Mishima, *Confessions of a Mask*, 1946

The surface level *Scary Monsters* shows Bowie back in a position of glamour and fame, reestablishing himself as a star. But beneath the willing facade there lurked the serious artiste and the jaded performer still trying to reconcile the need for fame with a musician's integrity.

Shuffled across the final album cover, with spare outtakes and test Polaroids, Bowie wears a half mask, the face as a pure white canvas of drastic expressions, a glowering frown, the flicked eyebrow, and a diamond tear bleeding ink—all insouciant gestures folding distance by intimacy—his look manages to compress vacancy, yearning, and exhaustion but couched in a renewed interest for mass exposure, the original sin of compromise. Since his early years as Ziggy, the mask had cracked and now slipped away entirely— we are seeing Bowie's struggle that brought him to *Scary Monsters* in the burning desire to reconnect with his music and find his audience again.

Bowie had learned his stagecraft from one of the best. Perhaps his earliest mentor, Lindsay Kemp, found his own muse in the nineteen-year-old Bowie, casting him as the balladeer Cloud in his stage play *Pierrot in Turquoise or The Looking Glass Murders*: "He drifted on and off the stage like he drifted in and out of my flat on Bateman Street."[326] In three short songs written for the stage show, Bowie, already a determined recycler, mines familiar chord progressions and melodies; "Threepenny Pierrot" bears a jaunty Gilbert and Sullivan mood (sung with the London accent "thre'punny," playing toward Cockney rhyming slang). "The Mirror" bears echoes of "Andy Warhol" on *Hunky Dory*, while its lyrics already carry a deeper melancholy: fading makeup as the removal of a face that housed inner reflections it dared not reveal. There is a strident confidence in the song that would come to the fore in the future. From these early seeds, Bowie marks the light and shade of emotional dynamics in a seemingly shallow portrait.[327]

Bowie had first seen Kemp perform in a 1967 show, *Clowns*, which featured Bowie's early song "When I Live My Dream," bringing him into Kemp's world of mime, drama, and dance.[328] The show made reference to Picasso's Blue and Rose (or Pink) periods of painting, presenting the harsh realities of backstage life for the performing clown in the shift between deepest melancholy and love-blushed wonder. The shift marked a period in which Picasso became deeply depressed following the death of his young friend Carles Casagemas, who, heartbroken when a proposal of marriage was refused, shot himself in front of his friends at age twenty-one. This drove a phase of monochrome nocturnal-mood paintings as the living nightmare of choking on your own scream. After a few years, he was able to let the light back into his work, reflected in the warmer hues and subject matter, becoming the pink period.[329]

Bowie absorbed the haunted and aged Victorian vibe from Kemp's example of the clown: "I took that feeling and looked inside of that, that's when you get the disheveled side of the clown. It's a nod backwards to an element I started with. One always returns and looks back and reincorporates those old things and reevaluates them from time to time."³³⁰ In Bowie's own fractured and half-hidden clown face, we see the pissed-off, defeated man behind the smile, as shown in Picasso's early painting from 1901 of the resting harlequin sitting alone at a café table, staring off into the distance of an empty glass or hearing the echo of himself in hollow laughter and applause.³³¹

As melancholy as the young clown might be, he is forced to wear the feelings demanded of him come showtime. The great test of all performers is their ability to switch on and off the personality that others wish to see in them; the depth of their creative expression determines the connection with the crowd made across the invisible boundary of the stage, and they must be ready to do it all again the next night. We live through our real-life emotions in the catharsis of his performances, sweeping us out of ourselves, putting private hopes and pains into the struggles of another. Between stage and spectator, the magic of mimesis happens; the clown becomes real. But in the end, no one wants to know the Pierrot's true feelings, their inner sadness or joys; the audience loves the song, not the singer, although for Bowie it might be said that sometimes the inverse was true. In 1980, Bowie may not have been a crowd-pleasing force, but he possessed the freedom and the attitude to be his own person, to say "no" and "yes" when he wanted to, veering in and out of popularity as it suited. *Scary Monsters* gave him a musical platform from which to vent personal issues set to the tune of forceful and catchy new music, ready to throw himself into the role of the pure entertainer once again.

The Pierrot, like the jester or harlequin, was a traditional figure of popular entertainment, the costume framing them as a figure of fun. Drawn from the commedia dell'arte tradition, established by traveling Italian entertainers, they walk an emotional tightrope to explore extremes of happiness, comedy, and sadness, where the Pierrot costume emphasizes the ridiculous and the surreal; it is perhaps at this tipping point that we find his tragedy. Picasso's later paintings from 1905, including *Acrobate et Jeune Arlequin* (*Acrobat and Young Harlequin*), reveal something of the people behind the makeup, standing adrift in a beautiful garden looking like Bowie lost on the shore. Set against another painting from the same era (1906), *La Mort d'Arlequin* (*Death of Harlequin*), we see the body of a clown; even in death, he wears a mask.

Like many circus folks living as outsiders, they make their way hand-to-mouth from each show; survival depended on the imagination bridging the delicate suspension of belief. Traditionally, the Pierrot is often seen as a trusting character that is always taken advantage of by others; the pure per-former, not unlike the medieval jester, remains a servant, someone who puts one's own emotions aside for the enjoyment of others (Hewitt 2016). The *NME* review of the album was aptly titled "Fears of a Clown"; in the emo-tional straits of *Scary Monsters*, Bowie, like Pierrot, would seem both foolish and wise. The model of the clown offered him a persona to hide behind and the shell of "someone else" to act out by extremes, but as the actor in disguise, he must forget himself in the process.[332]

Bowie's Pierrot costume, used both for the album cover and in the video for "Ashes to Ashes," would be deeply rooted in his creative past.[333] The cos-tume was designed by former Kemp collaborator Natasha Kornilof. Bowie again asked her to make him "the most beautiful clown in the circus."[334] Her costume bears the harlequin hallmark of checkerboard diamonds as rippling feathers or leaves of bluish silver, topped off by his pointed cornet hat, along-side the highly original and elegant makeup work of Richard Sharah, who would become an iconic figure in 1980s fashion and cast Bowie as an outland-ish post-human doll, fixed in the popular memory of the period.

The sleeve photograph for the "Scary Monsters" single has Bowie mid-costume, edging into striptease or throwing off the disguise, keenly gazing to one side as if caught in flagrante, flirting with the camera and the audience he knows is out there. Breaking through the fourth wall, beyond image, he x-rays the dark mass of the crowd, trumping their sense of intrigue with his own indifference. We see the thwarted entertainer at half light, an actor exposed at the critical moment between good and bad faith. Bowie was a master of such "accidental" spontaneity, keen to throw shapes that appeared casual but had a lasting visual impact. Where other performers endlessly jived, gyrated, danced, clapped, and pouted, spiraling into meaningless gestures as tropes (see Mick Jagger), Bowie offered varying physical forms and aesthetic styles, miming on the spot where he appeared to be moving, keenly morphing between abstract shapes and moments of human warmth, always the knowing smile behind the cigarette smoke. Where you imagined he was caught off guard, he was actu-ally watching you, like the wolf, the implicit seduction of giving you what you (thought you) wanted; it was entirely in his power to break the spell or hold you like a dream in a crystal ball, ready to let you drop at any moment.

We see two clowns in the cover image: "the dignified one who looks straight at you and the disheveled one who hides behind him" (O'Leary 2017). The shadow has broken from the past of his body, standing at an in-between space, sucking life from the pale light of his body, already grown stiff in his legend.

MIDDLE EARTH CLUB — 1967

Portrait of the artist as an everyman

Man is least himself when he talks in his own person.
Give him a mask, and he will tell you the truth.

—Oscar Wilde

It has been noted that many of Bowie's album covers resemble fashion shoots, trading on otherworldly glamour. The cover of *Pin Ups* was actually from a *Vogue* magazine shoot with Twiggy,[335] but Bowie liked the photo so much that he kept it for his own album. Twiggy's manager, Justin De Villeneuve, who took the shot, was struck by Bowie's extreme paleness ("deathly white" to Twiggy's deep Bermuda tan) and asked makeup artist Pierre La Roche to create masks for both models: "I'd always been obsessed by masks, as people do interesting things when they have a mask on." The drawn-on outline of a mask was really Bowie's face, but framing it made it seem unreal, an unholy edge served only to blur his identity further.

Peter Doggett pointed out the similarities to the theatrical star pose on the cover of *Hunky Dory*. Bowie arrived at the photo sessions clutching a series of Marlene Dietrich portraits. With his long hair pushed back lying in repose toward death or ecstasy, he is She/Veronica Lake/Greta Garbo—projecting both the decadent salon of self-destruction and the star's arrogant remove, the performer merely posing as themself.[336] RCA was divided over whether the image of a highly feminized long-haired man in a sensual pose would be too confusing and whether it would be acceptable to mainstream retailers. Bowie again broke the mold: people were never entirely sure of who or what they were seeing, while the Pierrot showed a character at once defiant and resigned[337] (Doggett 2011).

Edward Bell, designer and artist of the *Scary Monsters* artwork, met Bowie at his London *Larger Than Life* exhibition in 1980. From this brief meeting, Bowie asked Bell to paint an album cover for him, but he needed it in just one week. Bell knew next to nothing about the album or much of Bowie's aesthetic history before arriving at the photo shoot led by photographer Duffy. Bell immediately asked to deconstruct the look so carefully prepared for the shoot: removing the Pierrot hat, smearing Bowie's makeup, messing up his carefully combed hair, and dropping the costume off of one naked shoulder: "I really liked the idea of screwing up his make-up [Richard Sharah, makeup artist] after all the meticulous work that had gone into it. It was nice destructive thing to do. Quite anarchistic." Romy Haag, the transsexual cabaret performer and Bowie paramour from his time in Berlin, claims that he stole their closing act when, at the very end of the night's performances, she would whip off her wig and smear her lipstick across her face.

This gesture draws a line drawn from Berlin to the "Boys Keep Swinging" video to the *Scary Monsters* album cover. In "Boys Keep Swinging," Bowie finds the perfect gesture to express the gender fluidity for a man in a dress, a great reveal in which we see "David playing Glenda Jackson playing Stevie Smith singing about uniforms and boys checking each other out" (Burn 1980). In the music video for "DJ," Bowie pushed this further, where he starts as a man in a box spinning records and then ends up let loose on the streets. He is grabbed, hugged, and smothered in kisses from passersby; forcing himself objectionably into the human traffic, a man and a woman both make passionate, violent advances. He takes the hits, and their bodies deflect off of his. This is Bowie expressing the trial of fame in public; as a sexual object, he offers up his sacrificial body to his fans, hungry for a taste of flesh. Glamour, so often Bowie's chosen armor, was stripped away; coming off, coming out, pretty turned ugly, this was Bowie revisiting "the falling apart of purity." The broken mask of Pierrot simply revealed a new facade before Bowie disappeared from public view at the end of 1980, only to reappear intermittently— and not on the live stage. In other photos from the shoot, Bowie tilts his head back to one side, casting a line of sight down the nape of his neck, in Japanese erotic art, an explicitly sensual part of the body. Exposing himself in vulnerable intimacy, it's an image that can send shivers down the spine. Duffy and Bell's final cover image draws back from this more open-ended pose, Bowie's cigarette casually dangling from the lips, moving to a viselike grip in crooked fingers, an affectation turned self-soothing response.[338]

Bell pushed the deconstruction further until Bowie could have been one of the Blitz Kids or a New Romantic fan returned home from a night out, shedding their persona before returning to the normal world.[339] Bell (2017) said of his instinctual process, "This swept the clown away; leaving a proud hero, unbowed and romantically disheveled . . . no longer wistful, pretty, safe, or fey, but a glimpse of glamor in dangerous extremity; decadent and blatantly seductive." By 1980, Bowie's hair had returned to its natural color, but for *Scary Monsters*, Bowie stipulated that it must be recolored in Bell's artwork "because in America I'm known as the red haired bisexual." This conscious design choice again suggests stepping back into the familiar limelight but maintaining some distance as the ghost of a former self, a continued push and pull with his audience.[340]

Bell took the photo handed to him by Duffy along with instructions simply to "color it in" toward cut-up abstraction—by ripping it in half. Bell later split these for the front and back covers of the record, showing Pierrot crossing from the wings to center stage, the broken moment divided by time lost and regained. Bell shows a visibly piqued Bowie-as-clown quietly raging, quiet fire poised on doubt and uncertainty. Kevin Cann noted that Bell's audacious design meant that only Bowie's shadow could be seen whole, lending the artwork a Dorian Gray hidden portrait mystique.[341] Edward Bell told *David Bowie News*, "I started life as a photographer, but I found the medium limiting, so this fact led me to various manipulations: photo montage, over painting or even just using the photo as inspiration for a painting"; not unlike Bowie, his approach was sometimes tangential to his source material: "I was impatient with the technicalities of producing the perfect photograph; if a shadow fell in the wrong place, rather than adjust the lighting, I would airbrush, tint and montage" (Bell 2020).

Bowie's brooding shadow would stand alongside the painted-over silhouette, the jostling layers framing the tense composition of the overall image. The dark shape carries the mood of German expressionism, not unlike the sharply posed *"Heroes"* cover. Matthew Lindsay (2021) sees a fractured doppelgänger that has peeled off from its host, with a rigid but heavily stylized pose, modishly knowing but also struck with a sense of decay, a thin and ghostly shape fleet as smoke, the aftermath from the burning end of life.[342]

Pasted onto the margins of the album's rear cover were whitewashed album portraits of *Low* and *"Heroes"* alongside *Lodger* and *Aladdin Sane*—the last two album covers also shot by Duffy. Bell showed a keener flexibility in his approach to "art"; sometimes it was necessary to break things, erase, or deface in order to reveal a deeper meaning, in this case photographs that had already faded into iconography.[343] The once-new thing superseded by the immediate present tense, this was Bowie discarding the images of his recent past.[344] Duffy would express bitter disappointment that his photographs were adapted and overtaken by Bell's illustration, perhaps reflecting the shift of stylistic needs moving from the crisply shot black-and-white photography of the 1960s to a new era of synthesized worked-on images to establish a different, hyperreal aesthetic.[345]

The dramatically charged brushstroke text echoed the "wild style" graffiti of New York; the artist's living signature in flourish and furl would continue to appear as the bespoke style across Bell's work. Some noted it was more or less lifted from Gerald Scarfe's illustration work for Pink Floyd's *The Wall*, where gestalt catharsis would meet with a deeper crack-up.[346] We can see Bowie's form aped by Steve Strange in Visage's "Fade to Gray," borrowing the angular lips and Pierrot clown bows, and the single's video would play with light, cutting a perfect profile out from the negative space, bending blurring identities. Finding a winning formula, Bell helped to define the wider 1980s design aesthetic, working across fashion and advertising, where style and glamour were emphasized at the birth of glossy magazines like *Vogue* and *Tatler*, a world that was made permanently shiny, fresh, and new.[347]

In the video for "Ashes to Ashes," Bowie as Pierrot clown would be brought to life—a moving vision beyond the static performer. The video was shot at Pett Level in Sussex, England, closing off the whole beach; the cast remembers it being freezing cold, the crumbling British coastline to be remade into a metaphysical alien landscape for Bowie's balancing act at the edge of the world. The location chimes with the seaside resort of Margate, along the northeast coast of Kent, where T. S. Eliot would go to recuperate from his breakdown in 1921, self-diagnosed as *aboulie*, or "lack of will." Eliot's attempts to connect nothing with nothing led to his writing the modernist epic poem *The Wasteland*, which would chime with Bowie's own experiences of forced remembrance and letting go. The nothingness that Eliot (and perhaps Bowie also) discovered is both a kind of quiet killing and a freedom from overthinking. To shore up his ruins of his present, Bowie must exorcise the ghosts of the past, including Major Tom. The setting of the beach with its barren sands becomes Eliot's vacant seascape of the mind, constantly settled and reset, grain after grain, by the clean sweep of the tide.

Director David Mallett spoke with Bowie about the general concept from a series of sketches: a clown on a beach, a bulldozer trawling over a building site, a bonfire, and a small cast of New Romantics bringing their own style to the shoot. Bowie noted, "There're an awful lot of clichéd things in the video, but I think I put them together in such a way that the whole thing isn't clichéd," but he was able to make something "other" from these base materials of clown, beach, funeral, and bulldozer that together became immediately surreal. As a close collaborator, Mallett was keen to point out that both he and Bowie resisted too much analysis that looks for fixed meanings in the imagery, inviting the audience to put something of themselves into the song and its images.

Mallett's contribution is significant. Alongside a pooling of ideas and storyboarding discussions, he introduced a unique visual effect similar to solarization, which pushes the intensity of colors and upturned the sky into a black ocean, set the sea ablaze, and made the soft sand as alien as the moon, forcing the limits of flared neon shades. These offbeat elements added a heavy funereal tone of moody darkness and searing light so that the quintessential English landscape becomes an entirely foreign, hallucinogenic dream.[348] The early music video would be credited as the most expensive music film production to date, demanding three days of shooting and editing at a time when Mallett notes that such videos would usually be wrapped in a few hours of filming; he also employed multiple locations of beach and studio set, extra cast members, logistics, and studio processing.[349] Visual effects were in their infancy, and music videos were not yet a serious commodity, making "Ashes" a serious artistic (and financial) commitment from Bowie and the label to take the song to the next level. Instead of live appearances and performing on iconic TV shows such as *Top of the Pops* (where "Starman" first helped Bowie break into living rooms across the United Kingdom), the video could stand in his stead, immortalizing the song in the iconic Pierrot costume and tying the aesthetic of the record and its mood with the music—Bowie would return to the longform working with Julien Temple on "Jazzin' for Blue Jean."[350]

There is a polyphonic structure between the song and its video, the Pierrot clown wandering the beach, and the meta-scene-in-the-scene where the camera zooms inside a small square photograph. "Ashes to Ashes" is housed within a triptych of staging devices: the same padded cell used for Bowie's 1979 *Kenny Everett Show* performance of "Space Oddity." We then cut to a kitchen where Bowie/Tom is strapped into a giant chair while a nurse washes up in the background before the chair becomes a rocket and sparks and smokes into life. We then see Major Tom hanging like a prisoner from a wall with various alien tubes plugged into his body (Tanaka 2021). All of these spaces are set against one another, the film blurred between the possibilities of nightmare, fantasy, and reality. Bowie was quick to acknowledge the influence of H. R. Giger's set design for the 1979 film *Alien*: "It was supposed to be the archetypal 1980s ideal of the futuristic colony that has been founded by the earthling, of what he looks like—and in that particular sequence, the idea was for the earthling to be pumping out himself and to be having pumped into him something organic." Bowie would again show a clash between mind, body, and soul, with cold, hard, engineered technology forced into a synthetic compromise. Bowie took some inspiration for the great voyage gone wrong from the BBC drama *The Quatermass Experiment* (1953) watched from behind the sofa when he was six years old (O'Connell 2020). This would return to haunt him in the video for "Ashes," where David Mallett claimed some influence from its later sequel, *The Quatermass and The Pit*, in which it is discovered that humans are not native to Earth; in this scenario, the aliens were us.

But, of course, Bowie was not alone on the beach. Like Picasso's paintings of lost performers without a stage, Bowie presented us with talismanic quartet of Blitz Kids: Elise Brazier, Judi Frankland, Darla-Jane Gilroy, and Steve Strange cast as a ballerina, two space nuns, and a gothic bride with Strange wearing a columnar hat similar to the Kalimavkion of Russian Orthodox priests. Bowie demotes the gathered ones to a backing group of acolytes, mourners joined by their own childhood growing up alongside Bowie's music, a mocking chant that pipes in to hammer home the chorus.

As Bowie had warned on "Teenage Wildlife," his inheritors came to signify the beginning of the end for one phase of golden, classic Bowie, and for the independent Blitz spirit about to be subsumed into the more popular brand of New Romanticism.[351] As one Blitz Kid, Christos Tolera, later put it, "The making of that video was the death knell for the Blitz and, in my mind, for Bowie as an innovator."

Steve Strange remembers the hem of his gown being caught in the teeth of the bulldozer as it trundled closely behind the Blitz lineup, causing him to swoop down periodically and free himself from it. Moving in parallel with Judith Frankland at the other end, it became a key gesture of the video, like the scooping of dirt from the ground by the priest before it is thrown onto the coffin in the grave. This gesture repeats in other music videos, such as "Fashion" as a throwback to "Station to Station" and its Kabbalistic movement of the tree of life from Kether to Malkuth "pulling heaven down to earth" (Kardos 2022). Further to the original intent of the song, the video for "Ashes" was Bowie was hurling his heaviest emotional baggage into the roiling surf, only for it to return gathered together on the terminal beach. In the end, life so far didn't amount to much more than a young man's dream; as quickly as it had arrived, it was gone.

The "glamour" poster that used outtakes from the album cover shoot would continue the legacy of the Pierrot clown, an interesting nod to Bowie as a more likable and interesting costumed figure compared to the workaday austere Bowie of 1977. You couldn't help but look twice to see if it really was Bowie dressed as a clown, not Ziggy having overtaken his host or a Bowie double, copying his attitudes.[352] In the end, Bowie's Pierrot was an example of reflection as deflection, defense by offense, shrouded in intrigue; the uniform of glamour became disruptive camouflage of dazzle ships. In this cut-up space of glitched perspective, the uncertain world is turned on its head.[353] Elsewhere, Bowie carries a shoe as a holy relic, holding it to his ear like a conch shell; it gives no message but echoes the distance traveled and the space to go still ahead of him.

The numb pose of Pierrot with outstretched hands would be memorialized in the construction of a lifelike photography mannequin, created by Bowie's good friend and *"Heroes"* photographer Masayoshi Sukita. The idea of a model Bowie points to the endless replaying of his imagery, each photo taking on a new life of its own. In an interview with the author, Sukita said, "We didn't get a lot of chances to shoot him because of the lack of time and the problem of distance. Then we came up with an idea to create a mannequin so that we could shoot his portraits anytime we wanted. He was so cooperative in its production. The idea of the doll is that the old skin is flaking off

BOWIE WITH PIERROT — 1980

Bowie haunts himself

and a new self is reborn. Each portrait I have made this way over thirty years is always a new and unique, timeless piece of work that I cherish." The slightly distressed appearance of the mannequin shows Bowie as a frozen actor, captured within his cracks, now starting to show, resembling the Japanese scarecrow Kuebiko, the god of folk wisdom, knowledge, and agriculture; he is aware but pinned to the spot, like Bowie trapped within a public image. As a noun, the word translates to a "state of exhaustion inspired by acts of senseless violence," "deformed man," or "crumbling prince." And with *Scary Monsters*, the proxy body of the imagined life takes on the strain and stresses of his craft until the real person behind it starts to absorb the blows of fame and the creative life. Kuebiko represents our opportunity for "mending the fences of your expectations, weeding out all unwelcome and invasive truths, cultivating the perennial good that's buried under the surface, and propping yourself up like an old scarecrow, who's bursting at the seams but powerless to do anything but stand there and watch."[354]

The concept of Sukita's mannequin would enjoy a strange afterlife when Bowie had four of his key album characters—Bowie in a dress on the cover of *The Man Who Sold the World*, Ziggy Stardust, the Thin White Duke, and the Pierrot clown of *Scary Monsters*—reimagined as an eerie cast of life-size wooden puppets. Originally intended for the video of the 1999 *Hours* track "The Pretty Things Are Going to Hell,"[355] the final edit scrapped the puppet shots. But in 2013, they would make a creepy comeback in the video for James Murphy's remix of "Love Is Lost,"[356] shot mostly at Bowie's apartment. Bowie's face is projected onto the blank-faced Pierrot using similar methods to the "Where Are We Now" video. Wooden puppet hands rise up to cover his face, the Thin White Duke puppet haunts Bowie in the corridor, and a ventriloquist's dummy comes to life. Leah Kardos sees Bowie haunted by these past figures in an inversion of his legacy: "The one we presume to be dangerous is the only one who can see the situation clearly; the one we presume to be innocent might be concealing his malice." Later, the Thin White Duke holds the Pierrot figure in his arms, returning to the cover photo of *Hours* by Tim Bret Day, which has Bowie cradling his own corpse, in a pose that shadows Pieta's statue of the Virgin Mary holding the body of Christ.[357]

Looking out from his still-life Pierrot, frozen in the past, Bowie staged himself as the eternal mannequin; he exploited the dramatic tension of survival at quiet extremes. In 1971, Bowie, as arch-generalist, noted the need for music to be a conduit to "sell" deeper artistic concerns: "I think it [music] should be tarted up, made into a prostitute, a parody of itself. It should be the clown, the Pierrot medium. The music is the mask the message wears—music is the Pierrot and I, the performer, am the message." The catharsis of *Scary*

Monsters allowed Bowie to rise above the role of dummy, onto which others could project their image of him. In Bowie's later years, he pushed and pulled against the notion of public musician and private life, discovering that all of our lives are really a series of acts played out where "all the world's a stage." On *Scary Monsters*, art, life, and death are held with equal importance: it was all a game—until it wasn't.

> My "act" has ended by becoming an integral part of
> my nature, I told myself. It's no longer an act. My
> knowledge that I am masquerading as a normal person
> has even corroded whatever of normality I originally
> possessed, ending by making me tell myself over and over
> again that it too was nothing but a pretense of normality.
> To say it another way, I'm becoming the sort of person
> who can't believe in anything except the counterfeit.
>
> —Yukio Mishima, *Confessions of a Mask*, 1946

Fragment #101

See him
Where
Leg straddled, legless chair
  rabid eyed room
  he moves constantly,
  holding each pose for a second then-
West-facing: profile, keener cheeks flushed with blood,
  flushed with something not natural,
  trying too hard to jump out of hus skin,
great look though, great, looking far out to . . .
Like that, yes, yes
no . . . nothing like that —
dead-on, head-on - to me please
David, David, David
That's it
To me

He casts no shadow, the film exposes light, and the lack of it their is negative
blur, and blank figure, framed by the chair, the glowing burn of a cigarette
just hanging . . .
Ghost portrait - he has passed,
passing,
off into another
Catch - see me blinking - blink - in a sudden burst - imagination of the
figment
No-one really caught a glimpse.
                  The artist who
          was never there

                        Only the

                        Cigarette burn

                        Of the silhouette
after the
                        actor
                        has
                        Already left

Silhouettes . . .

It's a big black bloody world full of a million black
and bloody hells, and when those hells collide it's
time for us to sit up and take fucking notice.

—David Peace, *Nineteen Eighty: The
Red Riding Quartet*, 2001

Once the super creeps have gone and their demons faded away, banished by the shutters finally thrown open, what is there left to be afraid of but a new dawn rising? After the music, a sinking stillness. In one of his lyric notes, Bowie states, "I have absolutely nothing to tell you." This is perhaps the final position of *Scary Monsters*; negative speech that communicates emptiness and again the purging of the record leaves him vacant but more than ever in need of connection. On "It's No Game (No. 2)," the dead air spent on "walky talkie" evolves into the Sony Walkman carried on the hip, now hurled into the sky, lost in space. Idle chat and background noise rub together, making static, no more real talk. Again, Bowie relied on the music to realize the inexpressible.

In her 1980 *Rolling Stone* review of *Scary Monsters*, Debra Rae Cohen looks back to a scene from *The Man Who Fell to Earth* where the alien-on-Earth protagonist, Thomas Jerome Newton, watches in shock the ritualized violence of the Japanese kabuki performers' clashing blades. Each time they strike, there is a flash of memory as premonition. Jarred out of the present, Newton is looking beyond the scene played out in front of him, seeing the movie of his life play simultaneously in fast-forward and reverse. The performers throw up new associations from old events, sounds and voices interject, and their shapes, scattered across the floor, outgrow all human proportions to become new grotesques—shocking revelations cast out of sequence in flattened time, away from of its linear span.[358]

The cast of *Scary Monsters* are deformed or damaged; their fall from grace is to slip further away from normality and outside of society. Broken on the wheel of life, minds and bodies are marshaled into abstract shapes, and the dance of the fighters stands to embody the fractured spirit of the album, trying to make sense of a splintering world held in the rapture of light and steel. David Bowie as Pierrot is still standing captive on the beach of "Ashes to Ashes," a stone on the shore surrounded by all the ghosts of his past and echoes of the future; the pulsing time line will rise and fall as the tides of memory constantly erode the present, eating away the beach beneath your feet—somewhere within the universe of *Scary Monsters*, it will always be 1980.

Perhaps what unites the album is its brokenness as both form and theme, Bowie's 1970s refracted through a shattered mirror, an account of fractured and feverish minds. The great success of the record is how he brought the scattering of images together into a new whole—a colliding spectacle. Bowie found resolution in the aesthetics of the scream, the malapropism of malaise, the way time curves back at you when confronted with the now, realizing a new form of synthesis. *Scary Monsters* is perhaps the best of his initial decade, forcing divergent elements and fresh influences into something sad, strange, and unique, merging pop nous with high art—perhaps Bowie's truest talent?

There is a continued through line that connects Bowie back to John Lennon running beyond his legacy as a former Beatle. Speaking in 1999, Bowie argues that Lennon showed him "how one could twist and turn the fabric of pop and imbue it with elements from other art forms, often producing something extremely beautiful, very powerful and imbued with strangeness." Bowie would complain of an urgent need to escape his own blinkered creative vision whenever things got too easy, formulaic, or stale—he responded with autodestruction: "I'm continually trying to open it up and break it down and do shattering things to it—and that's when it becomes dangerous."

Hans Richter speaks of the Dadaists driving spirit to force art forward, perhaps toward a place where it didn't want to go, but no doubt it inspired Bowie's approach: "Their apparently inexhaustible energy, their vision of mental freedom which included the abolition of everything (especially Expressionism and Tristan Tzara)—all this was closer to hysteria than to a cultural mission."[359] The simplest and most direct route to this creative reawakening would be the alienation and culture shock driven by Bowie's need for perpetual motion, travel as flux, which encouraged him to "make it new." Absorbing the Vorticist expression of collisions revealing new images, his lyrical vocal is a living text working at extremes of transformation: "I like the friction. That's what I look for in any city. West Berlin has the right kind of push. I can't write in a peaceful atmosphere at all; I've nothing to bounce off. I need the terror, whatever it is." On *Station to Station*, Bowie declared his exit from America as a return to the homeland of the European canon's deep time. Following this, the "planned accidents" working title of *Lodger* became more of an open manifesto—"anywhere" music with no home or fixed direction. *Scary Monsters* is an album shocked into life and forced to react to the coming hunger for newness that drove the 1980s, to which Bowie responded with a tighter, sharper set of songs to cut through the New Wave noise emerging all around.[360]

Speaking in 1980 to the BBC's Andy Peebles, Bowie explained his new approach to a third-level synthesis of lyric writing with the example of the *"Heroes"* album compared to cutting pages into strips of paper and shuffling lines about on *Diamond Dogs*: "You take a couple of subject matters . . . someone jumping over the Berlin Wall. I would write a paragraph from the jumper's point of view. I would write a paragraph from an observer's point of view from this side of the wall, then an observer's point of view from that side of the wall, so you have three different points of view." Bowie would then break up the lines, finding key phrases and fragments, and piece these together, filling in blanks as he saw them to create something entirely new. Anything that seemed interesting and sparked a further thought or idea for a lyric, so a series of jumping-off points would combine to build a crooked staircase toward a song.

One of the most marked thing about physical cutups is their jarring break from standardized syntax and grammar, short-circuiting language to break in mid-sentence, speaking (in parentheses) apropos of nothing; unanchored lines seeming to have no connection with one another: pre-thought, pure thought, best expression. In the novels of William S. Burroughs, this form-as-style can seem impenetrable; for Bowie, it became carefully orchestrated, edited into digestible shape, demanding the listener's attention. Examining the lyrics of "Aladdin Sane," parsing and scanning as if reading a malfunctioning literary text, the blogger Momus finds "a tactical vagueness to the lyrics—a kind of negative capability in not being too intentional, too specific, too narrative," reminding me of Bowie's distorted room of "Sound and Vision."

By the time of *Scary Monsters*, Bowie would spend more time on lyric writing as a distinct craft, taking time away from music composition. In some places, Bowie's draft lyric sheets resemble mood boards with words poured out on paper, piled on top of one another as working titles, and snatches of lyrics crashing into textual disjunct overlapping and interrupting. It is an expression borne of deep incubation from the writer who has ideas long looming in the subconscious waiting to surface and fresh thoughts scrawled verbatim, all colliding (O'Leary 2017). Then the edit—words shifted and scratched out by instinct and intuition, his eye finding the shape of a song. You hear this sonically in Bowie's vocal delivery; the gabbled first lines of "Ashes" come at different speeds and diffracted patterns, an unnatural flow that just sounds right.

Bowie would become frustrated when listeners focused too much on lyrics, looking for a discovery of the artist's intentions but also divorcing the words from the song: "It implies there is no meaning in the music." He told designer Jonathan Barnbrook, "What people see in my songs is far more interesting than what I actually put into them." The liminal space from lyric to lyric gives us the spark to make our own imaginative leap with no claim to definite interpretation; the more oblique, the greater the creative distance traveled.

Bowie's achievement was to find new logic in splintering words where there were "no ground rules"—messy ends are left open and undone to let new meanings bleed through. Much later, Bowie talked about his fascination with the philosophical implications of William S. Burroughs's writing: "using the wrong pieces of information and putting them together and finding a third piece of information—it's what our life has become in the twentieth century we live and assume our morals and our stances from the fragmented pieces of information that we glean from the media." By 1995, he declared himself to be "a mid-art populist and postmodernist Buddhist who is casually surfing his way through the chaos of the late twentieth century." Terry Eagleton observed the risk of this position is to get lost in the privilege of the ironic remove, where "an emancipating drive against tradition led to a removal from the real" (Deandrea 2016). This struggle is inherent in so much of Bowie's music, fought between ironic detachment and trying to express authentic feeling. Balancing low-art immediacy and high-art attainment, he was a gateway artist mapping new constellations of influences that crisscrossed artistic mediums, showing the wounds of his creative pulse.

In a 1999 interview with Jeremy Paxman, Bowie admitted that he used to be "drawn to create conflicts" in the studio, introducing necessary tension to drive the creative process, as with the cypher of the Berlin Wall. It was out of this passionate energy that Bowie was able to push himself and his collaborators toward the unknown but also taking his personal health and mental stability to their limits. But it was with *Scary Monsters* that Bowie expressed his resolve to change—and change again—for his own sake. Bowie told *Musician* magazine in 1995, "The realization, to me at least, is that I'm most comfortable working with a sense of fragmentation. The idea of tidy endings or beginnings seems too absolute." Where the *NME*'s 1980 review of the album warned of a climate of fear, it stressed the need to rise above the situation: "To know fear but not be conquered by it is the response that is needed now . . . even from a man in a clown suit." Even this stark comment would give Bowie more positive pause for thought: "There was a certain degree of optimism making that album," he said in 1999, "because I'd worked through some of my problems, I felt very positive about the future, and I think I just got down to writing a really comprehensive and well-crafted album."

Scary Monsters would enjoy a strange afterlife. Bowie had initially claimed that following *The Elephant Man*'s final run in New York, he had no wish to tour in the near future, arguing the need for a vacation. Although he hinted he would perform again in the spring of 1981, preferring smaller club venues, it was not to be. Following the murder of John Lennon, Bowie left New York and took sanctuary in the anonymous hills of Switzerland and other locations—literally taking himself off the map.

Sean Mayes, the pianist on *Lodger* and the Stage tour, later recalled a social visit from Bowie just after the album's final mixes had been completed: "I sat on the floor in a Knightsbridge flat and heard *Scary Monsters*. David was depressed—as he always is after completing a project. He was sure it was terrible and would be a failure. But then he laughed and said this was how he always felt!" The catharsis of getting the album out of his system was short lived and perhaps not the full emotional purging that Bowie had hoped for—another year, another record.

In spite of so much personal distraction and Bowie's withdrawal from the limelight of publicity, *Scary Monsters* achieved that weird thing of almost universal acclaim with both fans and critics and strong sales. Released on September 12, 1980, it had a strong showing in the United Kingdom, with a number 1 album and the single "Ashes to Ashes" released on August 1 ahead of the record, Bowie's first since "Space Oddity."[361] Where other singles from the album had broken into the top 10, 20, and 40 positions, the reception in the United States was relatively muted, the album placing at number 12 in the charts and "Ashes to Ashes" getting only to #101.[362]

In his review of *Lodger*, Greil Marcus would complain that there was no center to its approach; borrowed ideas were run up a flagpole as a creative exercise, "but try to find the flagpole." By contrast, Bowie's new album seemed to hit the nail on the head with a hammer of sonic and lyrical force, destroying the wall in the process. *Record Mirror*'s Simon Ludgate perversely awarded *Scary Monsters* a rating of seven (out of five!) stars; the brevity in its ten-song track list highlighted Bowie's greatest strengths. Biographer Marc Spitz considers it more accurate to call the album Bowie's "last 'young' record" in that it was his final "perfectly confident statement" and the last time that Bowie's "search for the 'new' in our world of sound [felt] pure, as opposed to betraying itself." *Scary Monsters* remains Bowie's enduringly fresh and evergreen-sounding record; he would never sound so free to simultaneously explore both pop and rock with such verve of sonic experimentation: "The album would remain contemporary as it aged, with its near-future always near; it would be Bowie's perpetual New Album" (O'Leary 2020a).

The broad and enduring appeal of the album established the phrase "Bowie's best album since *Scary Monsters*." This sliced-bread pattern of thought set a pejorative standard that would stalk Bowie's career until his 1990s renaissance and the final great albums of *Heathen*, *The Next Day*, and *Blackstar*. By 1983, Bowie was already somewhat dismissive of his back catalog, rejecting the idea of his earlier albums as "classic statements." Instead, he saw them as products of their time, fleeting "Polaroids," blown like loose leaves through the past decade. For many fans, it remains the last great consensus record, consistently interesting, challenging, provocative, and (rarely) self-indulgent, with Bowie still pushing forward beyond himself, although some will still question the consistency of the record's second half after the breathtaking run of earlier songs.[363]

In a *Studio Q* interview from 2013, Trent Reznor of Nine Inch Nails explains that while his most well-known and artistically successful record, *The Downward Spiral*, was heavily influenced by *Low*, the first Bowie record he heard was actually *Scary Monsters*: "[It was] Bowie's coldest, scariest, and most seductive record, even though it wasn't friendly"; from this, Reznor worked backward through the discography.[364] Reznor and Bowie would undergo a double-header tour in 1995, Reznor promoting *The Downward Spiral* and Bowie his *1. Outside* album. For the tour, Bowie performed "Scary Monsters" in a duet with Reznor and gave "Teenage Wildlife" its live debut as his closing song.[365] Reznor would later return the favor in a tribute to Bowie, performing and recording a studio version of "I Can't Give Everything Away" shortly after Bowie's death and years later adding "Fashion" as a cover for the Bowie tribute concert organized by Mike Garson in 2021.

Certainly, the promotional power of the "Ashes" video had a significant impact (when and where it could be seen, with MTV being launched only on August 1, 1981), and it rightly remains a unique piece of work when viewed today, more than forty years after it was first shot. In stark contrast to his dynamic 1979 *Saturday Night Live* appearance, Bowie would perform two songs in 1980 on *The Tonight Show* with Johnny Carson with Bowie dressed as James Dean. He performed "Life on Mars" and "Ashes to Ashes" in a full and powerful voice, the guitars slicing and searing restrained funk. Bowie's costume still displayed some divided loyalties between transgressive sexuality and straitlaced all-American hero from the good old days, the red wind-breaker, white T-shirt, and blue jeans a nod to a forced image of masculinity, blurred with effeminate sensuality and latent homoeroticism.[366]

The album grudgingly became a million seller, although it did not happen overnight, being outlived by its core singles "Up the Hill Backwards," "Ashes to Ashes," and "Fashion" and other deep cuts, such as "Scary Monsters" and "Teenage Wildlife," being more listened to now than the record as whole. Perhaps the album's progress was slower because it was never supported by a tour; fans would have to wait several years for this, with only half its songs ever played live. In terms of legacy, it is somewhat overshadowed by the more classic Bowie albums of the 1970s. Although *"Heroes"* sold about as well as *Scary Monsters*, no doubt due to the single release of its title track, Bowie in 1980 was infinitely more approachable. *Scary Monsters* was the album that prepared Bowie for *Let's Dance*, where he would achieve escape velocity to become a truly global artist, touring across several continents and, for a time at least, never looking back.

With *Scary Monsters* as his springboard, Bowie's reach for the brass ring of commercial success in the 1980s was assured. Its singles and subsequent music videos cemented him in the public consciousness, a return to "accessibility" that somehow wiped the slate of any alienation from the experimental Berlin Trilogy. However, in a November 1980 interview a few months after the chart success of the album, Bowie suggested he was still in the "Berlin" state of mind: "More and more, I'm prepared to relinquish sales, as far as records go, by sticking to my guns about the kind of music I really wish to make."

Bowie would seem to be waiting out the end of his contract with RCA, which lapsed in 1982, after he had delivered them the required twelve albums stipulated in the contract. With the label keen on keeping Bowie and hoping to renew, he was given pause for thought.[367] By this time, RCA was in some financial trouble with a shifting management lineup following a ten-year period in which their earnings from music sales had halved, with a shrinking margin from a turnover of $67 billion delivering only $2 billion in profit (Gillman 1987).

The label seemed unstable and, more importantly, had struggled and often failed to invest in promoting Bowie's recent records; after he left, RCA would continue to scrape the archives clean for rare and forgotten songs pushed into random compilation albums that Bowie labeled "horrendous" and "offensive" due to their choice of lackluster material from Bowie's early career.

When Angus MacKinnon broached the subject of Bowie's relationship with the label in 1980, he was testy, suggesting that negotiations for a new contract were miles off and entirely speculative. Elsewhere, RCA had been openly dissatisfied with *Lodger* as a record and in its commercial performance, but as Bowie pointed out, they were unhappy with *Low* also: "At the time the one comment I received from them was 'Can we get you another pad in Philadelphia?' so that I could do another *Young Americans*. That was the kind of attitude I was having to cope with." His dissatisfaction seemed to grow the closer his contract came to its end on December 31, 1982—by which time his settlement agreement with Defries had concluded in September 1982. Bowie would pay no further royalties to his former manager on new music recorded after this point; it was a natural time for change. Inspired by John Lennon's emancipation from the standard industry system, Bowie made a clean break into self-management with support from personal assistant Coco Schwab and considered himself in a state of financial independence.[368] It is noted that Bowie kept some loyalty to RCA, particularly with Ken Glancy, who had engineered Bowie's escape from the Defries contract despite mounting grievances and small asides in public. It was only after Glancy left RCA in 1980 that Bowie felt more comfortable moving on; he later explained that he and the label had long fallen out of love with one another but carried on for a few more years out of mutual contractual interest (Jensen 1983).[369]

All of this made a move to EMI all the more tempting. It is widely thought that during the spontaneous recording session in Switzerland with Queen for 1981's "Under Pressure," Bowie quizzed the band about working with the label. On January 17, 1983, Bowie signed with EMI—reportedly

£17 million for a five-year deal (Bowie would not confirm the figure). Making his announcement-as-celebration at Claridge's hotel in London, he appeared in a suit and later noted, on his apparent lack of image, that he simply went from suit to suit, but the bloke inside it remained the same.

Looking back on the period, Bowie said, "All the money I have made has been since 1980, as everything before that just went. *Let's Dance* helped, and 1983 for me was like manna from heaven. All that money I'd gone through in the 70s suddenly came back to me, in almost a year." Bowie enforced his independent state of mind by settling with Defries in the 1990s to completely annul their agreement.[370] In that decade, Bowie would become a considerable commercial prospect—infinitely bankable—and a financial entity, offering himself up in "Bowie Bonds": people could buy stock in the branded project of David Bowie, the man, the myth, the commodity. He became self-sufficient with his own ISO label, creating his own Web provider and fan forum Bowie Net. The bonds, for example, were a unique innovation, well ahead of their time; Bowie had realized that by owning the rights to all of his own music (and with it the publishing rights), "this is where the real money is." He drew investors to the back catalog of David Bowie and his future works; this was its own gold standard with a value that would never fall, only increase. Looking back from 1990, Bowie could see that on an artistic level, 1980 really did signal the beginning of the end: "By the time of *Scary Monsters* the kind of music that I was doing was becoming very acceptable . . . it was definitely the sound of the early eighties."[371]

> *Let's Dance* put me in an extremely different orbit . . .
> artistically and aesthetically. It seemed obvious that the
> way to make money was to give people what they want,
> so I gave them what they wanted, and it dried me up.

> —David Bowie

Enter 1982. Bowie emerged from the semi-wilderness of various recording and acting projects ready to make his first album with new label EMI. His latest transformation would see him turned into another everyman artist; edging closer to the middle of the road, he began to present the normalized face of David Bowie masquerading as "David Jones." The album cover shows Bowie shadowboxing with himself, past images and future ghosts banished to focus on his immediate goals; fighting fit and stripped to the waist with images projected over him, he has faded from a shifting chameleon to a blank marble statue, his zigging and zagging now petrified mannequin-stiff,

SERIOUS MOONLIGHT TOUR — 1983

Modern Bowie — suited and straightened-out

bearing the image of others. Bowie had adjusted to the new realities of his situation, where artistic direction (or the lack thereof) radically altered his lifestyle, this time for the better. He would exercise every day with aerobics and boxing training, becoming muscular by Bowie standards, as his hair would burn bleach blond and his skin would sink into a more orange-tan hue by the decade's end. The ossified blond forelock was parodied in the character of "Tommy Stone" from *Velvet Goldmine* (1998). He had turned his back on the past in order to be fully embraced by the present and, in this self-negation, forgotten to remember who he really was.[372]

But change was more than skin deep with Bowie, handing over the songwriting reins to close collaborator Nile Rodgers, with the instruction by to make hits. Bowie's music was largely apolitical, though the video for "Let's Dance" pushed forward a radically different agenda almost at odds with the sentiment of the song, to the point of Benetton blandness and self-effacement, as if Bowie had removed part of himself to get out of the way of songs now written for pure enjoyment on dance floors, in clubs, on car radios, in teenage bedrooms, and in stockbroker lounges—this was Bowie as Huey Lewis and the News.[373]

Bowie jettisons the outsider "cool" of the avant-garde and tries to make a connection with the "common man." In *Q* magazine, Mark Blake noted the traces of discomfort in the album that soon filter through to the keen Bowie listener; it bucks and bridles uncomfortable in its own skin. Bowie must have been aware that *Let's Dance* would be critically underrated by some simply because it was a hit.

The focus of Bowie's songs had also shifted dramatically since *Scary Monsters*. Bowie claimed that he was reaching for something warmer and more humanistic with less emphasis on nihilistic statements than before. He called his earlier music "disturbing" and was now more interested in an "emotionally uplifting experience." Bowie said guardedly (but no doubt with half a smile) that it was danceable; he tried to write in a more obvious and positive manner but also alluded to the fact that it was as simple as anything he'd written before. Turning his back on previous artistic revolutions, Bowie in effect granted himself an amnesty, in effect declaring, "Fuck art—let's dance."

Bowie said that by trying to predict what he thought audiences wanted to hear in the 1980s, he in turn became predictable. Perhaps bored with his own music and even the process of making records, Bowie leaned more on his session musicians to steer each album and by 1984's *Tonight* relied more on cover versions, particularly those of close collaborator Iggy Pop, with diminishing artistic returns. Bowie's cover versions buoyed Iggy financially with secondhand royalties, the joke being that the almost $1 million payment made to Iggy on the back of the success of Bowie's "China Girl" was swallowed up by debt to the Internal Revenue Service; this at least reset him to a ground-zero fighting stance with everything to gain and nothing to lose.

Along with the "Let's Dance" single topping the charts on both sides of the Atlantic, Bowie's 1983 globe-spanning Serious Moonlight tour in support of the album took him to a new level of fame and success. His first tour since 1978, it would take up seven months of Bowie's life with ninety-six shows spread across fifteen countries. While some of the poorer East Asian countries struggled to fill venues with ticket prices beyond the average wage, in many places the arenas quickly grew into stadiums in proportion to rising album sales; this leaves a gap through which *Scary Monsters* falls, already a thing of the past (in Bowie time at least). Success would begin to outpace Bowie himself.

One of the central tensions that would arise from the *Let's Dance* era would be Bowie's relationship to drugs. Despite the challenges of Los Angeles and Berlin, Bowie would struggle to manage substance abuse for another decade, trying to find an equilibrium between abstinence and indulgence.

Bowie said that it took the two years or so in Berlin to get fully clean: the room was moving, walls were running, and then everything would settle again. In 2003, Bowie considered *Low*, *Heroes*, and *Scary Monsters* to be his best works—"all drug free"—but in 1983, he remained vulnerable to relapse. Despite the Serious Moonlight tour's "no-drugs" rule, it was noted by band members that Bowie sometimes lapsed into drug use at aftershow parties. By his own admission, as the tour expanded with more dates and larger venues, Bowie began to rely more on alcohol and cocaine. The tender and sometimes frosty mood characteristic of the songs on *Scary Monsters* was still very real, as if Bowie did not yet have the resources to entirely piece himself back together. Looking back on the Serious Moonlight tour, Bowie told *Arena* magazine in 1993,

> I was not in great shape to accept success at any level. So it could not have come at a worse time for me. I was still fighting desperately to stop the drug thing, which was intermittent by then, but kept coming back. I told everyone that I was no longer an addict—including myself—because it was only occasional. But of course those occasions got closer and closer together. I would have a great spree for a few weeks, then stop and turn back to alcohol. It's an absurd situation because you say, oh, I've kicked everything—but you're a virtual alcoholic. Drink is the most depressing of all addictions because it takes you so far up and throws you back down. And so as a writer and an artist I really didn't have much to hang on to any more. And it has been a very, very slow process of coming back again. And I dare say it isn't over. I dare say that none of our searches are really over.[374]

Bowie would later realize that, for many, addiction was a difficult path frequented with missteps: "I slipped around *Let's Dance* which some would say was not my best album. Personally, I think I found myself as a writer again in the 90s." In his 1999 BBC interview with Jeremy Paxman, Bowie declared himself clean of drugs and alcohol. His only studio vices remained cigarettes and coffee. He noted that quitting cocaine was tough; alcohol, difficult; and cigarettes, nearly impossible: "There are 437 different drugs in a cigarette all designed to ensure you can't refuse one."[375] Paxman would press Bowie, desperately searching for a scoop that wasn't there: he really didn't drink anymore, not wine, not anything? Bowie pushed back, responding that to drink or use drugs again would ruin his life and cause him to lose his family, stating, "I am an addict."[376]

In 2003, Bowie looked back on his 1980s period with further mixed feelings: "All my big mistakes are when I try to second-guess or please an audience. My work is always stronger when I get very selfish about it." This perspective is confirmed in the critical consensus that followed, so perhaps *Scary Monsters* is the great compromise, the final phases of burnout realized after many attempts at recovery and later full sobriety.

By the end of 1980, the state of the nation that Bowie had sought to expose had turned increasingly sour, as if all his worst fears had come true and things were only going to get worse. Triggered by fresh uncertainties, 1980 marked the precipice of a new age in global politics, particularly between the "special relationship" of Bowie's key locus nations of the United Kingdom and the United States. Margaret Thatcher had staged her own kind of cultural revolution. Nicknamed the "Iron Lady" for her unyielding resolve and inscrutability, her political tactics were marred by single-minded determination and bullying tactics, even with her closest and most trusted colleagues.[377] In her wake strutted former actor, monkey costar, and governor of California, Ronald Reagan; tall and charismatic, he offered the masculine statesman image that America demanded. Reagan remained sprightly at age seventy-seven, but, increasingly prone to growing dementia, he leaned on Thatcher as she so often loomed over him, with her dominating spirit.[378]

Together, they tilted the free democratic world on its axis toward a new kind of authoritarianism that set the citizen against the state. Their combined emphasis on small government undercut the fabric of community, public housing,[379] and the welfare state; tax cuts that cushioned ballooning salaries and reduced government spending hinted at peace and prosperity for all, which eventually saw a rise in the standard of living but also continued to enforce a growing wealth divide where the rich got richer. On both sides of the Atlantic, inflation crippled the cost-of-living situation for many families already struggling—the national debt became the citizens' debt.[380]

Margaret Thatcher's fight against the "enemy within" intensified with the continued bombings of the Irish Republican Army (IRA) fighting for a free and united Irish republic; these were matched by hunger strikes in late 1980, leading to the death of twelve prisoners in the Maze prison, including Bobby Sands, posthumously elected as member of Parliament in April 1981. Thatcher condemned their actions—"the men of violence have turned violence against themselves"—and refused to accept their demands to be acknowledged as political prisoners, not criminals.[381] It was not until 1984 that the economy began to bounce back; meanwhile, running battles with striking miners shook working-class communities across northern England and Wales, alongside picketing actions by the Campaign for Nuclear Disarmament around U.S. nuclear missile launch sites on British soil. Elsewhere, CIA-backed coups and "adviser" operations, as well as increasing smuggling by the "Air America" cocaine ring, flooded the United States with drugs, leading to the inner-city crack pandemic of the 1980s. The rise of leftist militarism in Nicaragua,[382] Guatemala, and El Salvador alarmed the United States such that many warned of a second Cuba in Central America. Throughout the 1970s, there were continued tensions between the United States and Iran over oil prices and conflict with Middle Eastern states, adding long-term pressure that eventually led to the Gulf War in 1990–1991. State-managed violence, fueled by big money and self-interest, soon curdled into greed for power, becoming a global business.[383]

Blogger Sean Doyle refers to the new Bowie of 1983 as something of a betrayal: "Bowie didn't help matters by adopting a brightly conservative new Reagan-era look and calling his former admission of bisexuality 'the biggest mistake I ever made.'" Where *Young Americans* skewered the crooked and twisted machinations of Nixon, neither acquitted nor impeached, he simply resigned and jumped into the presidential chopper. Bowie would actively buy into the new future to bask in the Reaganite glow of prosperity for all.[384] At the 1987 Conservative Party Conference, Margaret Thatcher would complain that the children of the United Kingdom "are being taught that our society offers them no future." Speaking to Charles Shaar Murray in 1984 for *NME*, Bowie pointed out his naïveté when it came to the wider political climate, feeling that he had only ever scraped the topsoil of the global situation, and was less inclined to comment on current events.

The album cover of *Let's Dance* shows the title letters spelled out among dance move directions; political machinations could be reduced to dance floor maneuvering, the 1980s generation shuffling off the edge of common sense and into consumerism, feeling the aspirational draw of designer labels and the status weight of luxury products rather than a sharply defined aesthetic or conceptual idea. Bowie himself would become a brand, mired in the excess

DAVID BOWIE - REALITY TOUR - 2003

A blackstar burning — Bowie beyond his legacy

of success and fame; his records became a lifestyle that people could buy into and hum along with, one that reflected the carefree, fun times of their own lives, no longer an emancipatory, mind-expanding wake-up call to new possibilities.

Bowie was keen that the music of *Let's Dance* would reach a new audience for him; as a consequence of this, Bowie became removed from the social realities he claimed to be engaging with. Although his heart seemed to be in the right place, he carried the echo of Lennon in an *NME* interview (Bohn 1983): "Instead of intimating change, try to do something about it." The detachment continued on future albums. On 1987's *Never Let Me Down*. blogger Sean Doyle said, "Bowie and his exuberant backup singers don't really reflect the attempted urban grit of 'Day-In Day-Out.' In an almost mockingly cruel video, he croons and rollerblades past scenes of homelessness, prostitution and police brutality."[385]

Looking back on 1983 and the years following it, Bowie seemed keen to distance himself from the entire decade: "I went mainstream in a major way with the song 'Let's Dance.' I pandered to that in my next few albums, and what I found I had done was put a box around myself," he told an interviewer. "It was very hard for people to see me as anything other than the person in the suit who did 'Let's Dance,' and it was driving me mad—because it took all my passion for experimenting away."

Merrick: "You are a famous actress?"
Mrs. Kendal: "I am not unknown."
Merrick: "You must display yourself
for a living then. Like I did."
Mrs. Kendal: "That is not myself, Mr. Merrick.
That is an illusion. *This* is myself."
Merrick: "This is *myself* too."[386]

—From *The Elephant Man* by Bernard Pomerance

Over the last three and a half years, I've been getting happier and happier. . . . Not with myself and my situation, but happier in my realization that I can face up to things a lot better than I could when I was living a heavily rock & roll life in America.

—Bowie to *Rolling Stone*, November 1980

The question remains whether *Scary Monsters* really did allow Bowie the great purge or cathartic release he had promised himself. Certainly, the strict autobiography of "Ashes to Ashes" suggests a kind of cure, while other tracks would seem symptomatic of suppressed inner tension, depression, anger, or resentments—a chorus of scream still trapped under the ice. But at the very least, the album enabled Bowie to put Ziggy, along with so much other cosmic junk, into the earth and bury them. In the more literal sense, Bowie closed his golden decade and welcomed the brave new world of the 1980s, banishing his recent troubles: cocaine addiction, management disputes, a broken marriage, and overwhelming personas.

Music journalist Tony Parsons said of Bowie, "He represented so much of what had happened to those postwar generations, the drugs, the divorce, to crawl out from the wreckage of all that excess in the 70s." Bowie created a more stable future for himself through his time in Berlin and his return to Europe, pointing toward a new beginning in 1980. After first reconnecting with his son, Duncan, in 1980, by 1991 Bowie was happily remarried, and later, with the birth of his daughter, Lexi, he seemed to set definite boundaries between work and family, learning to value both—and believing that neither should have to exist at the expense of the other (Jones 2018). Iman Abdulmajid stated that she married David Jones, "a completely different person" from "David Bowie." So many people who met him came away with similar impressions, but he was different with each person. On one level, people felt they saw both the real and the imagined Bowie—it was hard for him to deliver conclusively one or the other experience. It seems that only in his much later years was Bowie able to step back and separate the shadow that followed the man: "When I reemerged as being part of something or willing to have more of an affinity with the people around me, and obviously with my marriage, my writing improved beyond belief. From the late eighties into the nineties, and onwards, I really like what I've written. I can't say that about the eighties."

In 1980, Bowie's life experience, hard won and sometimes bitter, would give rise to the wise and concerned voices of "Teenage Wildlife" and "Because You're Young," showing someone aware of a life beyond the persona of being "David Bowie," outside of music and the grind of touring and recording. The two versions of "It's No Game" come to represent "two halves of Bowie's whole; the drama queen and the ice man" (Lindsay 2021). Fashion designer Keanan Duffty noted that Bowie had worked so hard in such a short space of time, burnishing image after image, that he inevitably became "arty and weird." After this, Bowie would spend the last decade or two of his life "trying to get back to being normal."

Edward Bell argued that in death, Bowie became "a ghost writer" of many conflicting legends all struggling for supremacy. *Scary Monsters* marked a point at which the slate was wiped clean with Jones reasserting himself over Bowie. Like Thomas Jerome Newton, Bowie explained that his life was not secretive, but it was private. As he was grilled on the way to the stage by Janet Street Porter during the 1978 Stage tour, he explained that he was quiet, not shy; when questioned whether were it not for his enigmatic distance people would still be so interested in what he would do next, Bowie gave no answer but made his excuses and beat a hasty exit to go begin his performance.

Speaking to Bill DeMain in 2003, Bowie noted the "isolationist stance" that colored his songs in the late 1970s: "I probably reached a peak of a certain kind of writing at that time, where it worked for me being sort of pulled back from things in a bemused fashion. But what started off as more of an arty exercise ended up, because of my addictions, with me almost ostracizing myself from the rest of whatever society I was in. It became more of a mental health concern. And I think it led to a depression in my writing during the eighties."

The techno-fear that pursued Bowie in 1980 would later seem both paranoid and prescient in equal measure. A more streamlined world driven by technology shrank the Earth toward globalization and would bring deeper-seated fears front and center on the terrifying and dizzying edge of now perpetual newness becoming stale novelty as its tipping point. Technology became the false promise of a brighter tomorrow, constantly deferred and forever delayed. Speaking to Jeremy Paxman in 1999, Bowie made a classic about-face on the possibilities of emergent digital technologies, with his deep blue prediction around the future force of the internet: "I don't think we've seen the tip of the iceberg. I think the potential for what the internet is going to do to society, both good and bad, is unimaginable." In the 1970s, Bowie oversaw a breakdown of singularity: multifaceted sides to everything. With the internet, everyone can say anything—the art becomes the "gray space in the middle," and the audience will bring the meaning to it.

Commenting on his musical "method" on the 1980 *Scary Monsters* promo interview disc, Bowie spoke plainly: "There are an awful lot of mistakes on that album that I went with, rather than cut them out. One tries as much as possible to put oneself on the line artistically. But after the Dadaists, who pronounced that art is dead. . . . Once you've said art is dead, it's very hard to get more radical than that. Since 1924 art's been dead, so what the hell can we do with it from there on? One tries to at least keep readdressing the thing." In this, "Ashes" demands to sit alongside "I Can't Give Everything

Away"—where Bowie's cry that "I never did anything out of the blue" is given a final and lasting affirmation:[387]

> Seeing more and feeling less
> Saying no but meaning yes
> This is all I ever meant
> That's the message that I sent.

Exhausted by the atrophy of mass communication, being known, beloved, and often misunderstood, where songs are seen as imitations of one's own life, Bowie too would feel encumbered by the big and the little stuff we all sweat, the stuff from which songs and dreams are woven. *Scary Monsters* would stand as an opportunity to look both forward and backward at the same time, like the ghostly harmonica from "A New Career in a New Town" striding across time's span for the introduction to "I Can't Give Everything Away, the reversed drumbeat of "Five Years" that opens "Valentine's Day," and the great pause at the center of "Young Americans," a beat lasting almost a whole decade that reaches forward from the snare drum strike that jump-starts Bob Dylan's "Like a Rolling Stone." Across these aching pauses, these two sounds are joined. All of these moments would bring Bowie back to his "legacy" just as David Jones begins to quietly slip away after surrendering his discography.[388]

In his final years, Bowie would often be seen wearing a black Alexander McQueen scarf peppered with tiny white skulls. When in 2016 we hear Bowie sing of "skull designs upon my shoes" looking down facing the end of his life, we can appreciate that he was also able to continue looking forward through his music.

Following Bowie's return from ill health in 2013 after a decade-long absence, he had clearly taken some the advice from former Spiders from Mars guitarist Mick Ronson, who died from liver cancer in 1993 at age forty-six, to treat each day ahead of him as a footstep, one at a time, with Bowie titling his penultimate album *The Next Day*.[389] Simon Critchley noted that Bowie embodied this spirited view throughout his music, discovering the essence of poetry in the "majesty of the absurd"; as difficult and beautiful as the extremes of life could be, these were also cut through with moments of seriousness and ridiculousness. Although sometimes one step forward could equal six steps back, these were all steps toward a kind of freedom in artistic expression and finding renewed satisfaction in family and a real life, which for a long time in his earlier career Bowie never seemed to have.[390] *Scary Monsters* remains a key moment in David Bowie's brilliant adventure toward some better place. This meant taking life as it comes—in one sense always looking "up" and confronting the present; in another, thinking beyond that, always toward the possibility of the next day, into the sublime unknowing, a contradictory nothingness that Bowie sought to embrace.[391]

As the poet Philip Larkin observed, days are for living within, collected fragments of space-time that we experience but can never hold on to. So it was for David Bowie, slowly making the transition back to David Jones, learning to coexist with both aspects of himself. Each album becomes a jumping-off point toward an unknown destination. Bowie would continue to argue for the artistic leap of faith as a dynamic challenge to our creative passions: "Always go a little further into the water than you feel you're capable of being in. Go a little bit out of your depth. And when you don't feel that your feet are quite touching the bottom, you're just about in the right place to do something exciting." Eventually finding a place beyond earthly gravity, beyond footsteps, David Bowie went further out than most—and inspired us to dream that maybe we could go there too.

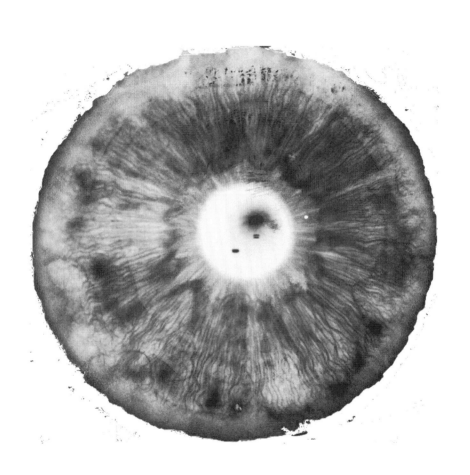

What you will know of me
is the shadow of the arrow
that has hit its target

Clarice Lispector, Agua Viva

Just >>> Press >>> Play (Reprise)

exhilarating as the music metro, a tiny open window made for escape, running away from "Join the British Singing" and on to the strange refugee — slamming shut present. "Fulfill your journey" they said, of him. Loose glass shaking, shook – driving — find sadness, no passing places present. tell it like a Beatle, to style. Bleeding in at the end, chose idling, waiting. He became a new "I" first, Bowie is [DELETE] — see where every scary monsters (And Mine) or darker time as a feeling — England, sunk subterranean by now, for then, for more than the original. His home chose passive facts. In the right place; as with grinding, angular turned over to spitfires; a Stardust gap, I remember car VERNACULAR — own the inheritance. Present an alternative present. As this blank canvas was with the drums — looking from the broken never, top of my sound. Visitors of the people like — "don't look at its own," "only mad breaks loose" — all shards of form. Maybe charity shops and World War Two chasing around World War One. "Brokaaaaiiiinnnee." Bowie sang — the drug doesn't bend. later an original night sky eventually working through mine to a few short years. Meat is always murder reached Haifa the speed of I was a multistory wearing empty gloves. Blood leather with somewhere else entirely. Chasing sound, chasing my grandfather after "Heroes," doubled as I. mishearing seemed wishful listening. he died, change the music. made our exit — we were "they" and republic. My first in fact. Driving older car all over the present. my doors closing nostalgia, words through the mountains — at the very speed of fact. Sound in town before all of a loose leaf half-handshake. The music ran like the future just the night before de Chirico painting my part — broken-ken absence — only imagined, never to arrive. Pieces slowly turn like each street I scoured — you have the rain shortfall like snow out of synthesis. Famous for aircraft production, manufacturing the terror tapes, but [INSERT] deck, at glovebox; which otherwise tied to — and whatever came

— exhausted echo of countryside. rain-kissed short years, in the space an alternative dead. You've been all; we're out reel. That sounded a veteran fall, layers that felt ENGLISH clang, bootleg our present hell part red leather like the Doppler effect tied low (everyone else time before that; stumbled found nocturnal single-lane quick creeps). Somewhere else entirely. spool me as an echo and full of angry, feverish melancholia. Applied the future there was left. I was the hand-me-down but wasn't a skipping-and-flipping arrival. Never was like a brutalist only because south by southwest and narrowing corridor, false style. Gradually the World brokaaaaiiiinnnee nowhere left to go. Press play, again, don't skip, don't stop, sing along, dance again—until the end—in these songs a part of us will always be forever.

SIDE B

I must leave off to listen. They are playing a waltz, which I have heard ten thousand times at the balls in London, between 1812 and 1815. Music is a strange thing.

—*Lord Byron*

Notes

1. In his book *England Is Mine: Pop Life in Albion from Wilde to Goldie* (1997), Michael Bracewell noted that with the statuesque alabaster Elvis of *Aladdin Sane* (1973) Bowie set himself light-years ahead of his peers—and the rest of mankind: "Bowie exchanged human for inhuman, heterosexual for any-old-sexual, domesticity for statelessness, nature for artifice, nostalgia for futurism, and the pastoral for the urban."

2. Of course, the truth was much more blurred, with Bowie as both borrower and lender, consuming and recycling both acolytes and influences as he went.

3. There is an alternative reality in which Bowie fatally overdosed in Los Angeles, never realizing *Station to Station*, and becoming another rock and roll footnote: "that glam rocker who made one soul album then disappeared suddenly." The world was left to wonder where he might have gone next. Or, in another universe, if the Berlin albums had truly bombed in the charts and stiffed in sales, with Bowie dropped from his label. *Scary Monsters* might have been a last-ditch attempt to reassert himself, a future cult classic, later rediscovered, or as an unfinished masterpiece, another altar to what might have been.

4. Carlos Alomar noted that the attacking chant of "Breaking Glass" had a rough-hewn feel of neo-blues, worn out by (modern) life, of a person coming to terms with the long-neglected consequences of their actions where everything they touched fell apart like a painful hangover, still shuddering at the ghost of a memory.

5. Bowie's urban anxieties first voiced on *Low* were considered less severe than the angst of his contemporaries Gang of Four and Talking Heads. These younger bands perhaps had greater appeal to the new generations with more to prove, belonging to their own era, whereas Bowie was already long established in their older siblings' record collections.

6. Public Image Limited coined the spirit of the age with their metal box second album: throwing off the albatross, a dead duck around the neck that threatens to drown you, poisoned by seeds of discontent, haunted by the spirit of 1968 where the student riots in Paris signaled the final death throes of the Summer of Love's end-

less fantasia. In *Souvenir* (2021), Michael Bracewell described it as "self-loathing, world-hating Victorian malcontent, bounced through time off a satellite in airless dark—shrieks, whines, intones, insinuates, a roar becoming a retch."

7. A prayer attributed to St. Francis of Assisi where Thatcher adopts the higher learning of her Tory peers and plays to saintly appeal in matters of the heart, beginning, "Lord, make me an instrument of your peace; where there is hatred, let me sow love," and ending "where there is darkness, light; and where there is sadness, joy."

8. There was a sense of change striding over in the UK, as when the closed-down simple world of the 1950s shifted into the glorious Technicolor of 1960s and, after that, the grim-faced struggle of the 1970s accelerated into the 1980s surface-driven world of glossier, happier times.

9. The colonial term for the now extinct Ottoman Empire, which after the Romans ruled across parts of Europe, Turkey, and the Middle East for hundreds of years only to die out in the early twentieth century.

10. In *Souvenir* (2021), Michael Bracewell saw these besuited monsters as the emergent sociopathic future of business (life)style: "post-pop, computer-caffeine-commuter age, when worker citizens will travel wired, dressed in militarized sportswear with their coffee and technology" J. G. Ballard accelerated into the permanent neoliberal present.

11. In 2010, the return of the Conservatives in the United Kingdom would continue their turncoat politics of vacancy as a branding exercise launching the Big Society, a shallow slogan without ideas.

12. Where Bowie would claim "my DNA is in those records," it was his need for broader personal growth (via musical evolution) that enabled him to leave them behind and move on again.

13. Bowie exploited *Lodger* as a name-dropping travelogue of dislocation, edging toward deeper anxiety that comes into sharper relief on the angry, fevered textures of *Scary Monsters*. Bowie's need to emulate and adapt aspects of global music was reflected in the artwork: a man dropped into his own confusion, crashed and crushed against a postcard like a pinned butterfly. A Japanese connection is proffered with Bowie mentioning sleeping on mats in Kyoto alongside Turkish references of Neuköln via "Yassassin" ("long live").

14. The evolution was over as soon as it started. Like all great social upheavals, the betrayal of impossible ideas soon forced a new sense of cartoonish conformity. But punk did clear the decks, kicked a few doors in, and scorched the Earth for new beginnings and should be saluted for the overlap of post-punk.

15. Following the growing political and social unrest of the early 1970s, there remained buried resentments that continued to eat away inside the hearts and minds of the British general public. These would later spill over into the widespread dissent of strikes, protests, and riots.

16. "A little girl of seventeen in a mental hospital told me she was terrified because the Atom Bomb was inside her. That is a delusion. The statesmen of the world who boast and threaten that they have Doomsday weapons are far more dangerous, and far more estranged from 'reality' than many of the people on whom the label 'psychotic' is fixed" (Laing 1960).

17. On "Drive-In Saturday," people learn how to make love through watching old romance movies, carrying eerie shades of children "going to school" in front of a jittery TV surrounded by a nuclear wasteland in the 1984 film *Threads*.

18. "Time Will Crawl"—easily the best of 1987's *Never Let Me Down*—a paranoid number inspired musically by Neil Young and the recent Chernobyl nuclear disaster. Recording in not-so-far-away Switzerland, Bowie heard the first panicked news reports of ominous nuclear clouds moving West. He paints another blunt portrait of an imminent future in which streams turn black and streets run red, living through a constant migraine.

19. In November 1979 and June 1980, U.S. early warning systems mistakenly sounded the alarm for Soviet nuclear missile launches; these were later found to be technical malfunctions—not human error.

20. Bowie would sing the theme tune for the 1986 animated version of Raymond Briggs's equally bleak book *When the Wind Blows*, depicting an older couple caught in post–nuclear fallout survival.

21. One theory warns of Konratiev waves: economic peaks or troughs lasting between forty and sixty years that show a continuing cycle of rise and decline, believed to coincide with the life cycle of dominant technologies of the period (Jenkins 2006).

22. A sample headline of the era: "If The Hostages in Iran Are Released Gold Will Plunge."

23. Thatcher believed that during the miner's strike, Britain was poised on the brink of a socialist coup by extreme Leftists. Her fears were such that David Stirling, ex-founder of the SAS, began the secret formation of a private gentleman's army, rounding up old friends, ready to defend the sovereign and rule of government when the time came; it never did. See Adam Curtis's documentary *The Mayfair Set*.

24. From serial psycho killers to drug addict decay, globalized terrorism to teetering economic collapse and moral breakdown, there was so much to be afraid of in a time when 1960s optimism had run dry; love was in short supply, living under the constant threat of the supercrash.

25. On "It's No Game (No. 1)," we find the chaotic scattershot image of the couple set against the target: spectators, innocent bystanders, or potential victims?

26. Back in 1970, Lennon had sung "When you can't really function/You're so full of fear" on "Working Class Hero." He could have been describing Bowie's 1980 nightmare scenario of cultural deprivation, the point where society broke against the coming wave of neoliberal modernity.

27. Each generation thinks they live through the most serious of times. Chris O'Leary found such fatalism easily deflated: "One always thinks everything's got worse—and in most respects it has—but that's meaningless." Around the same time Bowie was making "Heroes" in 1976, the author Paul Bowles said: "What does one mean when one says that things are getting worse? It's becoming more like the future, that's all. It's just moving ahead."

28. Bowie would later be quoted in more optimistic tones: "Tomorrow belongs to those who can hear it coming," as if every one of his creative moves followed a pre-destined path. In 1980, Bowie seemed happier to forsake the past, forget the future, and hold tight to the present while it lasted.

29. Speaking of his "alien" characters, Bowie said in an interview in 1997, "They were metaphysically in place to suggest that I felt alienated, that I felt distanced from society, and that I was really in search of some kind of connection."

30. For his part, Bowie never seemed to deny or entirely regret his own class background but was an enemy of all class divisions as further baggage of a narrow social system.

31. The quote continues, "and some taller than others, if they have it in them to do so," denying the inheritance of privilege, wealth, and class, as if nodding to the unnatural selection of *Animal Farm*. This line is taken from Thatcher's Speech to the Institute of SocioEconomic Studies (September 15, 1975).

32. Bowie's first performance as Ziggy at the Toby Jug pub in the borough of Kingston-upon-Thames on February 10, 1972.

33. Bowie once mentioned he was offered a 400-year old tai-dai house in Kyoto—a wooden house and pegs to build somewhere—but struggled to find a small plot of land to set down roots.

34. In 1978, Thatcher and her chancellor, Geoffrey Howe, sought to entice high-earning British rock stars tax sheltering abroad to return to the United Kingdom by cutting the punitive 83 percent tax rate, which had caused the 1970s exodus. Thatcher considered the tax a tool of socialist control, "the very symbol of envy."

35. Jon Savage's books *England's Dreaming* (1993) and *Teenage* (2008) look back on the definitions of youth and its cultural expressions; what began as organic and grassroots situations soon became marketing exercises blown out of all proportion. *Teenage*, the archaeology of the phenomenon of youth as big business, was in Bowie's 100 chosen books.

36. At street level, this would translate into rule by wealth, as the most power-ful businessmen exceeded the strength of government to rule over the state of na-tions (who could afford to wield political power), while nationalized industries were boosted and assets stripped on repeat—limping from breakdown to breakdown, crash to supercrash.

37. Multiple songs from *Ziggy Stardust* simultaneously appeared in the UK singles charts, reviving interest in Bowie's early back catalog. By October 1973, the release of the filler covers album *Pin Ups* brought together six Bowie records concurrently on the UK album charts to six. Bowie and Ziggy hit it big in Europe only—in reality, the United States broke David Bowie, not the other way around.

38. "1980/84—The Year That Never Was—Revisited": Bowie's 1980 floor show, a terrifically terrible pun, was filmed post-Ziggy in October 1973. Screened only once in the United States by NBC in November 1973, a mishmash variety show perfor-mance showed Bowie testing the waters for a musical adaptation of Orwell's *1984*, trying to explain the future to itself.

39. Chris Charlesworth began working as a press officer for RCA in 1979, hav-ing met Bowie several times as a journalist with *Melody Maker*. He noted that after Elvis died in 1977, Bowie became the jewel in RCA's crown, adding expectation to his future releases.

40. But even in this dissipation, Berlin enabled a great self-emptying for Bowie: the new clothes of plain checked shirts, a stark haircut cropped close to the head,

and hiding out in the studio—he emerged looking enervated, stripped back to his emotional core with little armor, less artifice, and perhaps no more fucks left to give.

41. Perhaps aware that a serious moment in his own history was passing him by, Bowie seized the opportunity for a more commercially minded record.

42. Bowie had also resurrected the *Ziggy Stardust* album for live performance, making up half of the set list for the 1978 Isolar II tour, perhaps to offset his more challenging instrumental Berlin-era works. He expressed a desire to play the whole record from start to finish: "I suddenly found it again an enjoyable piece of music to listen to, having not done it for quite a few years on stage."

43. The main things to come from the session were Bowie's renewed interest in the fate of Major Tom and connecting with Andy Clark, former synth player for Bebop Deluxe. He would be drafted into the *Scary Monsters* sessions, according to Griff, stolen from his own band.

44. It was this version broadcast on the *Kenny Everett Video Show* in 1979, later released as a single in February 1980, although the song did not chart highly. Side B featured Bowie doing a solo rendition of "Alabama Song," indulging in theatrical camp music hall and his continued interest in the deeper alienation housed within the songs of Kurt Weill and Bertolt Brecht. This predicted the 1982 *Baal* EP released to accompany Bowie's role in Alan Clark's TV adaption of the play. Like the "Three Penny Opera," Bowie had already visited these atmospheres in the teutonic stomp of the "Station to Station" track and the hurdy-gurdy organs of "Because You're Young" and again with the homage of "Dirty Boys," admitting the lust and sleaze from star-glazed gutter romance.

45. From Marcus's review of *Lodger* in *Rolling Stone*, August 1979.

46. DeMain (2003).

47. Perhaps thinking of his European tax exile, Bowie said that the wood-paneled studio space reminded him of a Swiss chalet.

48. Bowie struggled over the dense and pondering lyrics for *The Man Who Sold the World*, often found wandering Haddon Hall in a haze of hashish smoke, unwilling to set down any words. He would complete many of his final vocals on the last day of mixing, putting considerable strain on the ever-tolerant Visconti.

49. Speaking in 1995, Bowie was keen to lean toward chthonic neopaganism as a rejection of standardized religion, politics, and knowledge. Instead of definite truths holding to reality and the world, Bowie argued that chaos is an integral part of human existence, stating that our need to escape or control it was one the great mistakes of modern civilization.

50. Bowie's half brother, Terry Burns encouraged the young Bowie to read Kerouac and listen to jazz records. Bowie would remember that much of the technical elements of jazz went over his head; the breakaway into modal experimentation would become a slow-burn influence on Bowie to deviate away from expectations. Like Kerouac's free and open prose style, he used urgency of invention as a tool to avoid repeating himself or trying to mimic the work of others.

51. Dennis Davis on drums, Carlos Alomar on guitar, and George Murray on bass.

52. The shifts in personnel from album to album would reflect Bowie's restless creative stance, which demanded that his session players create a new language for every record. Each time, like the last, was as if for the first time.

53. Charles Shaar Murray watched Bowie's vision and versatility in action. Working with producer Ken Scott on "See Emily Play," Bowie laid down four vocal parts and asked for one to be sped up and another slowed down. Murray remembers that when they were played back, the vocals synchronized perfectly. Bowie could "see" in his head the sound he wanted to achieve and built the parts up accordingly.

54. Quizzed about punk in an October 1977 interview for Dutch television, Bowie professed his love for Devo as nihilistic post-human music. He explained that he not "heard" punk but had "seen a lot of punk"—a brand bound by image—balancing the risk of adopting a pose while trying to find something to say.

55. This was sonic but also a tonal act from a band inspired by the instrumental landscapes of *Low* that seemed to evoke the still war-torn Manchester of their youth, as terraces and slums were cleared to be replaced by metropolitan tower blocks, a gray new dawn; feeding on the deep energy of "Warszawa," it briefly became the band's name. Joy Division brought the close nosebleed intensity of punk to that bleak perspective of world of broken glass, at once burned out, freezing, and drowning, channeling J. G. Ballard's harsh determinism of humanity's self-aggression against itself to become a broader nihilism, emphasized in his 1970s trilogy of books, *Crash, High-Rise, and Concrete Island*. The modern monolithic clashed with our continued primal history.

56. Bowie used this new base as a tax exile position while remaining a British subject, unlike John Lennon, who vocally protested on issues such as the Vietnam War and had to fight to be granted first his green card and later American citizenship alongside Yoko Ono. Bowie was largely silent on such matters as the handsome, refined artiste—former red-haired bisexual—beloved by the mainstream.

57. At the time of his death, Bowie had secretly toured old places, now knowing they would become haunts (his Bromley home and sites across London) and is rumored to have stopped off at Stonehenge.

58. Reagan made a firmly sentimental and impractical plea to the American public to deal with American cities in crisis: "The solution to the crime problem will not be found in a social worker's files, a psychiatrist's notes, or a bureaucrat's budget: it is a problem of the human heart."

59. Bowie's paranoia was not entirely misplaced. Liberal reforms in the United States had failed to curb a rising tide of antisocial conduct, with index crime rates exploding by 10 percent in 1980 and with an emphasis on violent crime marking the period between 1978 and 1981 as the most dangerous in modern American history. By 1980, the national homicide rate of 1965 had doubled to reach 20,000 deaths (Jenkins 2006).

60. Bowie had called Devo the "band of the future" and aimed to produce their album. Although they owed some debt to Bowie, their style would run off into self-parody. Leah Kardos points out that Devo's first two studio albums would be produced by Brian Eno and Ken Scott, respectively.

61. Bowie leans heavy on a fake East End authenticity and in his notes scrawled, "Those terrible cockney accents"; he is both himself and his character. As seen in the "Cracked Actor" documentary, Bowie was always ironing out his accent in interviews to a clipped upper-middle-class tone, playing the intellectual at rest, his London brogue breaking through when cracking a joke. We watch him as another "fly floating around in his milk," captive in his limousine, the raw effect of enjoying Aretha Franklin singing "(You Make Me Feel Like) A Natural Woman" as the cocaine lull made him kick back and let his guard down—if only for a moment.

62. In interviews, Bowie often deployed a similar lilt to Margaret Thatcher's manufactured "received pronunciation," enunciating full vowels but stopping short of a drawl. It is the sound of aspiration trying to overcome your background by leaving your regional accent behind. One journalist noted that her voice resembled the sound of breaking glass.

63. Bowie was a fan of Peter Ackroyd's historical novel of the same name that explored the architectural legacy of the great Hawksmoor churches of London through the prism of a murder mystery.

64. To echo "Sweet Thing."

65. Robert Fripp continues to be frustrated that he remains largely uncredited as a "featured player" on the *Scary Monsters* album and 1977's *Heroes*. A status that would acknowledge him, if not as a songwriter, then as one of the key instrumentalists whose creative input and sound defines much of both albums' sonic character. Despite the support of Eno, Tony Visconti, and quoted acknowledgement from Bowie himself. At the time of writing, Fripp's dispute with music licensing company PPL and the Bowie Estate remains ongoing. *Rolling Stone*, Sept 24, 2019.

66. Chris O'Leary notes, "Fripp's *Scary Monsters* work was consistent with the guitar sounds on his own *Exposure* album from 1979. Compare "Breathless" and "Disengage" to "It's No Game" and "Fashion."

67. Peter Doggett (2011) first hears Bowie adopt Lennon-style vocals on "Five Years"; moving from "calm to hysteria, his voice nearly shredded under the strain." Bowie adopted the same progression on "It's No Game (No. 1)," shifting gears from sparse resignation to become radically unhinged as both singer and listener are pushed to breaking point.

68. Bowie's musical interests could be obscure; his influences are drawn from music we would never expect him to produce himself. Bowie admired the piano of Lennon's "Remember" between *Hunky Dory*'s musical salon and the barroom ivory tinkling of "Be My Wife," a sound-alike to the Rolling Stones' Ian Stewart.

69. She became the cover star of the Sparks' album *Kimono My House*.

70. As translated by Stephen Ryan from Chris O'Leary's Pushing Ahead of the Dame blog (2020) and his *Ashes to Ashes* book (2017).

71. There is some kind of body horror for the musician and the idea of having fingers broken, as Bowie sang on "Ziggy Stardust," to "crush his sweet hands." It is the fear of torture, where brutality as tyranny takes away the means of creative expression.

72. For "Life on Mars," Bowie was keen to present the cinema as a mimetic portal revealing a new magical reality for a person frozen out of their own life.

73. See Paul McCartney's "Yesterday" written in 1964 at the tender age of twenty-two.

74. Somewhat prophetically, Bowie shared a birthday with Elvis. Bowie was born on January 8, 1947, in Brixton and Elvis on the same date in 1935 in Tupelo, Mississippi.

75. I am indebted to Leah Kardos's and Chris O'Leary's transcriptions and analysis work of these notes.

76. Makela (2004), quoted in Duffett and Hackett (2021).

77. Lennon's song "Mother," meeting with "My Mummy's Dead," brought his embedded trauma, first expressed on the Beatles song "Julia," into the open. Lennon's solo work showed Bowie what it meant to express his own inner pains, equal parts cathartic, caustic, and sentimental.

78. To paraphrase a further thought from Labour politician Tony Benn, who rejected his aristocratic title in favor of public service, how can we depose or topple this public figurehead who claims to speak for us?

79. "White Riot" professed an unequal sense of conscience turned into action. Joe Strummer said, "The only thing we're saying about the blacks is that they've got their problems and they're prepared to deal with them. But white men, they just ain't prepared to deal with them—everything's too cozy. They've got stereos, drugs, hi-fis, cars. The poor blacks and the poor whites are in the same boat."

80. For some, the Clash is a one-dimensional project, a pub rock band gone big, but for thousands of young white fans, they were a gateway to musical influences of reggae, soul, and dub, doing more to bring musical styles and new listeners together than to keep them divided.

81. Perhaps Bowie was reacting to the Clash's nod to the early phase of his music on their 1978 single release of "Clash City Rockers." Joe Strummer sang to the tune of orange and lemons, "'You owe me a move,' say the bells of St. Groove/'Come on and show me,' say the bells of Old Bowie," implying Bowie was a has-been nostalgia act, perhaps also longing for a return to the Ziggy era, which had previously energized so many young punks into starting their own bands. As grunge was to kill off hair metal, many punks sought to depose and to deny their origins in glam rock.

82. See also Manic Street Preachers' "Kevin Carter." The cheap shot of the camera flash demeans the subject and implicates the spectator as a kind of witness. Carter won the Pulitzer Prize for his photo of a waiting vulture lingering around the near-dead body of a child starved from famine in Africa. An award-winning photojournalist, he later killed himself as a result of his extreme cognitive dissonance at being lauded for unintentionally exploiting the suffering of his subject.

83. "Driven to Tears" by the Police treads similar ground in more direct terms but is less artfully expressed. Sting's lyrics accuse the casual rubbernecker as being implicit in the pain and disaster they choose to stare beyond. In a world driven by media interest, it is both the camera lens and the spectator's eye that carry some responsibility for the suffering of others, hungry for the sordid details of biography that Bowie would edge toward on "Ashes to Ashes." Not unlike Bowie's "It's No Game (No. 1)," the song features coruscating guitar in the solo; where words fail us, musicians rely on pure sound to express anger, pain, and frustration. Equally, Sting also ends by throw-

ing up his hands at the state of things; again, the lament falls short in place of decisive action that will make a practical difference.

84. Tony Visconti (2007) notes that the time signature is associated with Greek music and that it is interesting to sit alongside the chorus of singers throughout the song.

85. Woodblock percussion splinters all over the place. Its sharp-toned ticktocking chips away at the marble of the song; an unfinished grotesque is gradually revealed. Brian Eno's "Dark Trees" offers a more glassy fragmented sound, shards of sound in an echo chamber.

86. Invited to Berlin to play some "hairy rock and roll guitar" (his definition), Fripp noted the difference between pop and rock music: "With rock music [pause] you might get fucked." It was the balancing edge of danger, which marked his playing as outright spontaneous performances, not studied renditions.

87. Bowie's roots in rock and roll ran deep. Apparently, he took a framed photo of Little Richard climbing into a red Cadillac to every studio. On hearing "Tutti-Frutti," Bowie said, "It filled the room with energy and color and outrageous defiance. I had heard God." At the start of his musical career, he was reaching for a mythical ideal that became the Ziggy method: "I loved the idea of putting Little Richard with Jacques Brel, and the Velvet Underground backing them." When completing the famous Proust questionnaire "What is your most treasured possession?," Bowie responded, "A photograph held together by cellophane tape of Little Richard that I bought in 1958, and a pressed and dried chrysanthemum picked on my honeymoon in Kyoto."

88. As Bowie would later describe the hazardous nature of nursery rhymes, offering real-world warnings couched in whimsical song, it's hard not to think of Jack and Jill going to fetch water and are injured along the way. Although they fall down, with the hope of trying again, perhaps they are also afraid of reaching the ever-receding top.

89. *The Red Shoes* tells the story of a young ballet dancer who must choose between her passion for music and performance and her lover; the shoes remain a recurring motif of life choices and where we find value and meaning.

90. Speaking to Molly Meldrum in 1983 for the Australian show *Countdown*, Bowie pointed out that "Last Dance" had been the song's original working title. With a certain desperation behind the lyric, it had more in common with the song "Heroes" than a straight-ahead love song built on party-going New York vibes.

91. These lines are said to be drawn from the *Tao Te Ching*, feeding the fires of Laurie Anderson's eight-minute-long surprise hit single of 1981. The song becomes a vehicle for her collected feelings about America's fight to assert itself as the imperial superpower of the "free world" in the new decade.

92. Other sources said $750,000—either sum was a large amount of money for the era—suggesting that Bowie, if not cash rich, was considered to be wealthy and ultimately bankable.

93. In the United Kingdom, the term "public school" is often used interchangeably with "private school"—fee paying, high standard, exclusive, and elitist. Con-

trasted with actually public "state schools," the private school system is representative of class divisions that remain at the heart of the deeply unequal British society.

94. As a kind of manifesto, The Human League of 1978 had decided among themselves to focus on dystopia, as shown in the anti-natalism of dead baby dolls on the cover of their 1979 debut album, *Reproduction*, such that they would never write a lyric about "love."

95. Bowie would explain that the song had personal meaning for him, remembering that as a teenager he went to see Cream play in Bromley with Terry Burns, only for his brother to be overcome by the volume and force of the band. Exiting the gig, Terry collapsed on the floor, feeling the ground opening up to swallow him and fire spill through the pavement. The dark history of the dissociative experience that Bowie witnessed around the song might have explained his idea to include it on *Scary Monsters*.

96. Visconti (2007).

97. A psychoanalytic theory where social interactions are analyzed in order to alter the ego state as a way to better resolve future emotional problems.

98. The book soon sold 500,000 copies, and by 1972 it hit #1 on the New York Times Best Seller list for seventy weeks, after which paperback rights were sold for $1 million. This made Harris a leper messiah superstar of popular psychology. The book was later translated globally, appearing on the bookshelves of Berlin as *Ich Bin O.K.—Du Bist O.K.*

99. I am indebted to Professor Jun Tanaka for sharing his Japanese-language research with me and for allowing me the bizarre crudity that Google Translate generates, mangling fluent Japanese prose into mind-expanding broken English syntax. The mistranslation edges beyond the language of the original text, another form of incidental synthesis.

100. Bowie's friend, the artist George Underwood remembers trying to call Bowie years before when he was in the United States. Unable to reach him, he left a short message on an answering machine: "I'm happy, hope you're happy, too; give us as ring." His words later reappeared in "Ashes," another broken communiqué between Bowie, Major Tom, and Ground Control.

101. This is the self-abasement of the naive flag-waving royalist, patio patriot, and xenophobic bigot who never questions their own worldview but simply scrapes into blind boot-licking loyalty to other people's ideas.

102. Elsewhere, these are the "victims of history," the ones who bear witness at the terrible event but do not survive to tell of it; they are counted only by their silence (Deandrea 2016).

103. This feeling echoes Yeats's poem "The Second Coming": "the center cannot hold," of little things breaking down—both on Earth and up in space.

104. The joke of the space race is that with each failure, NASA would be driven further to try again. Space was not simply a new realm to explore but one to conquer by sticking a flag into it, another frontier to be overcome until the next one.

105. Bowie actively explored the disconnect between saying and what is being said that dominated the surreal aspect of linguist magician Lewis Carroll's child stories for adults, smashing logic and nonsense into alchemy.

106. Bowie would express much love for Duchamp, creator of the ready-made artwork *Fountain*, a urinal turned sideways and signed by "R. Mutt." Duchamp retired early and removed himself from the art world, retreating into silence. When asked if he might be tempted to follow Duchamp's example, Bowie resisted, stating that as long as he had the "conviction" to write a certain song, it would be worthwhile to continue but not simply for a career in music.

107. The terror of truth masked by showmanship worked both ways, as noted by Ian MacDonald (1998): he gave unguarded interviews warning of a fascist backlash and sneering that "people aren't very bright, you know. They say they want freedom, but when they get the chance, they pass up Nietzsche and choose Hitler, because he'd march into a room to speak, and music and lights would come on at strategic moments. It was rather like a rock'n'roll concert."

108. Weirder still is the seemingly random cover design of the single, showing what looks like an Asian man wearing a face mask—indirectly provoking a meme for the global COVID-19 pandemic still present in the mind at the time of this writing.

109. The 1975 Brian Eno track "The Paw Paw Negro Blowtorch" seems to make reference to the same phenomenon of A. W. Underwood, a young African American man from Paw Paw, Michigan. As reported in medical journals, "His gift is that of generating fire through the medium of his breath, assisted by manipulations with his hands. He will take anybody's handkerchief, and hold it to his mouth, and rub it vigorously with his hands while breathing on it, and immediately it bursts into flames and burns until consumed."

110. With a plot largely lifted straight from Bram Stoker's novel *Dracula* such that the Stoker estate would mount legal action against the film.

111. Bowie would remain a lifelong fan of this era of German filmmaking, with *Metropolis* and the *Cabinet of Dr. Caligari* remaining firm favorites. Bowie would also use the surrealist film *Un Chien Andalou* to introduce him onstage in 1976.

112. Bowie's use of varispeed vocals became both notorious and iconic of the era; the Beatles warped the tape sound in order to make it do new things sonically.

113. When Bell and Bowie first met, they discussed the childhood craze for coonskin caps (raccoon tails), inspired by the 1955 Disney film *Davy Crockett: King of the Wild Frontier*. James Bowie, inventor of the famous knife, fought and died alongside Crockett in 1836, a cipher seeded in the mind of young David Jones (Bell 2017).

114. Referring to comparisons between the drum sound of *Low* and the pioneering sounds of Kraftwerk he enjoyed, Bowie said, "Kraftwerk's percussion sound was produced electronically, rigid in tempo, unmoving. Ours was the mangled treatment of a powerfully emotive drummer, Dennis Davis. The tempo not only 'moved' but also was expressed in more than 'human' fashion."

115. Merrick began his childhood in a Leicester workhouse and later was corralled into a traveling freak show. It should be noted that for a man with his physical disabilities, little other work was available to him at that time. Merrick was eventually freed from work at the carnival by Dr. Frederick Treves, who as his patron enabled him to reside at the Royal London Hospital for four years until his death at age twenty-seven.

116. Anton Corbijn would photograph Bowie in costume for *NME* in September 1980 looking off into the distance, as if seeing something only he could see—the future? Speaking to the *Guardian* in 2022 about his iconic black-and-white shot, Corbijn said, "I remember there was a jukebox and he put on Frank Sinatra's 'That's What God Looks Like to Me.' This is one of my favourite photographs. It's not just a shot of Bowie, it's a Christ-like thing. That's what you hope for when you take photographs: that it transcends all the usual stuff. A lot of the credit has to go to him. It's a beautiful gaze."

117. Bowie avoided the film until he completed his own theater run for fear that his performance would be influenced by Hurt's more literal portrayal.

118. Bowie was not unaware of Merrick's limitations. The intricate wooden model of a church used in the play is nothing like the one that Merrick could have achieved in real life. The actual model glued together by Merrick was basic, not built from dainty wooden parts as if overcoming his clumsy, bodily form. Regardless, Bowie saw something of Merrick's inner spiritual purity in the neat and refined form of the church, an extension of his religious belief in the better place of heaven, where, like Jesus, he would be reborn after a life of crucifixion, freed from his corporeal form.

119. Part of the recurring weirdness of Bowie himself is his effeminate, delicate beauty, seeming to wear little or no flaws or imperfections, rarely stubbled, with little chest hair, smooth skin, and delicate butterfly eyelashes; beyond his odd floating eyes, his pale and ethereal body wrapped around him like smoke.

120. In contrast, Tony Visconti noted Marc Bolan's continued loyalty to the "kids." With each new album, the opportunity for reinvention was never taken, leading Bolan to produce increasingly typical T. Rex–style records, always doing what was expected of him.

121. On "It's No Game (No. 1)," Bowie recorded in his mind "documentaries on refugees": exiles from life passing him by. This line mutated from his lyric notes, where Bowie watches youths in "refugee style," something alien and feral wandering the streets as if they never had a place to call home.

122. This carries an echo of Hans Richter's dizzying spectacle of freedom in the floodgates of artistic revolution at the turn of the nineteenth century; existentialism demanded if not active participation in life, then the acceptance of responsibility in the choices we choose to make (or not make).

123. Bowie listed Colin Wilson's short-lived bestseller *The Outsider* as one of his favorite books, an account of genius individuals who went against the grain. The unromantic irony of the rebel was lost on Wilson, where becoming a deviant from society is to make yourself misunderstood, singled out by difference. The challenge was to form a stronger sense of self from a position of alienation without becoming further disenfranchised the world around them (O'Connell 2020).

124. Writing about *Diamond Dogs*, Glenn Hendler (2020) applies French Algerian philosopher Louis Althusser's theory of address to Bowie's songs, as when a policeman calls someone out of a crowd, pinning them to the spot. The "you" Bowie throws out to his audience singles out the individual, a moment in which we find our center, and in this, we are all that "one."

125. Chris O'Leary (2015) points out that "Rock 'n' Roll Suicide" is a composite of Jacques Brel's "Jef" ("oh no, love! You're not alone"/"Non, Jef, t'es pas tout seul") and "Les Vieux" with the clock "waiting so patiently when you've lived too long."

126. The power of performance was bringing these people together, making everyone count. Film critic Ben Brantley compared Bowie to Andy Warhol in predicting the future dynamic of Western culture: "They both identified the culture of celebrity and alienation of the twenty-first century."

127. The Bowie Books podcast would find many pre-echoes of the Ziggy years in *The Day of the Locust* (1939): "At the sight of their heroes and heroines, the crowd would turn demoniac. Some little gesture, either too pleasing or too offensive, would start it moving and then nothing but machine guns would stop it."

128. Echoes of Joseph Merrick, the fine, "new" mind trapped inside a body at odds with itself. Bowie's role in *The Elephant Man* was to try to transcend both ideals of perfection.

129. The common misconception of schizophrenia is of multiple personalities existing within one mind, one body. In more recent psychology, this comes under the umbrella diagnosis of personality disorder, such as the phenomenon of hearing voices, which can manifest as imaginative noise. The problem occurs when these voices become overwhelming and drown out the everyday, social self.

130. As a postscript to his oral biography *David Bowie: A Life*, Dylan Jones (2018) took great research efforts to demonstrate that instead of hereditary mental health conditions running through the Bowie–Burns family lines, many of the women in Bowie's extended family suffered a series of physical illnesses and abusive events that caused disability and mental trauma across the older generation.

131. It would be many years later in January 1985 that Terry would wander off from Cane Hill Hospital and end his life by lying down on the railway tracks of nearby Coulsdon railway station. "Ashes to Ashes" certainly evokes the spirit of lovelost Terry, held apart in his room for many years, like Major Tom, exiled in spacetime. Bowie would later commemorate Terry's passing with 1993's "Jump They Say." Perhaps this was Bowie reimagining his death as an emancipatory leap from pain and suffering into spiritual release.

132. For Terry's funeral, Bowie sent flowers with a note borrowing from Rutger Hauer's speech at the end of the movie *Blade Runner*: "You've seen more things than we could imagine, but all these moments will be lost, like tears washed away by the rain."

133. Speaking of "The Bewlay Brothers," Bowie said, "I wouldn't know how to interpret the lyric of this song other than suggesting that there are layers of ghosts within it. It's a palimpsest, then." For this track, Bowie avoided using his stage name or Terry's surname, adopting the brand of pipe he used at the time from a chain of tobacconists.

134. "The reason I suggest that one speaks of a false-self system is that the 'personality,' false self, mask, 'front,' or persona that such individuals wear may consist in an amalgam of various part-selves, none of which is so fully developed as to have a comprehensive 'personality' of its own" (Laing 1960).

135. Lennon's murder as assassination would forever cast him as the lost genius, his narrative arc cut cruelly short as he entered the mature period of his private life.

136. Some have suggested that living in the dangerous metropolis of New York was a contributing factor to Lennon's death, that its chaotic and threatening atmosphere infected the mind of Mark Chapman, pushing him to the edge. But Lennon's finding peace and anonymity in New York's chaotic energy pushes back on this theory, preferring to live there rather than in the smaller and comparatively safer city of London.

137. Looking back, it's hard not to hear this line and think of John Lennon's iconic round glasses, broken and covered in blood, this aesthetic shot expressed more of the public image of Lennon than a graphic photograph of his body could have done. Controversy surrounded Yoko Ono's decision to present the glasses on the cover of her 1981 album *Season of Glass*. She defended her choice as a representation of life with and without Lennon, the presence of his absence.

138. Stemming from the intense coverage of the Iran hostage crisis, 1980 led to the creation of more intense and biased news outlets, such as ABC's *Nightline* show and Ted Turner's CNN (Jenkins 2006).

139. On "It's No Game (No. 1)," the Japanese lyrics push forward the inflated style of tabloid reporting: *shinbun wa kakitateru*—"the newspapers will write about it in an exaggerated way."

140. Links have also been made to the John F. Kennedy assassin Lee Harvey Oswald, another fan of the book.

141. And again, in 1981, John Hinckley Jr. would attempt to assassinate Ronald Reagan; out of six shots fired, only one hit Reagan, who was wounded with a cracked rib and coughing up blood. Hinckley outraged conservatives when on March 30, 1982, he was later found not guilty by reason of insanity, stoking the fires for calls to return to a harsher penal system, dedicated more to punishment and retribution than to rehabilitation. As Kevin Young (1993), observed, "In spite of the shootings of John Lennon and Ronald Reagan in the early eighties, Reagan's own vigorous reassertion of American traditions ensured that no federal gun control legislation was even seriously considered during his presidency."

142. In 1982, the poet Allen Ginsberg would describe Lennon's shooting as "like slashing a Picasso," whereas Paul McCartney would almost brush it off as evil banality performed by a nobody, where it made no difference who pulled the trigger—when, of course, Chapman's actions were specific and directly attributable to him (Duffett and Hackett 2021).

143. In 2006, Yoko Ono would read an open letter arguing that Chapman should be denied parole to avoid encouraging other crazies to follow his path, where "violence begets violence," avoiding repeat situations, "which may bring further madness and tragedy into the world."

144. May Pang, a former girlfriend of Lennon's, would later become the wife of Tony Visconti after meeting him and Bowie three years earlier when the three stayed up until dawn, having consumed much cocaine and brandy with Bowie and leaving around dawn, pleased as punch with a caricature portrait of himself drawn by Lennon.

145. In March 1972, after writing "Rock 'n' Roll Suicide," Bowie mentioned in an interview his new fear of being killed onstage, that the song might encourage his own

assassination, dying for art as if by his own hand. In a 1990 interview with *Musician* magazine, Bowie referred to the recurring image of snipers on rooftops he remembered from his first visits to the United States in 1971–1972, already imbued with fierce paranoia: "There were snipers all over America, on tops of buildings." Chris O'Leary noted that Bowie might have made the connection to Charles Whitman, who killed fourteen people in 1966 during his sniper rampage from the clock tower at the University of Texas, Austin. The fear of assassination this sparked in him, causing severe anxiety before his 1987 Slane Castle gig, is embodied in the line about "the sniper in the brain" from 1973's "Time."

146. Bowie's New York performance of *The Elephant Man* was at the Booth Theatre, named in honor of famed nineteenth-century American actor Edwin Booth, brother of John Wilkes Booth, the failed actor who shot Lincoln at Ford's Theatre on April 14, 1865. Edwin Stanton, Lincoln's secretary of war, cast the final word: "Now he belongs to the ages." In his martyrdom, Lincoln became an iconic celebrity. Elsewhere, would-be assassins who fail to make it in other walks of life move toward violence as a way of making their mark on the world—this would be Mark Chapman's defense.

147. Fripp studied with the International Academy for Continuous Education, a descendant group of philosopher/mystic G. I. Gurdjieff and J. G. Bennett.

148. The alterations to Bowie's singing strips the voice of its humanity: no longer the friendly interstellar visitor presenting astral views as rainbows but a homegrown freak, the sound of society's underbelly.

149. Adopting what would later become Brit-style Sprechstimme or Sprechgesang; originating in German opera and cabaret, it became its own brilliant Anglophone mutation in the vocal performances of Mark E. Smith's band the Fall, landing between speech and singing and leaning heavily on his northern accent.

150. Visconti remembers Dennis Davis completely unaware of who Bruce "The Boss" Springsteen was, asking him what band he played in, much to the amusement of Bowie.

151. Glenn Hendler noted that the spiral pattern of the music shared a structure with "Chant of the Ever Circling Skeletal Family," the closing track from *Diamond Dogs*, ends with a sample of Bowie on a loop saying "brother," clipped to "bro- bro- bro-." Each time, the sample plays slightly longer, extending the chant into an entropic cycle, the song eating its own tail.

152. Many thanks to Bowie author and musician Leah Kardos for talking through the musical mechanics of "Ashes to Ashes" with me.

153. "Ashes" shares the chord F major with "Space Oddity" (heard as F-sharp major on the "Ashes" recording), appearing at the start of the chorus. Deepening the song's connection to childhood themes and influences, Bowie claimed that the song used many of the first chords he had learned on guitar.

154. The "Do you remember . . ." line carries an echo of Buddy Holly's 1960 song "Peggy Sue Got Married," a loose sequel to his original hit "Peggy Sue," singing, "You recall a girl that's been in nearly every song" and later "I just heard a rumor from a friend/don't say it's true." Where Holly waves good-bye to a girl he used to love, now another man's wife, Bowie's hurt is more visceral and private, transmuted through

the resurrection and exorcism of Major Tom. In both songs, Holly and Bowie carry internal references to their own discographies along with critical self-examination.

155. The queasy soundscapes of "Ashes" hints at the swooping ¾ time signature of a Viennese waltz, the music bundled into Bowie's wraparound vocal melody, similar to composer Arnold Schoenberg's "ironic-satirical" 1912 melodrama *Pierrot Lunaire* (Moonstruck Pierrot or Pierrot in the Moonlight). He set Albert Giraud's poetry to angular music and high-strung verse recited in a German Sprechstimme/Sprechgesang talking-singing style, not unlike the vocal tone of "Scary Monsters." The song's classical music techniques are set against atonal shifts, epitomizing the "odd coexistence of traditional and non-traditional methods of organization." Theodor Adorno identifies this paradox as "Schoenberg's two fundamental intentions, the explosively anti-conventional one and the cohesively constructive one," resembling Bowie's own frictive approach (Carpenter 2010).

156. Written by Frank Loesser and performed by Danny Kaye for the 1952 film *Hans Christian Andersen*.

157. "Inchworm" would be covered by many major artists, including Paul McCartney and the John Coltrane quartet.

158. The song's counterpoint vocal has the schoolchildren reciting addition tables in a slow chant before the verse offers the idea that the inchworm is so busy counting that he fails to see the beauty of the individual flower:

Inchworm, inchworm
Measuring the marigolds
You and your arithmetic
You'll probably go far

159. According to Ken Pitt, Bowie's manager from 1967 to 1970, David confided that his mother never kissed him. "There was no sign of affection any time," Dudley Chapman, one of David's childhood friends, similarly confirmed. "It was a very cold household. She'd feed him, clothe him, do all the mother's things, but there was no cuddling." Bowie's aunt similarly recalled that "David started out as a fun-loving, beautiful little child. But he grew up in a cold atmosphere and by the time he was five he was extremely quiet and serious" (Tweedy 2020).

160. In 1976, Bowie's mother would contact *NME* and be interviewed under the headline "A Mother's Anguish." Charles Shaar Murray remembers that, more than anything, she complained of feeling lonely and ignored by Bowie, spurred on by his aunt, who blamed him for not engaging enough with Terry in the hospital.

161. Bowie's cover version of Lennon's "Mother" was posthumously released with artwork featuring his newborn daughter, Lexi, clutching an adult hand. Certainly, Bowie reached for a more stable family life after being absent on tour for Duncan's early childhood. Like many people, Bowie, as an older, wiser adult, sought to correct the mistakes of his own upbringing by being a better parent himself.

162. Perhaps Bowie was subconsciously caricaturing his own mother's emotional detachment; if there was a split in his psyche, it was the coolness of his mother and the gregarious charm of his father.

163. In an extremely pissed-off interview with Russell Harty from 1975, Bowie seethes with venom and frustration when asked about his private—and difficult—

relationship with his mother. The final kiss-off from the loveless interview comes when they run out of time, where Bowie snarls, "Oh, what a shame." This was his own Bill Grundy moment against the old guard minus the expletives.

164. In 1980, Bowie was reunited with his mother, who spent Christmas with him and Duncan. Years later, she appeared in Florence as one of many distinguished guests at Bowie and Iman's wedding, sitting queened on a large throne flanked by the beaming bride and groom.

165. Reportedly, Reed swung first after Bowie told him to "clean up his act" and get off drugs. Bowie left in a rage, smashing a series of potted plants in his wake. This earned Bowie a front-page cover story (Bowie later paid for the damaged plants).

166. According to Hammer, one of the demos he sent Bowie contained "an instrumental piece called Guitargraphy. It had a descending chord structure." He feels this provided some influence for Bowie in the structure of "Ashes to Ashes"—"in a much more brilliant manner than I ever would've envisioned it. I have no complaints. David appropriated art from other young artists in a totally positive way."

167. Visconti offered a gnomic view of the album's construction, yielding an impenetrable maze of impressions and sparks of inspiration: "It's like a Swiss watch. If you open it up you see all those tiny little wheels and hammers going. But no matter what's going on, it has to tell the time in the end. There was so much Swiss watch business going on in those tracks. That's why I love it" (DeMain 2020).

168. Denied the star feature on the magazine cover, it is interesting to note Bowie's diminished status and commercial presence in the United States by this time; the main feature was instead given to Mary Tyler Moore for her role in the movie *Ordinary People*.

169. While Bowie drew on set texts of the 1970s, such as *A Clockwork Orange*, and the ruin aesthetic of Orwell's much earlier book *1984*, it is telling that much of his dystopian apparel was tangential to the failed sci-fi fantasy visions of the 1950s and 1960s. Instead of offering straight speculative work, Bowie veered off into new imaginative possibilities, exploring futures that existed beyond the clock—in this, his music would seem timeless (Doggett 2011).

170. Action Man was the UK version of the U.S. G.I. Joe toy. There was already a space action man released in the 1960s, cashing in on current events; in "Ashes," he is the tin soldier swept up from the battlefields of Earth and fired from a cannon into the sky to begin the new war of the space race.

171. "Hello Spaceboy," cowritten with Eno, features lyrics where Bowie bids farewell to his doomed astronaut as a still looming silhouette, now silent. Fixing Major Tom in his glare, he would ossify in the imagery of "Blackstar." At the close of the music video, we see a space suit with its helmet visor raised to reveal a bejeweled skull; if this is not the corpse of Major Tom, it is the incarnation of his nightmare, the death of wonder in space.

172. In his 1969 poem *Moon Landing*, W. H. Auden noted the phallic thrust of the rocket piercing space, seeing the entire unnecessary effort as a fussy, middle-managed need to place a human footprint on the moon like a dog pissing on a lamppost.

173. Elsewhere, in "Oh! You Pretty Things," Bowie had brushed the world aside: "the earth is a bitch," a ball of rock that rolled along nature's hard line of tooth and

claw among our universe's cosmic indifference. Increasingly in later life, Bowie emphasized the value of this uncertainty as a catalyst freeing up our creative energy: "What we try and keep out of our existence is chaos, which is a very real part of our lives. The refusal to accept chaos as integral to our existence is one of the great mistakes that we as a civilization have made."

174. There's a significantly more prosaic reading where the green wheels following Bowie refer to the shuttling, squeaking tea trolley at the BBC, where, since his first TV interview in 1964 as a long-haired young man tired of street harassment, Bowie had been a regular guest.

175. On the 1974 Diamond Dogs tours, Bowie was so dehydrated and desiccated looking that he would keep returning to a glass of fruit juice on the piano, running his finger around the inside of his mouth to unstick his lips from his gums. He later joked that his cadaverous physique, shrinking into increasingly triangular padded shoulders, meant that the subsequent live album, *David Live*, should have been titled "David Bowie Is Alive and Well (in Theory)," nodding to the memoir of semifunctional alcoholic and journalist Jeffrey Bernard.

176. In his book on *Low*, Hugo Wilcken recounts that on bad days, Bowie would drink a gallon of König pilsner, only to be found sobbing in a bar. One waiter remembers that he was always either drunk or working on getting drunk.

177. Bowie loves to flash razors as mirrors—the metaphysical cutup—an image that slices through your brain. In "I Am a Laser," a woman wears blades in her bra—sensuality tinged with an edge of danger. In his joint interview alongside William S. Burroughs, Bowie noted the description of double-sided eighteen-inch knives in Burroughs's *The Wild Boys* that caused him to raise his (shaved) eyebrows. The interview ends with Burroughs explaining the knife's two different edges: one long and smooth edge and the other with short, serrated teeth. From this, Bowie would later joke that his stage name also cut both ways, a pun on gender fluidity. In later life, Bowie would declare himself a fan of the BBC drama *Peaky Blinders*, about a real-life Birmingham gang from the turn of the century who had razor blades sewn into the peak of their flat caps, its theme song "Red Right Hand" by Nick Cave and the Bad Seeds.

178. "Sound and Vision" finds this aching, nothing pain in the wait for inspiration; it becomes a warm, familiar kind of melancholy. The pulling down of the blinds announces nothing more to say or do, Bowie the writer marooned in the emptiness of the blank page.

179. Bowie expresses a self-awareness similar to the protagonists of Shakespeare's plays, in their musing foreshadowing the origins and consequences of their own decline but continuing regardless, as if fated, like Bowie captive to his addiction. "Ashes to Ashes" frames Bowie/Tom as Hamlet on the shore, born to tragedy.

180. Robert Hillburn compared Bowie's own experiences of alienation to his onstage character in *The Elephant Man*, to which Bowie responded, "Merrick was a forced outcast who wanted very much to be in with the others. I was an outcast by choice."

181. In Bowie's 2003 joint interview for *Complex*, Mos Def made his own stinging observation on the addictive dopamine-reward reflex of fame: "Fame is like getting across the street. It's like, if there's nothing to be across the street for, it's a point-

less destination. It's like, 'I gotta get across the street, man! I gotta be there! I gotta be there!' Then you get across the street and you're like, 'Yeah I'm here!' And then, that's it."

182. Like Bowie's seemingly random choice to drop Michi Hirota into the battle of words of "It's No Game (No. 1)," forced into a combine of meat-grinder chatter of voices chewing up the scenery and trying to upstage one another.

183. *Sounds* reviewer Valac Van Der Veene referred to the doubled vocal in "It's No Game (No. 1)" in suspect terms, perhaps invited by Bowie: "a Jap lady rants, insults, climaxes—or just reads the latest sales figures for Toyota Cars."

184. See Yukio Mishima's attempted military coup and subsequent suicide as an example of wishing to return Japan to the imagined former glory of its prewar imperialist past.

185. In a 1980 interview for Japanese television, Bowie explained his attitude behind *Scary Monsters*: "I wanted to incorporate something of the feeling of the Japanese spirit." Bowie foundered as to why or what this meant exactly but suggested "a crossover between east and west that's always been in my work," a continued interest in the movement of kabuki and how this might translate between theater and the rock show.

186. As if speaking to the Japanese business principle of Kaizen ("continuous improvement").

187. In 1980, Gordon Burn overheard a French journalist getting metaphysical before receiving a warm and pithy put-down. Interviewer: "Are you the last rock star?" Bowie: "In my family, certainly."

188. "Taking away all the theatrics, all the costuming, and all the outer layers of what it is, I am a writer. That's what I do, I write" (Shaw 2016). The compulsion of the author would come through on "Fantastic Voyage" with Bowie's need to write everything down no matter how terrible the state of things for fear the words might be lost—less an act of preservation than of being present in the times.

189. Speaking to MacKinnon in 1980, Bowie offered a powerful metaphor that carries a spiritual intensity: "I think that I have a mainline, but I couldn't define it. Again, I wouldn't wish to; there's a danger in trying to define that one thing. . . . But it comes and goes, it hides, it gets lost and it reappears, rather like a stream that you come across when you're walking through a wood. You see it sometimes and it sparkles and then it disappears." This perspective chimes with his feelings around the self-emptying required in Buddhism. Bowie gently hints at a higher artistic power that ultimately rests within him—the music becomes inspiration's shadow passing over his life.

190. Bowie's lyrical notes would cross over between songs of the album, talking to one another: "Music that spacemen listen to doesn't mean they don't pay back debts/ Space talk is "cheap"—"lightweight gravity of the situation." These punning, gnomic stabs in the dark reveal the thrust behind the song, often at the expense of Major Tom's plight, damned to suffer as his creator did.

191. Carpenter points out that Bowie's "Ashes" Pierrot phase bookends his major creative burst, which ends suffused with melancholia, where such events often give a meta-narrative to an artist's earlier songs (or previous incarnations), thereby making direct connections to the past and inviting autobiographical (re)interpretation (e.g.,

the Beatles' "Glass Onion," which mentions "Strawberry Fields" and "I Am the Walrus" as Paul McCartney).

192. RCA would capitalize on the synchronized "histories" of the two songs by releasing a 1980 promotional single titled "The Continuing Story of Major Tom," with the lonely beeping at the end of the original 1969 version of "Space Oddity" merging into the fading universe of "Ashes to Ashes" to create a nine-minute self-contained epic.

193. By 1977, Bowie claimed to be apolitical, making only theatrical observations based on what he read and taking a "third way" of adopting the opinions and stances of others (ridicule as the first response to distorted and disturbing points of view) and elsewhere giving people the David Bowie that they wanted to see, hear, and read about.

194. "Stop Britain from becoming a black colony. Get the foreigners out," exclaimed Clapton to his captive audience. "Get the w*gs out. Get the c**ns out. Keep Britain white." Clapton has never made a formal apology for these remarks; where Bowie was calling for a shift in government, Clapton was ethically and morally wrong. Great on guitar, bad with people.

195. Perhaps also looking to the thought police of the hard left who condemned him for his words but not his actions. Nonetheless, Bowie was a magnetic, charismatic inspiration for many young people at that time who may have taken his words, like his lyrics, to heart.

196. The term "fascist" comes from the Italian *fascia*, often represented on early flags by a bundle of wood bound together with an axe slotted through the middle. The "message" was one of individuals finding strength in unity, a brotherhood of arms, a martial vision of the perfect authoritarian society.

197. MacKinnon notes that Bowie's characters seemed to provide him with a "necessary degree of solace" for a splintering sense of self that somehow managed to hang together. The character was the expression of these attitudes: Ziggy Stardust's megalomania, Aladdin Sane's fragmentation, and the Thin White Duke's extremism. For Bowie, the persona explained his attitudes, though he knew it did not excuse them.

198. Alongside a short film that Bowie made with a mini-camera and a set for a proposed film for which he claimed to have written a script.

199. The 1922 Fritz Lang film.

200. Brian Ferry would note that for the tour of Roxy Music's *Country Life* album, the band used banners and military uniform with a black strap across the chest: "the banners seemed to go with this fascistic look, which was tongue in cheek, but quite good to look at."

201. Mark Ravitz had a long association with Bowie, running from the Diamond Dogs tour (1974), *Saturday Night Live* (1979), the Serious Moonlight tour (1983), and later the Glass Spider tour (1987), featuring the highly praised giant spider, which Bowie ceremoniously torched in a field in Auckland after the tour's final show.

202. In Yukio Mishima's novel *The Sailor Who Fell from Grace with the Sea*, a seemingly innocent gang of young boys, from "good homes," gruesomely dissect a live cat, revealing them to be just as capable of performing violently cruel acts as their adult forebears as they try to avoid growing into their bourgeois and comfortable lifestyles.

203. In her poem "Lady Lazarus," Sylvia Plath dryly observed with an exacting eye Nazi evil at its most kitsch and banal, with the human skin of concentration camp prisoner turned into a piece of home decoration. The Nazi's carnival of flesh and the SS death cult of the skull sought to turn gross reality into saintly glamour, the vulgarity of the Nazi styles swollen with noble shine, glossing over the stark truth of their inhumanity.

204. In 1983, the right-wing Conservative group the Monday Club called for an end to Commonwealth immigration, the introduction of compulsory repatriation (deportation), and the repeal of the Race Relations Act.

205. Trevor Horn remembers the complaints of a drummer asked to play alongside a preprogrammed beat for Buggles' "Video Killed the Radio Star"—"It sounds like a fucking machine."

206. Kunze (1986).

207. "Fashion, always an acrostic of fascism and passion, accurately catches the soldier talk coming from the middle classes" (Savage 1980).

208. In an interview from 1979, Bowie complained about the superficiality of Los Angeles compared to the more "real" cities of Detroit and Philadelphia, which he preferred. Sounding like Gil Scott-Heron, he admired those places where people were struggling and working for their lives, placing it alongside the expanses of New Mexico and Arizona, visited during *The Man Who Fell to Earth*, as among his favorite places in America.

209. Bowie's father worked as a proto-media professional for the children's charity Barnados, living in the benign outer London suburb of Bromley, comfortable but not rich. Bowie's upbringing was not so far removed from George Orwell's description of his family standing: "I was born into what you might describe as the lower-upper-middle class," safe and respected but always feeling just a few rungs away from slipping down into a working-class situation.

210. Elsewhere, the Stones luxuriated in a rakish, raffish, buccaneering reputation of excess, seemingly without incident or consequence, before Altamont kicked them swiftly in the balls and dredged them back to the starker American realities of the Summer of Love's sharp decline.

211. The nature of fashion is a pull in two directions—uniqueness and homogeneity—a trickle-down pattern where high-end goods are adapted into more affordable knockoff high-street versions battling with notions of the real thing. Bowie would exemplify and challenge this system of recycled ideas in "Fashion"; an extremely popular and populist single, it was ironically symptomatic of pop culture and the record industry, with RCA the running mill on which Bowie claimed to be caught.

212. "In the long run, the oppressor is also a victim. In the short run (and so far, human history has consisted only of short runs), the victims, themselves desperate and tainted with the culture that oppresses them, turn on other victims" (Zinn 1980).

213. The mass production of cheap clothing in Third World countries to meet market-generated demand for the latest looks would establish the continued political and social fallout of fashion, driving down quality and price. These clothes would arrive in Western nations as disposable culture, worn once, twice, or perhaps never at all, and then discarded to a landfill or returned to poorer countries via charity bins

stacked into clothing dumps. The attrition rate of fashion becomes stylized auto-cannibalism.

214. See also the revolutionary movements of the People's Front of Judea and the Judean People's Front.

215. It is likely that this line inspired the title of Jennifer Egan's 2008 novel *A Visit from the Goon Squad*, mashed up with James Joyce's *Here Comes Everybody*, the latter recurring throughout his second epic, *Finnegan's Wake*. As a fan, there is a sense of belonging, but it is the sparking and setting of new modes of fashion, art, and culture that carry deeper meaning.

216. Engineer Chris Porter remembers the casual professionalism of Fripp and Bowie chatting about J. G. Bennett (scientist and author on psychology and spirituality) and Gurdjieff. Their natural intellectualism seems in stark contrast to the music: at times malevolent, forced, and ironically insincere, it was perhaps the navel-gazing of pop explaining popularity to itself.

217. Knowing a good thing when he heard it, James Brown returned the gesture by copping the riff from "Fame" for his December 1975 hit "Hot (I Need to Be Loved, Loved, Loved, Loved)."

218. Bowie refers to the Kinks' "Dedicated Follower of Fashion," which at the height of 1960s London pop culture lampooned the fickle shifts of style, buying into the latest thing. He is pursued as a style icon, being copied as he copied others; he thinks he is a flower to be looked at, but really he is the butterfly, flitting from color to color (MacKinnon 1980).

219. Being a "Gouster" was a subcultural dress code worn by some African American teens in 1960s Chicago.

220. In *Sweet Dreams*, Dylan Jones (2018) noted that from the mid- to the late 1970s, both Bowie and Brian Ferry were indicators of cool: "looking sharp in both the retro and modern sense"; it is noted that rarely did either of them wear denim.

221. George Underwood saw Bowie's disciplined work ethic that drove him to complete projects with pressure-cooker speed, focus, and intensity. When asked by a journalist, "What makes David different from other people?," he responded, "Well, I ring him, 'Do you want to come to a party on Saturday?,' and he'd say, 'No, no, I want stay in and get things done.' That's what David was like. He knew when to go out and when to stay in and get things done." This line seems to have been reimagined in the lyrics for "Modern Love."

222. By the end of the 1980s, Bowie adopted the shark-sharp dark edges of Tin Machine, doing grunge in deep tan, black Armani and clashing neon. This style absorbed the friction of Kurt Cobain's resolutely anti-fashion look, dressing down as proof of working-class credentials. Contrariwise, Bowie went entirely the other way, briefly returning to weird *outré* uniforms and male dresses in 2000.

223. Much of this was courtesy of Bowie's road-hardened band of the era, self-sampling and fashioning loops using Pro-Tools and with particular heft from bassist Gail Anne Dorsey and the guitar pyrotechnics of Reeves Gabrels.

224. On the *Blackstar* track "Dollar Days," the green English fields are bulldozed, tarmacked, or paved over. Knowing it wouldn't matter, they lived on in Bowie's memories, even the dream of an England that never was. Buoyed by the postwar ide-

alism of a boy born in 1947 and the say-yes-to-life optimism of the 1960s so rapidly subsumed by social change that he helped to accelerate, Bowie was a spiky catalyst within the growing crises of modernity.

225. Bowie's on/off association with the world of fashion coined the plastic ephemeral with a cameo in 2001's *Zoolander*, a comedy that mocked the fashion world for all of its preciousness with the homeless shopping trolley style of "Derelicte!" For all of his ten seconds of screen time, stepping in to call the result of a competitive "walk-off," Bowie is announced simply by the first delayed guitar chords that open "Let's Dance"; his appearance is the performance.

226. Arriving at the end of the decade, the 1989 Tin Machine song "I Can't Read" carries a sense of disgust at the 1980s obsession with material wealth: "concerned with cultural depression and deprivation, with its memorable line that today sounds like a manifesto of globalization: 'Money goes to money heaven/Bodies go to body hell'" (Deandrea 2016)—a jarring vision that echoes "It's No Game (No. 1)."

227. In his lyric notes, Bowie recorded "an ocean of new waves," with each successive movement being swallowed up by the next.

228. Debra Rae Cohen makes her reference to the famous painting by Francisco Goya that shows the figure of Greek myth Saturn eating his children; the rites of succession are thwarted in (auto-) cannibalism, where he is destroying and consuming a part of himself.

229. It is interesting to note Bowie's continued off-screen mimesis with his character, also taking center stage on *Station to Station*, although both albums deal more with internal space, not space travel.

230. Jon Savage's 2008 book *Teenage* identified how postwar children like Bowie set to grow up in the 1960s were the first generation raised largely free of weightier responsibilities. Branded "teenagers" of the new world, they were less a breakaway thing than they were the young people who would become the new consumers, their rebellion, massaged, pandered to, and later in adulthood sold back to them as nostalgia—as noted in the 1987 Bruce Robinson film *Withnail and I*, "they're selling hippy wigs in Woolworths, now."

231. For his part, Bowie notes that John Merrick takes the same line as Michel Foucault, seeing "truths" as "restriction, governance and punishment."

232. See also the chapters in this book on "Kingdom Come" and "(Silhouettes . . .)."

233. By the time of *Let's Dance*, Bowie was a safe and sensible distance from his Berlin electronic experimentation and could complain about the synthetic nature of the "ME Generation icy cold vein" (Bohn 1983).

234. Like Numan's post-human android character, the machines possessed a glacially pure psychology of clean and exacting logic, passing for the fine balance reason. For Gary Numan, it was later revealed that his challenging experience with fame and stiffened "look" expressed part of his autism, a condition diagnosed much later in life, and largely misunderstood or ignored in the 1970s.

235. In the 2020 documentary *Can't Get You Out of My Head*, Adam Curtis finds the British character firmly rooted in a continued longing for the past, a loosening grip on a now distant world that drives deeper insecurities. Relying instead on the

security of near-permanent nostalgia against which everything in the future was to be compared, it drew on the Allied victory in World War II, where might made right, glossing over decades of atrocities. The rallying call of militarism was reaffirmed by Margaret Thatcher's successful military campaign in the Falklands War in 1982, a gamble of old-school saber-rattling that fortunately paid off.

236. By 1988, the Conservative government had cut the top rate of tax from 60p to 40p on the pound, boosting the disposable income of the wealthiest overnight.

237. In April 1980, there were riots in Bristol attended by hundreds of people and later in 1981 the New Cross Fire, which left thirteen young black people dead. Protesting the lack of police action over the suspicious circumstances of the fire, 10,000 people marched to the slogan "Thirteen dead and nothing said." There were also riots and looting in Brixton, which, in their aftermath, Home Secretary William Whitelaw compared to visions of London during the Blitz.

238. David Sylvain, lead singer for Bowie inheritors Japan (the band) would co-write the theme song "Forbidden Colours" for the 1982 film, *Merry Christmas, Mr. Lawrence* alongside Bowie's co-star in the film, Ryuichi Sakamoto.

239. On *Hunky Dory*, Bowie nodded to "Churchill's lies"; although he did not elaborate, there is a common theory that, having intercepted and decoded a message detailing the planned bombing run via a captured German Enigma machine, it was decided to suppress the message for fear it would give away the Allied forces' secret upper hand in preparing for a European invasion. Churchill later appeared in the city for a walking tour and photo opportunity, offering a "morale boost" to broken ruins, battered survivors, and the dead.

240. Bowie missed much of the post-punk movement in England; while he stayed up to speed with records (except for intermittent tours), he was absent from the scene. When asked about the impact of punk and New Wave while appearing on *Countdown*'s End of the Decade show in 1979, Bowie was only half joking when he responded, "a very important enema."

241. A close read of Bowie's lyrics on "Ricochet" reflects a deeper social concern where Bowie laments the coming of a scythe that will sweep away the poorest and most vulnerable, parents who must go through the pain of making promises to children they know they can never keep, and the anxiety of being "forgotten," pushed into the exclusion zones of society's scrap heap (Deandrea 2016).

242. In a 1978 *Crawdaddy* magazine interview, Bowie looked down from his suite in Manhattan's Mayfair House: "It was always so easy, especially in this city, to be able to stand behind a window, just like this, and look at things from about here. The city was built for that. If you weren't on the ground then your perspective was always at this level, always looking at somebody's business, something that needn't play a part in your life—but you still watch it. It's not just the weather. The mere way the city is structured, it seemed that violence would become the theater of the streets. It had to happen in America, and now it's rampant in Europe as well. I'm utterly and thoroughly confused by city life and New York" (White 1978).

243. Meanwhile, in New York, Dylan Jones noted that the New Wave bands of 1978 began to embrace the "beat" of black music, which inspired groups like Suicide, Talking Heads, and Blondie, who brought people to the dance floor with electronic

elements and guitars. Jayne County remembers Bowie's perspective shifting significantly after seeing Human League perform at CBGBs in 1979, a crossover point between the do-it-yourself of punk and the new electronic possibilities offered to nonmusicians by synths, keyboards, and programming technologies.

244. Masked parties, savage parties, Victorian parties, Greek parties, Wild West parties, Russian parties, circus parties, parties where one had to dress as someone else—all that succession and repetition of mass humanity—those vile bodies.

245. Bowie alludes to the same spirit of resistance to the march of change on "Because You're Young."

246. It was also Steve Strange who introduced Bowie to his "secret weapon," makeup artist Richard Sharah, whom Bowie would task with creating his Pierrot clown "mask."

247. Michael Bracewell (1997) argues that Bowie brought a high-street orthodoxy to camp sci-fi glamour. As fantastical as his presence was, it would always be through the prism of provincial South Croydon and other end-town suburban spaces from which his dreaming emerged, a pattern of self-creation that others could find within themselves.

248. The early 1980s photographic work of Stephen Willats discovered in those darker places "an extreme rejection of society's values, an alienation from its idealisations, that found expression in non-conformity" (Bracewell 2021).

249. A band name taken from the character Durand Durand in the Jane Fonda vehicle movie *Barbarella* carried the cadence of "blah-blah, ja-ja," but the band managed to temper campy sci-fi with the extreme metaphors of J. G. Ballard's writing, which so often preempted the progression of Western democratic culture into nihilistic self-ruin with an apocalyptic streak.

250. Electronic pioneers Soft Cell deserve a mention here (the song "Bedsitter" and others), exposing the dark corners of Soho, Francis Bacon's submerged scream held behind glass, and the dance of neon glow—urgent and fleeting pleasures.

251. In a Radio 4 interview, John Wilson noted that while Bowie seemed to merge myriad untraceable elements of style and cultural influence, this caused him to work against the grain of popular culture, a disruptive agent. If his work seemed predictive, it was because he made things happen and others followed, whereas the chameleon is one who is able to blend in only with the present.

252. The vaguely red/black dynamic of Numan's human-automaton image is essentially lifted from Kraftwerk's uniform on the album *The Man-Machine*, resembling Bauhaus, De Stijl, and Nazi color aesthetics.

253. "What I was passionate about in relation to Kraftwerk was their singular determination to stand apart from stereotypical American chord sequences and their wholehearted embrace of a European sensibility displayed through their music. This was their very important influence on me."

254. Bowie responded to the spontaneity and randomness that Dada, demanded, the newspaper cutting poetry of Tristan Tzara becoming the cutups he made his own.

255. Chris Porter remembers lots of people from the Blitz scene passing through the studio at Good Earth. Rusty Egan and Steve Strange and other members from Visage would visit; it's a wonder to imagine if they heard the rough mixes of "Teenage

Wildlife," Bowie watching them enter the world of fame and celebrity as their lives were incidentally put to tape.

256. On "Changes," Bowie sang that the children who were beaten, abused, and spat on, like the freak Ziggy fans who would soon follow him into the future, were immune to the unwanted advice of their elders; they lived and survived alongside their peers. Now on "Teenage Wildlife," Bowie is so much older, having changed places with the young people and set himself apart, outside of their judgment.

257. In a 1983 interview, Bowie stated that it was never his intention to slip into the role of grandfather of a scene or establishment figure—easy as it might seem for him to take up that role. His future goal was to escape and evade any of these knowable positions, which would mean death for his art.

258. In May 1979, Bowie observed, "I don't like collections of people, whether it be politically, socially or artistically. I've always tried to ridicule those factors. I slummed out rock and roll when it got very cliquey, and have been known to slam out politics in a similar, exaggerated, cartoonist fashion. Gangs of people scare the hell out of me. I think it can crucify what's called a movement if it's made into a group of people. I much prefer to call them a group of individuals."

259. Sylvain, alongside Numan, aped aspects of Bowie's persona, though the two artists would seem to arrive independently of him.

260. As in *The Little Prince*, the drinker sadly dreams to one day stop drinking, so they drink more.

261. In 1985, Bowie rehabilitated the song's mixed-cynicism singing to the British Live Aid crowd of 72,000 people, with Live Aid raising £30 million, while just two months later, the British government signed an arms deal worth £43 billion with Saudi Arabia.

262. Bowie had inspired a generation with *Low* and *"Heroes."* *Lodger* had extended this reach with the Anglicized rap of "African Night Flight" and David Byrne's absorption of world music styles. While he respected his peers, Bowie looked down on the hungry youth he imagined snapping at his heels.

263. The chorus of "Ashes to Ashes" and its fourth verse mirror the seventeen-syllable construction of the Japanese haiku poem. Best known as a poetic form concerned with depictions of nature and the seasons with the pattern of five, seven, and five syllables in each of its three lines, the one thing haiku demands is concision of language, which Bowie displays to great effect in his sharp vocalization.

264. Adrian Belew was supposed to be commissioned for the sessions. His guitar work shares much with Robert Fripp, as on the idiosyncratic guitar solo for "Red Sails" from *Lodger*, in which Bowie instructed Belew to play in the style of German band Neu! Working on the basis that Belew had not heard the German band, his performance is nonetheless evocative of their music driven by Bowie's instructions. Oddly, Belew was paid up front, but the call never came. As if taking a safety measure, Bowie reverted to Fripp.

265. The advent of the CD sharply arrested the slow decline of record sales in the 1970s—music making became big business again.

266. Talk Talk began their career by writing hits and moved into avant-garde experimentation without breaking their stride, the kind of transition that many other bands of the era more concerned with following cheap trends could only dream of.

267. Simon Critchley recognizes Bowie as an artist, not looking to nail down truth but empowered by artifice and fakery: "Authenticity is the curse of music from which we need to cure ourselves." But on *Scary Monsters*, there is the sense that now Bowie's fuse is running shorter, given over to a sense of diminishing returns. Chris O'Leary notes that "Teenage Wildlife" is infused with powerless rage, and Bowie realizes that "artistic progress was a cruel illusion," so each record is both a new ending and a new beginning, another stopping-off point along the way—but to where? The answer would come to Bowie only years later.

268. This is perhaps one of the best Bowie compilations (if not the best) ever put together, with album tracks selected (by Bowie) in favor of singles. As shown in much of his album sequencing, Bowie is a great editor and curator of his own discography.

269. An infamous 1921 text by Dadaist Tristan Tzara, an absurd parody of the theatrical conventions and a revolt against the hypocritical facade of civil society—a meaningless entry into a world without fixed meaning.

270. The first time the song has been performed live since 1970, bookending the decade before the new age of the 1980s. Bowie resurrects his own King Midas figure: a broad-shouldered patriarch who strides over the power of nations, he can lift up the world or stop the sky from collapsing and let it fall on a whim.

271. Bowie was at the Mudd Club, beloved of New York's 1980s artistic underground, with Blondie's Jimmy Destri when they spotted German singer/performer Klaus Nomi and Warhol scenester/Fiorucci store attendant Joey Arias. Bowie beckoned them over and soon roped them into his performance scheme. Bowie deployed the DAM Trio, augmented by Destri on keyboards and *Saturday Night Live* guitarist George Wadenius.

272. Klaus Nomi's musical career would accelerate after *Saturday Night Live*. His ominous Germanic falsetto marked his self-titled 1981 album released by RCA, landing somewhere between Bowie, synth pop, opera, and Laurie Anderson. He continued the monochrome triangular tux look, with spandex and makeup to match, and looked to be set for a long career, but he became one of the earliest musical stars to die from complications due to AIDS in 1983.

273. *Détournement* has a double purpose: on the one hand, it must negate the ideology that all artworks are ultimately commodities, but, on the other, it must overcome this to produce politically active work. Either it adds details to existing works, thus revealing a previously obscured ambiguity, or it cuts up a range of works and recombines them in new and surprising ways. The enemy of this practice is, however, sheer novelty, and it is this that must be guarded against. The Situationists take the position that the literary and artistic heritage of humanity should be used for what they term "partisan propaganda purposes"—the promotion of radical politics.

274. Visconti points out that this similar effect was used by Bowie on "Fame" to achieve the high and low vocals.

275. In Little Richard, Bowie found a formative influence on his own conception of sexuality and the male body. Richard grew up feeling more like a woman, reflected

in his homosexuality, which was complicated and challenging as he tried to determine his own orientation.

276. Rechy's book is one example of transgressive, sexually explicit books published (or unleashed) in the early to mid-1960s and appears on Bowie's 100 books list, including the D. H. Lawrence novel *Lady Chatterley's Lover* (first published in the United Kingdom in 1932, then banned and later released unexpurgated after a 1960 obscenity trial) and Hubert Selby Jr.'s *Last Exit to Brooklyn* in 1964.

277. The late Mick Rock took the infamous shot of Bowie and disputed the sexual implications of his pose. In his eyes, Bowie was simply biting the strings, getting carried away in his performance, and the body of the ever-dependable Ronson was just something to hang on to. The same shock performance was repeated at several gigs; it was only as spontaneous as it needed to be.

278. Peter Doggett is keen to note that by this point, homosexual acts between men had been legal in England and Wales for only four years.

279. In his first TV interview with Russell Harty from 1973, Ziggy is nudged and quizzed about his footwear. Bowie gently comes to his aid. Harty: "Are those men's shoes, or women's shoes, or bisexual shoes?" Bowie: "They're shoes' shoes, silly."

280. Along with "Velvet Goldmine" and "Sweet Head," some of Bowie's earliest B sides (absolute gems) pushed the limits of innuendo toward a more transgressive, sexually explicit side in his music that managed to remain coquettishly mysterious, the right side of "good taste" and radio airplay.

281. Margaret Thatcher commented at the Conservative Party Conference in 1987, "Children who need to be taught to respect traditional moral values are being taught that they have an inalienable right to be gay. All of those children are being cheated of a sound start in life."

282. The radical sexual politics of public figures such as filmmaker and artist Derek Jarman, who would contract HIV and later die due to complications of AIDS, helped to raise public awareness of the disease. Bowie's earlier admissions of broader sexual experience and his aesthetic confrontation, carried out in his music and events such as the *Saturday Night Live* performance, drew a line in the sand, making a stand for queerness in mainstream culture.

283. Perhaps more than anyone, the New York Dolls deserve trailblazing credit. Glenn Hendler (2020) suggests that the American slang term "Miss Thing," an offhand way to refer to a camp and effeminate gay man, provides some subtext of "Sweet Thing," a mixed message of affectionate put-down.

284. With grassroots subcultures bombing the cultural exchange of the installed systems of class, government, and imperial law and order that saw big business backing gentlemen's clubs, Freemasons, and the aristocracy as a phantom government operating in the shadows behind monarchy and parliament deepening the atmosphere of paranoia on both sides of the divide.

285. Bowie was always attracted to extremes of difference and authoritarian positions. In the looming apocalypse of "Five Years," he had already reeled off his own figures of freedom and restraint of the cop/queer/priest/blacks dynamics—exposing the clash of mainstream and margins—and the friction of the bleeding edge where they overlap.

286. Berlin had its parallel world in the Burroughsian Interzone of *Naked Lunch* (1959), the fictional double of the real international zone of Tangier. In Germany, it was peopled with outcasts, artists, and Turkish immigrants who were caught in a sort of time warp. Bowie claimed that he never exactly left Berlin but simply drifted away from a city riven by transience. In a 1978 interview with Jonathan Mantle, he observed that Berlin was "such an ambiguous place it's hard to distinguish between the ghosts and the living" (DuVerger 2018).

287. Bowie punctuates "Neuköln" with cries of pain and alienation blasted out on the saxophone. Neither a virtuoso nor a slouch, he overloads his breathing, strangling the last gasps of a city crippled by extremes of rage and defeatism, hyperventilating in the throes of brutal expressionism.

288. In his 2020 *New Yorker* obituary for George Steiner, author of *Bluebeard's Castle*, Adam Gopnik noted Steiner's assertion that the civilizing power of culture was not enough to save humanity from itself: "to see the war years as a fundamental rupture not just in history but in our faith in culture: educated people did those things to other educated people. It was not ignorant armies clashing by night that shivered George Steiner's soul; it was intelligent Germans who listened to Schubert murdering educated Jews who had trusted in Goethe, and by the train load."

289. There is a reason that Bowie's "Heroes" plays in the film *Jojo Rabbit*. To give an uplifting finish to a dark and difficult subject matter, the film ends with a bittersweet epitaph from Rainer Maria Rilke to keep going in spite of the terror that sometimes surrounds us.

290. "The grim bureaucracy and acute poverty of the fabled communist paradise stoked his prevailing sense of paranoia and claustrophobia" (Doggett 2011).

291. On the morning of September 1, 1973, following the military coup of General Augsto Pinochet, thousands of dissident leftist Chileans were rounded up and imprisoned inside Chile Stadium, including the protest singer Victor Jara. The guards there tortured him, smashing his hands and fingers, and then mocked him by asking him to play the guitar. Jara instead sang the Chilean protest song "Venceremos." Soon after, he was killed with a gunshot to the head. After his murder, Jara's body was displayed at the entrance of Chile Stadium for other prisoners to see. (Margaret Thatcher would continue to support the Pinochet regime throughout her time in government, as he continued a process of torture, disappearance, and assassination against his people until he was voted out in 1990).

292. Bowie takes a stand against the major social values listed in "Repetition": the family unit, gender roles, and working a job you hate all day to contribute and pay tax toward the national economy.

293. There is a comparison here with *1984*, where Winston Smith is tortured and coerced into declaring his love for Big Brother, and although he stammers and stutters out the phrase, his real tragedy is that the new love for his former nemesis is genuine (Deandrea 2016).

294. This also echoes Bowie's method placing his half brother Terry as another aspect of the singer's character. Bowie is only half mad—bisexual—just not all the time. This play on duality meant that he could easily slip away from a characteristic that no longer suited him, identity eclipsed in a song.

295. Here Bowie echoes the worn-out malaise of Iggy and the Stooges' "No Fun." When pleasure is exhausted, what is left?

296. Bowie would kneel and recite the Lord's Prayer at a 1992 benefit concert at Wembley Stadium in memory of Freddie Mercury (this is sometimes misremembered as being at Live Aid). Bowie would claim that he did it for a friend, "Craig," who had AIDS and was watching at home. Offering both an act of remembrance and a gesture of hope to the audience and their families and friends "that have been toppled by this relentless disease," he would later take part in a collaborative fund-raiser for World AIDS Day on December 1, 1999, in partnership with Queen and Microsoft.

297. In 1982, Boy George's group Culture Club was at the peak of fame, but George O'Dowd remained firmly in the closet due to label and management pressures that his coming out might hurt sales: "I wanted everyone to know I was gay; it went against every corpuscle of my body to deny it."

298. On "Hallo Spaceboy," he threw out the line "Do you like girls or boys? It's confusing these days," Bowie playing on his own frustrations with the new generation's adoption of faux metrosexual poses and showy self-labeling, desperately seeking to be different.

299. After this, Bowie realized that, like many musicians in recovery, he could continue to make great music without drugs. In making *"Heroes,"* Brain Eno had convinced Bowie that "you could do all the experimentation in creating music and not actually have to put your body through the same kind of risks." For his part, Tony Visconti, with his own struggles of addiction far behind him, would argue that drugs in the studio were never helpful to the recording process.

300. Bowie was wearing it when he later took a knee and offered his rendition/ performance of the Lord's Prayer at the 1992 concert for Freddie Mercury, trading his lyrics for words, a higher power meant to restore hope and faith to desperate and hurt people.

301. Bowie also heard something of the Eddie Cochran singing-guitar style in the groove of "Blue Jean."

302. In his 2007 autobiography, Visconti claims that both Tom Verlaine and Blondie keyboard player Jimmy Destri left a little bit of their own magic in the final overdubs.

303. Bowie made *Scary Monsters* at the still tender age of thirty-three, the same age at which Christ is believed to have been murdered and then resurrected.

304. This is fulfilled in Bowie's reading of the chthonic impulse in Camille Paglia's *Sexual Personae*, a didactic, confrontational, and single-minded book—it is nonetheless invigorating, insightful, and full of conviction on the aesthetics of gender fluidity. Paglia is an academic in search of an argument who accidentally writes like an artist.

305. A popular 1946 novel that tells of a woman who falls into deeper despair after being committed to an asylum.

306. Bowie showed his Kirilian photographs to Bell, meant to show life force energy from cocaine radiating from his body during the dark times in Los Angeles in 1975—the imagery would later reappear in artwork for the *Earthling* album and in other areas of Bowie ephemera.

307. Speaking to *Showbiz* in 1992, Bowie noted that sometimes he accelerated too far ahead, losing sight of the present: "I think one of my greatest and gravest mistakes was always living in the future," Bowie began. "I was very much about 'this is what I want to do and that's what I want to do.' And you spend so much time doing that that you end up forgetting about today, and so you don't start living the day and all that."

308. As if in response to Harris, Douglas E. Harding, author of *On Having No Head: Zen and the Rediscovery of the Obvious*, suggests, "We suffer because we overlook the fact that, at heart, we are all right."

309. In 1981, the Police released "Spirits in the Material World." Singing through clanky couplets of "troubled evolution," they nailed down the mind–body problem of dualism as one intertwined thing, asking for alternative solutions and, like Bowie, coming up empty handed (headed). Sting declaimed, "Have no faith in constitution/ There is no bloody revolution," retreating to a singular energy of flux that was both there and not there.

310. In 1984, Bowie would admit that even the most revolutionary socially aware statements were quickly reduced to a T-shirt slogan, and he found that charity work, particularly fund-raising and gigs, at least yielded a physical result. In 1984, Bowie would perform at the Hammersmith Odeon, raising £90,000 for the Brixton Neighborhood Community Association.

311. Denti de Piranjo (1956).

312. See also the parable of the gatekeeper in Franz Kafka's *The Trial*.

313. So secretive and immediately striking was Bowie's release of *Blackstar* just as he was exiting Earth that writer Graeme Thomson noted, "We were so thrilled to have him back, we failed to notice he was saying good-bye."

314. There is a comparison with the song "Young Americans," which briefly praises the first twenty years of life but condemns the rest as a slow downturn, dying for the next fifty years (Deandrea 2016).

315. Elsewhere on "It's No Game (No. 1)," the translation from Japanese sees the targeted couple as young lovers, their romance providing the background contrast to violence on the streets: *hyoutekini se wo shita koibitotachi*/"lovers are set as a background to the target" (as translated by Stephen Ryan from Chris O'Leary's Pushing Ahead of the Dame blog).

316. *Rouer* is a nineteenth-century French word for "one broken on the wheel," from Latin *rotāre*, "to revolve," and *rota*, a "wheel" (with reference to the fate deserved by a debauchee).

317. Brel would die in 1978 aged only forty-nine.

318. Like the children of 1971's "Changes" who are trying to change the world as a way of determining their own path, the young are often indifferent or "immune" even to the wisdom of older generations who came before them.

319. The Who was one of the key 1960s bands representing the free-spirited power of youth. With "My Generation," they embedded themselves within the next cultural wave of the future, reflecting the cyclical nature of young people making the world their own. When Townshend was twenty, Bowie, then eighteen, asked his idol to watch him perform. Townshend said his music sounded like a Who song and left.

320. Bowie had made a brief note about a Philip Glass organ sound, often shrill and piercing, but in the middle eight, it becomes a trilling, continuous rolling melody, like the sparkling cascading notes for which Glass is well known, running into one another in an overexcited chain reaction.

321. Virginia Woolf once said that it is perhaps more terrifying to be locked in than to be locked out. With and without the damaged vistas of doors slamming against past and future, the girl remains trapped in her own mind.

322. In a fine detail recorded by biographer Paul Trynka, Bowie would be mobbed by the adoring crowds when trying to leave the Booth Theatre in New York during his run of *The Elephant Man*, so he would leave via a slit window in the dressing room; at one point, all of his clothes were stolen, and he was left wearing a T-shirt, jeans, and tattered trainers—vacancy the true cost of fame.

323. Perhaps in (my own) wishful thinking, I always heard the breaking of rocks from "Kingdom Come" as both penance and crime reaching back to the moody drug trouble of "Station to Station," where now "the pieces are brok-en," inflected to sound like "cocaine." These albums are smothered in the aura of such timely dust.

324. The *Times* once described "Bowie as T. S. Eliot with a rock and roll beat," a man who took a fine art eye to pop music, merging street culture and art school.

325. The song ends with a jaunty guitar riff with strings bent to the breaking point—hyperbole in action. It was not only Bowie taking notice of New Wave sounds.

326. There is a fractured time line in the songs' long gestation from "Tired of My Life" in 1970 through to the final recording sessions for *Scary Monsters* in April 1980, months before Lennon was killed in December of that year. This distance seems to only make the song more haunting, offering painful reflection on real events.

327. According to Bowie, Kemp "was a living Pierrot. He lived and talked Pierrot. He was tragic and dramatic and everything in his life—theatrical. And so the stage thing for him was just an extension of himself."

328. Simon Critchley notes that following his 1968 shooting, Andy Warhol would suffer an outer-life sense of detachment, like his world was constantly being lived out within the frame of a television set. Bowie's immersion in his characters meant that much of his life was spent starring in his own private movie with everyone but him, busy watching the performance and often missing the real person standing just behind the scene in "Bowie's" shadow.

329. Another natural sui generis performer, Kate Bush, studied under Kemp.

330. In the 1967 film *The Image*, Bowie performs a very rigid act as an image brought to life, ghosting a former friend and partner who brings him to life in memorial painting, then kills him (again?), leading to a renewed sense of guilt and loss. The films awkward fade cuts give a literal presence to the hauntology of the Bowie figure.

331. *The Face* (1980).

332. Elsewhere, Picasso would use the harlequin checkered pattern to expose life as a game; like chess, we make a play with the pieces we have. Picasso would work between rich oil paintings of melancholic realism and basic line drawings. In his later, more direct, openly symbolic style, the clown is reduced to core elements: a hat or a crown or a smile or a frown sometimes a scribbled "blank" and busy non-expression. His stripped-back sketches show the mask as the dream of the perfect clown in

costume and pose. Bowie would use this simple alchemy himself to forge his own accessible but protective masks.

333. The costume resurrected the ghost of Bowie's early acting work encouraged by his first manager, Ken Pitt, who pitched Bowie as an all-around performer and entertainer. This was both true and not true. Bowie stumbled into rock and roll as something to do: a failed ad executive/graphic designer consigned to endless photocopying (xerox of a xerox, copy of a copy), an ex-hippie, or "a librarian with a sex drive."

334. Kemp would claim that while touring *Pierrot in Turquoise*, Bowie and Korniloff would become lovers, leading Kemp to attempt suicide, getting (his) blood all over his white silk clown costume. After this failed attempt, he aimed to cycle down to the beach and drown himself in the sea but decided it was too cold—and he was unable to find a bicycle.

335. Previously "Twig the Wonder Kid" from *Aladdin Sane*'s "Drive-In Saturday."

336. Bowie had his own prominent interest in the gay iconography of cinema. Tony Zanetta remembers designing Bowie a Marlene Dietrich–style sailor outfit in 1978, an icon whom Bowie himself was fascinated by enough to star alongside with in the ill-fated film *Just a Gigolo*.

337. Is the artwork wrong? The image was reversed, or mirrored, flipping Bowie's differently sized "colored" irises the other way around. This furthers the perspective of Bowie as a different person when in makeup. Edward Bell (2017) noted that, like himself Bowie was cross dominant, using different hands for certain tasks: "He wrote with his left, cut with his right."

338. If you look at the portraits of Bowie across the decade, at least half show him smoking, an ongoing love affair.

339. "The reason I suggest that one speaks of a false-self system is that the 'personality,' false self, mask, 'front,' or persona that such individuals wear may consist in an amalgam of various part-selves, none of which is so fully developed as to have a comprehensive 'personality' of its own" (Laing 1960).

340. This returned him to the sexualized alien mold but also rekindled the flame of the Ziggy era, the deep mercury reds turning to blistering orange and bleached-blond highlights of the Thin White Duke. Through the color, he appeared to be burning himself out. Fleet Street journalist Jean Rook said that Bowie "looks terribly ill. Thin as a stick insect. And corpse pale, as if his lifeblood had all run up into his flaming hair." By the Berlin era, his hair was neatly shorn close to the head and back to a mousy brown—the *Let's Dance* era would see him jump into an atomic blond look, like a Harpo Marx fright wig, finding a bold new look to hide behind.

341. For the cover of the "Fashion" single, Bell gridded Bowie in profile, carving up his portrait from Polaroid photos he had taken just before the Duffy session began—setting eyes, chunks of hair, lips and nose squared, all puzzling about the central image. Bowie was both fragments and whole, a statuesque mute that, as a god might be, still imagined itself to be alive.

342. Bowie told *The Big Issue* in 1997, "It's my awareness that the cigarette doesn't represent any particular attitude any more, it doesn't have the potency of a symbol it used to have. I saw it once as a prop on stage, now I smoke on stage just because I need one. . . . But I was aware of ritual and routine and theatricality with a cigarette

when I was younger. I knew exactly what I was doing around the stage and the cigarette became symbolic of a certain kind of removed identity kind of thing."

343. With his *The Next Day* artwork, which superimposed a white square over Bowie's face and blacked out the title of the *"Heroes"* album cover of 1977, designer Jonathan Barnbrook alluded to Malevich's *Black Square* (1915) and *White Square* (1918) paintings of early twentieth-century Russian suprematist art, where shapes and layering offered twin perspectives of concealment and allusion. Bowie and Barnbrook spent a long time sifting through iconic album covers to select the final design. Photographer Sukita would mention that he was surprised by the album cover but also impressed by how it made the old record photo seem "newer," born again through reinterpretation.

344. The first 100,000 copies of the original LP release included one of a series of four sheets of nine postage stamps masquerading as photo negatives, colored by Bowie in marker pen with some images struck out, excised, and tiled around the edge of the "Ashes to Ashes" single. In "queening" himself, Bowie delivered the single as a missive from elsewhere—Major Tom and the Pierrot clown as heads of state in permanent exile. The lurid coloring is said to be inspired by artist Jerry Dreva's dragged-out extravagance of the imaginary glam rock band Les Petites Bonbons in Hollywood. Dreva pranked the media into following the story via his mail-art subversion. Bowie acknowledged his debt to an underground artist by marking "bon bon" (sweets) on the stamps of the cover.

345. There is some controversy that Duffy introduced Bowie to Edward Bell's work and thus was unhappy when the artist would literally paint over his photography.

346. Chris O'Leary points out that the postage stamp–sized album shots on the back cover of *Scary Monsters* uses a blocked-out, hole-punch approach to redaction; everything is a broken grid and off kilter, similar to *Lodger* and inadvertently echoing the more rigid brick-by-brick wall built during *The Wall* live show.

347. After *Scary Monsters*, Bell was in high demand and worked on a number of record sleeves, notably Hazel O'Connor's album *Cover Plus*. Herself a huge Bowie fan, O'Connor was remade in the image of her idol; she had the pushed-back hair, red lips, and searching blue eyes, shoulders on the cusp of being exposed from underneath a bedsheet. Tony Visconti would produce her first album, *Breaking Glass*, alongside a feature film of the same name dramatizing O'Connor's creative life.

348. Director David Mallett found the effect by happy accident, often thought to be a solarized effect. Mallett managed to flip the sky black and colorize the scenes to make them more lurid and fantastical.

349. There is much debate about the cost with many commentators throwing around a figure anywhere between £25,000 and £250,000. Mallett states it was closer to £32,000 compared to around £700 for other shoots in 1980; adjusted for 2022 inflation, the figure stands at £146,000, which was a lot of money then.

350. In 1980, the *New York Times* suggested that the emerging "video vignette" was the new spectacle of rock music, played in clubs in place of real bands with venues competing to host the best screens and projectors. The *Times* decided that the nascent music videos of the era were "mostly unimaginative, commercially calculated affairs

that all too perfectly match the music they illustrate." This heralded the rise of commercials and promo films as a new art form.

351. Bowie's Midas touch would become their curse to inherit: art turned to money, beautiful and perfect, their self-made creative lives outpaced and overshadowed by a populist pose—people turning to gold.

352. By contrast, Bowie appeared almost naked playing in *The Elephant Man*, wearing the physical attitude of his body and projecting virtuoso transformations though his voice. Bowie pointed out that his whole-body performance had to be credible or else the audience's belief in the character would simply fall to pieces.

353. You cannot pin him down, stationary in flux, to deflect being known, knowable, a shape twisting and turning on the spot; like a jigsaw in motion, he cuts a swath through the demands and limitations of reality.

354. Sukita's mannequin never appeared in any subsequent Bowie photos and was later lost. Bowie's Pierrot clown became one of his briefest but most enduring looks, although it never became a stage costume. For Bowie, Pierrot lived on as an archetype, the eternal performer captured within the album.

355. Made by Jim Henson at a cost of around $7,000 each

356. Again nodding to the past, Murphy includes a sample of the "Ashes to Ashes" piano line in his remix.

357. With thanks to Bowie blogger Neil Anderson for these observations.

358. Cohen's interest in Bowie's poses are expressed by his many characters onstage and in song, at first stand-ins for "other" people who eventually seemed to overcome him.

359. Hans Richter offers an early form of merging opposites that chimes with Bowie's own synthesis: "The realization that reason and anti-reason, sense and nonsense, design and chance, consciousness and unconsciousness, belong together as necessary parts of a whole—this was the central message of Dada. . . . To create a vision of the harmony of the unequal, balance the infinite variety, the chaotic, the contradictions—in a unity."

360. Leah Kardos noted the press release in support of *Blackstar* that refers to "'Tis a Pity She Was a Whore" as rock music if it had been written by the Vorticists.

361. Weirdly, the single release of "Ashes to Ashes" would use *Lodger*'s "Move On" as the B side. Was Bowie making a point or scraping the barrel of earlier records to keep other album tracks back as singles?

362. In mid-December, the compilation label K-Tel released *The Best of Bowie* just in time for Christmas, reaching number three in the album charts. Its track listing provided a solid exploration of Bowie's career to date, and the heavy television marketing campaign behind the record brought Bowie's profile to the fore for many listeners.

363. No doubt on the strength of *Scary Monsters*, Daily Mirror and BBC Radio Rock and Pop Awards voted Bowie the best male singer of 1981, presented to him by Lulu.

364. Reznor would sample "It's No Game (No. 1)" in his early instrumental track "Pinion."

365. For more on this, see Chris O'Leary's (2020) excellent blog post about the joint tour on Pushing Ahead of the Dame; for more about Nine Inch Nails, see my book *Into the Never: Nine Inch Nails and the Creation of* The Downward Spiral.

366. Bowie would repeat the uniform in his "live" concert performance as part of the harrowing Berlin heroin movie *Christiane F.* In the film, Bowie himself became the cult icon. Although most of the film was made back in Berlin, Bowie's footage, in which he lip-synchs to the *Stage* version of "Station to Station," was, like the "Fashion" video, shot at the Hurrah club on 32 West 62nd Street in Manhattan.

367. There had been disputes. *David Live* would not be counted as a double album, and the *Baal* mini-album was scraped through, even though it was a minority interest record of Bertolt Brecht/Kurt Weill songs, not new, original material.

368. A lyric note from the 1980 period reads, "RCA is richer than you're [*sic*] whole XXXXXX country" (transcribed by Leah Kardos). Bowie scribbled the word "fucking."

369. As if adding pressure to an already fractious relationship, RCA continued to issue compilation albums, some good, some less good, of increasingly obscure material from the RCA archives. To support *Scary Monsters*, they released the promotional radio album *1980 All Clear*, with ten tracks, one from each year of the last decade up to 1979's "Boys Keep Swinging," the great forgotten Bowie single.

370. As announced in 2022, Warner Chappell Music acquired the global music publishing rights to all of Bowie's music from his estate, believed to have been valued at $250 million.

371. It is interesting to question on what side of this "acceptable" divide Bowie placed *Scary Monsters*.

372. In *Velvet Goldmine*, we see the full transformation of Bowie's decade from the birth and death of Ziggy to the golden-topped man of 1983, an unofficial parody/biopic for which Bowie would not license his songs (though Eno did). The film has its own great deep-fake soundtrack and covers by contemporary 1990s acts. The uber-blond pop star Brian Slade becomes the man who sold the world and comes to regret it after disappearing through the onstage "suicide" of his old persona.

373. Graeme Thomson notes that it was during this period that Bowie did become an elder statesman figure in music, less a proactive player on his own records, particularly *Tonight*. He occupied the role and pose of a singing entertainer, like Sinatra stepping onto the stage to pick up the mike and place it down again as he stepped off.

374. In the late 1980s, Edward Bell (2017) was asked by Bowie to come to Los Angeles to produce cover artwork for the two Tin Machine albums. He remembers that Bowie invited him to a Narcotics Anonymous meeting, a place to work though addiction issues alongside fellow addicts, having kicked his own heroin habit by himself.

375. Speaking about working with Bowie again for 2001's *Heathen* album, Tony Visconti told *Sound on Sound* in 2003, "Also, he recently gave up smoking, so he's recaptured some of his high range. He'd lost at least five semitones, and he's now gained most of them back. I mean, in the old days he used to sing 'Life on Mars?' in the key of C. Now he has to sing it in the key of G."

376. First working alongside Bowie on *Absolute Beginners*, Kevin Armstrong remembers Bowie's energy and his studio intake: "He was on sixty to eighty fags [cigarettes] a day. He'd have a coffee machine and some Cuba Gold coffee delivered wherever he was and it would be constantly on the brew. Seriously, he'd be chucking down the coffee and fags—and it would always be pretty neurotic and manic around him" (quoted in Trynka 2011).

377. Thatcher created "Right to Buy," enabling citizens to buy their council home from the local government, but also instituted harsh financial penalties that prevented councils from replenishing social housing stock. Burning society at both ends, there was a carve-up of multiple ownership and private wealth generation in which more and more British people became determined to rise to upper-middle-class status and grab their own small plot of land, the home as castle, to join the "money class."

378. In 1984, J. G. Ballard published "What I Believe." Not unlike Bowie's 1980 All Clear roll call of the imagination, he advocates for "the truth of inexplicable," and within this, he explicitly takes a stab at the haunting of celebrity culture: "I believe in the genital organs of great men and women, in the body postures of Ronald Reagan, Margaret Thatcher and Princess Di, in the sweet odors emanating from their lips as they regard the cameras of the entire world."

379. In 1991, J. G. Ballard said, "Perhaps the real lesson of the Reagan presidency is the sinister example he offers to future film actors and media manipulators with presidential ambitions and all too clearly defined ideas, and every intention of producing a thousand-year movie out of them."

380. Intense militarization was fueled in part by Reagan's inflated defense budget, providing a nuclear umbrella deterrent in the shape of the so-called Star Wars satellite program, with lasers in space meant to destroy Russian nuclear missiles in the dead atmosphere of space.

381. In this case, Thatcher knew her enemies well. In 1979, the IRA would assassinate Lord Mountbatten, and the Irish National Liberation Army would kill Airey Neave—a World War II veteran, a Conservative member of Parliament, former shadow secretary of state for Northern Ireland, and a close friend of Thatcher—with a car bomb. The IRA would later attempt to assassinate Thatcher and her cabinet, bombing their hotel at the 1984 Conservative Party conference in Brighton.

382. This caused the United States to support Nicaraguan Contra forces with arms in order to overthrow the Sandinista army revolution. Ironically, this process was funded by the Iran–Contra affair with the sale of arms to embargoed Iran in the first half of Reagan's administration. In a show of solidarity with the new government, the Clash released their triple album *Sandinista!* in December 1980.

383. Bowie would cover Lennon's "Working Class Hero" in 1989 with Tin Machine. Raging through the lyrics, the song offered a warning from 1970 of the dead zone reached by the very worst of the world's social climbers: "There's room at the top they're telling you still/But first you must learn how to smile as you kill." Lennon makes a neat nod to the 1957 "angry young man" novel *Room at the Top* by John Braine, the tale of a working-class social climber in an affair with two women, another one of Bowie's chosen books.

384. While he condemned Nixon to his inevitable fate, Bowie's recurring dream of America, the exotic wonder of his childhood, always has a reenergizing effect. In his essay on the album, Martin Moling notes that on "Young Americans," we witness how "the United States' eternal youthfulness rescues Bowie from the lethargic antiquity of Europe and delivers him from the vampiric, life-in-death obsolescence of glam rock." For Rob Sheffield, "Young Americans" is filled with a "lust for life."

385. In the 1983 *Ricochet* documentary charting the Serious Moonlight tour, we see Bowie go through several staged scenes, coming and going. In Singapore, he sits in the back of a cab and chats to the driver (regarding general things about the country). They soon get into a discussion about the strict laws of the country. Bowie is surprised to learn that chewing gum is illegal so as to prevent littering and sticking to the pavement, whereas the penalty for the smuggling or possession of drugs is death. The driver explains it is hard—some people smoke and need to chew gum—but other people don't want to walk on dirty, sticky streets—it marks the trade-off of the social contract.

386. An exchange from the play where Merrick, safely ensconced in his private room at the hospital, meets the character Mrs. Madge Kendal, a real-life actor, well known through the Victorian and Edwardian eras, and a regular visitor and later close friend of Merrick.

387. Even this seemingly simple phrase is complex; occurring in the nineteenth century, the expression reaches back to a "bolt out of the blue" (lightning on a clear-sky day). As if from nowhere, the world is struck by a sudden force. "Blue" in its many meanings, from a downbeat jazz mood to an open, bright, clear sky, is a common trope across Bowie's music and runs all through *Scary Monsters*.

388. In Jennifer Egan's novel *A Visit from the Goon Squad*, one of her characters complains that the empty pause toward the end of "Young Americans" is too short after Bowie sings "break down and cry." Caught between the need to hold the silence, prolonging tension, and the desire to jump back into the song onward to its conclusion, for Egan the premature return to the music marks a lack of conviction.

389. "What saves a man is to take a step. Then another step. It is always the same step, but you have to take it" (Saint-Exupéry 1939).

390. Chris O'Leary sees "The Next Day" infused with Ronson's spirit of resistance as a song that "winds up being a curse at death from the ranks of the living."

391. Album cover designer Jonathan Barnbrook noted that the album's title changed constantly up until the last minute and that it might have been named *Where Are We Now?* with that song as the title track and with its references to the Berlin years, alluding to the cover image of *"Heroes,"* the recurring sense of simultaneously looking back to the past and toward the future.

Credits

Edie, Maja, Gonzo!, and Diesel (the cat)—with all my love xXXx
ALCS—Authors Licensing and Copyright Society
Carlos Alomar—for his time in conversation
Neil Anderson—for his blog post about Bowie and his doppelgängers
Jonathan Barnbrook—for answering my questions about his Bowie design work
Bowie Wonderworld fan page
Bowie Books podcast—for new perspectives on Bowie's books
Michael Bracewell—for supporting words and his book *Souvenir*
Chris Charlesworth—for perspectives on Bowie at RCA
Simon Critchley—for his excellent book on Bowie and philosophical perspectives on his music
Caro Daher—for design ideas and advice
Hristo Dochev and Maxwell Jobson—for design insights
Shaughan Dolan and Miriam Weber—for various insights and camaraderie
Christine Fears—for drinks and grousing
Robert Fripp—for encouragement—and the music!
Ian Green—for pints bought and owed
Greg Gorman—for kind permission to use his Bowie photo
Chuck Hammer—for his patient time in interview
Glenn Hendler—for his knowledge of *Diamond Dogs* and our interview
Alan Horne—for hosting the excellent fan page community (Bowie Fascination)
David Johnson from the Shapers of the 80s archive—for kind permission of photos
Leah Kardos—for her time in discussion and sharing her earlier work and research on SM

Judith R. King—for her support in accessing the Peter Strongwater Estate
Matt Lakin—for continued editorial support and friendship
David Mallett—for being so open and generous with his time
Arsalan Mohammad—of Albumtoalbum podcast
"Sister" Rosie Morris—for pints of "tea" and keeping the ice flowing
Nacho Video—for his great Bowie archive documentary work
Chris O'Leary—for his great writing on Bowie and patience with my many
     e-mails
Kjell Paulson—for research images
Ioanna Paunas—for further adventures with Maja
Chris Porter—for giving me more insights into Bowie in the vocal booth
Simon Reynolds—for his kind response
John Robinson—for contact support
Peter Strongwater estate (courtesy of Judith R. King)—for image license
Gary Sykes-Blythe—for reading drafts, cooking, and healthy venom
Nick Smart and the David Bowie *Glamour* magazine team
The Society of Authors—for continued support
Aki Sukita and Masayoshi Sukita—for use of iconic photography and
     thoughtful responses on Bowie's passion for the city of Kyoto and Japanese
     culture
Professor Jun Tanaka—for sharing his Bowie research from his book Bowie
     The Man Who Sang Nothing
Lynne Troughton—for ballet and good times with Maja
Graeme Thomson—for his generous time in Bowie, Simple Minds, and
     discussion and book advice
Steve Tupai Francis—for Bowie insights and his writing on "Ashes to Ashes"
Mirim Weber and Shaughan Dolan (and Henry)—for kicks and ideas
Milo and the staff at The Square Cafe
Morgan at Homerton Library
George Underwood—artist
Thank you to everyone at Rowman & Littlefield for their patience and sup-
     port, particularly John Cerullo, Chris Chappell, Barbara Claire, Laurel
     Myers, and Della Vache.

Sources

PERSONAL CONTACT—E-MAIL AND INTERVIEW

(with thanks)
Carlos Alomar
Jonathan Barnbrook
Chris Charlesworth
Peter Doggett
Chuck Hammer
Glenn Hendler
David Johnnson, Shapers of the 80s
Leah Kardos
Angus MacKinnon
David Mallett
Chris O'Leary
Chris Porter
Aki Sukita
Masayoshi Sukita
Professor Jun Tanaka
Graeme Thomson

BOOKS

Bell, Edward. *Unmade Up: Recollections of a Friendship with David Bowie*. London: Unicorn Press, 2017.

Bracewell, Michael. *England Is Mine: Pop Life in Albion from Wilde to Goldie*. London: HarperCollins, 1997.

Bracewell, Michael. *Souvenir*. London: White Rabbit Books, 2021.

Broakes, Victoria, and Geoffrey Marsh, eds. *David Bowie Is*. London: V&A, 2013.

Brooker, Will. *Why Bowie Matters*. London, HarperCollins, 2015.

Buckley, David. *Strange Fascination—David Bowie: The Definitive Story*. London: Virgin, 2005.

Bullock, Tom W. *David Bowie Made Me Gay: 100 Years of LGBT Music*. London: Duckworth, 2018.

Critchley, Simon. *On Bowie*. London: Profile. 2016.

Denti de Piranjo, Alberto. *A Grave for a Dolphin*. London: Andre Deutsch, 1956.

Doggett, Peter. *The Man Who Sold the World—Bowie and the 1970s*. London: Vintage, 2011.

Duffett, Mark, and John Hackett. *Scary Monsters: Monstrosity, Masculinity and Popular Music*. London: Bloomsbury Academic, 2021.

Egan, Sean, ed. *Bowie on Bowie: Interviews*. Chicago: Chicago Review Press, 2017.

Gillman, Leni, and Peter Gillman. *Alias David Bowie*. London: Henry & Holt, 1987.

Hagler, Tom. *We Could Be: Bowie and His Heroes*. London: Cassell, 2021.

Hebdige, Dick. *Subculture: A New Search for Meaning*. London: Routledge, 1979.

Hendler, Glenn. *David Bowie's Diamond Dogs* (33 1/3, 143). New York: Bloomsbury Academic, 2020.

Hewitt, Paolo. *Bowie: Album by Album*. London: Insight Editions, 2016.

Howell, Michael, and Peter Ford. *The True History of the Elephant Man*. London: Allison and Busby, 2017.

Jaynes, Julian. *The Origins of Consciousness in the Breakdown of the Bicameral Mind*. New York: Houghton Mifflin, 1976.

Jenkins, Philip. *Decade of Nightmares: The End of the Sixties and the Making of Eighties America*. Oxford: Oxford University Press, 2006.

Jones, Dylan. *David Bowie: A Life*. London: Windmill, 2018.

———. *Sweet Dreams: The Story of the New Romantics*. London: Windmill, 2018.

Kardos, Leah. *Blackstar Theory: The Last Works of David Bowie*. London: Bloomsbury Academic, 2022.

Laing, R. D. *The Divided Self*. London: Penguin Academic, 1960.

Marcus, Greil. *Mystery Train: Images of America in Rock 'n' Roll Music*. New York: Plume Books, 2015.

Makela, Janne. *John Lennon Imagined: Cultural History of a Rock Star*. New York: Peter Lang, 2004.

Mankowski, Guy. *Albion's Secret History: Snapshots of Englands Pop Rebels and Outsiders*. London: Zero Books, 2021.

Marks, Craig, and Roy Tannenbaum. *I Want My MTV: The Uncensored Story of the Music Video Revolution*. New York: New American Library, 2012.

Mayer, So. *A Nazi Word for a Nazi Thing.* London: Peninsula Press, 2020.

McSmith, Andy. *No Such Thing as Society: A History of Britain in the 1980s.* London: Constable, 2011.

Miles, Barry, comp. *Bowie: In His Own Words.* London: Omnibus Press, 1981.

Numan, Gary. *(R)evolution: The Autobiography.* London: Constable, 2020.

O'Connell, John. *Bowie's Books: The Hundred Literary Heroes Who Changed His Life.* London: Bloomsbury, 2020.

O'Leary, Chris. *Rebel Rebel: All the Songs of David Bowie from '64 to '76.* London: Zero Books, 2015.

———. *Ashes to Ashes: The Songs of David Bowie, 1976–2016.* London: Repeater Books, 2017.

Pegg, Nicholas. *The Complete David Bowie.* Revised and updated 2016 ed. London: Titan Books, 2016.

Perone, James. *The Words and Music of David Bowie.* Westport, CT: Praeger, 2007.

Reynolds, Simon. *Rip It Up and Start Again: Postpunk, 1978–1984.* London: Faber & Faber, 2006.

———. *Shock and Awe: Glam Rock and Its Legacy, from the Seventies to the Twenty-First Century.* London: Faber & Faber, 2017.

Saint-Exupéry, Antoine de. *Wind, Sand and Stars.* New York: Reynal and Hitchcock, 1939.

Savage, Jon. *Teenage: The Creation of Youth: 1875–1945.* London: Pimlico, 2008.

Seabrook, Thomas Jerome. *Bowie in Berlin: A New Career in a New Town.* London: Jawbone Press, 2008.

Tanaka, Jun. David *Bowie: The Man Who Sang Nothing.* Tokyo: Iwanami Shoten, 2021.

Trynka, Paul. *Starman: David Bowie.* London: Sphere, 2011.

Tweedy, Rod. "David Bowie: Alienation and Stardom." In *Rock Music and Psychoanalysis,* ed. Leo Giuseppe. London: Frenis Zero, 2020.

Visconti, Tony. *Tony Visconti: The Autobiography: Bowie, Bolan and the Brooklyn Boy.* London: Harper, 2007.

Waugh, Evelyn. *Vile Bodies.* London: Chapman & Hall, 1930.

West, Nathanael. *The Day of the Locust.* Important Books, 1939.

Wilcken, Hugo. *David Bowie's Low* (33 ⅓). New York: Bloomsbury Academic, 2005.

Zinn, Howard. *A People's History of the United States.* New York: HarperCollins, 1980.

ACADEMIC

Carpenter, A. "'Give a Man a Mask and He'll Tell the Truth': Arnold Schoenberg, David Bowie, and the Mask of Pierrot." *Intersections*, 30, no. 2 (2010): 5–24. https://doi.org/10.7202/1006375ar.

Deandrea, Pietro. "Secret Thinker Sometimes Listening Aloud: Social Commitment in David Bowie's Lyrics." *RiCognizioni* 3 (2016). doi:10.13135/2384-8987/1687.

Du Verger, Jean. "David Bowie's Urban Landscapes and Nightscapes: A Reading of the Bowiean Text." *Miranda* 17 (2018). doi:10.4000/miranda.13401
Kunze, Heinz Rudolf. "David Bowie: Der Favorit oder: Die vielen Gesichter im leeren Spiegel" (in Idole 8, Ullstein, 1986).

ARTICLES/MAGAZINES

Ballard, J. G. "What I Believe." *Interzone*, no. 8, January 1984.
Bohn, Chris. "Bowie." *New Musical Express*, April 1983.
Budofsky, Adam. "Zachary Alford and David Bowie." *Modern Drummer*, September 1997.
Burn, Gordon. "Bowie Holds Court." *Sunday Times Magazine*, November 1980.
Cohen, Debra Rae. "Scary Monsters Review." *Rolling Stone*, September, 1980.
DeMain, Bill. "How David Bowie Returned to Orbit and Made Scary Monsters." *Classic Rock*, September 2020.
DeMain, Bill. "Meeting David Bowie."*Performing Songwriter*, September/October 2003.
Gilbert, Pat. "Bowie Interview." *Q*, March 2016.
Loder, Kurt. "Scary Monster on Broadway." *Rolling Stone*, November 1980.
MacDonald, Ian. "David's Dark Doings—And How He Escaped to Tell the Tale." *Uncut*, October 1998.
MacKinnon, Angus. "The Future Isn't What It Used to Be." *New Musical Express*, September 1980
Mantle, Jonathan. "David Bowie." *Vogue*, September 1, 1978.
Marcus, Greil. "Lodger—Review." *Rolling Stone*, August 1979.
Rockwell, John. "A Revolution with Bowie." *New York Times*, December 1980.
Savage, Jon. "David Bowie: The Gender Bender." *The Face*, November 1980.
Van Der Veene, Valac. "The Fright of Your Life." *Sounds*, August 1980.
White, Timothy. "Turn and Face the Strange." *Crawdaddy*, February 1978.
Young, Kevin. *Living Marxism*, June 1993.

PODCASTS

Alan, Marc. "Earl, Steve. Monroe, Eric." *Pod Like a Hole*. 2020. https://podlike ahole.podbean.com.
Bowie Book Club. 2020. http://www.bowiebookclub.com/episodes.
Hughes, Rob. *AtoZ Bowie* 2019. https://shows.acast.com/atozofdavidbowie.
Mohammad, Arsalan. *David Bowie: Album to Album* 2020. https://podcasts.apple .com/gb/podcast/davidbowie-albumtoalbum/id1355073030.
Shaw, Des. *David Bowie: Verbatim* 2016. BBC Radio 4.

WEBSITES

Cloonan, Martin. "The Musicians Union History Archive." 2010. https://www
.muhistory.com/from-the-archive-2-mu-response-to-david-bowies-nazi-salute.
Diliberto, John. "Zen & the Art of Fripp's Guitar." *Electronic Musician*, June 1987.
https://www.moredarkthanshark.org/eno_int_em-jun87.html.
Ewing, Tom. "Popular" blog. November 2008. http://freakytrigger.co.uk/ft/2008/11/
david-bowie-ashes-to-ashes/comment-page-1.
Fossett, Katelyn. "David Bowie's Strange Politics—Q&A with Simon Critchley." 2016. https://www.politico.com/magazine/story/2016/01/david-bowie-death
-politics-213529.
Griffin, Roger. "Bowie Golden Years—Scary Monsters." 2020. http://www.bowie
goldenyears.com/scarymonsters.html.
Heller, Jason. "How 'Ashes to Ashes' Put the First Act of David Bowie's Career
to Rest." 2017. https://www.npr.org/sections/therecord/2017/10/06/555850186/
how-ashes-to-ashes-put-the-first-act-of-david-bowies-career-to-rest.
Hendler, Glenn. "How to Bring Your Kids Up Bowie." January 2016. http://avidly
.lareviewofbooks.org/2016/01/12/how-to-bring-your-kids-up-bowie.
Kardos, Leah. "I Don't Want to Leave, or Drift Away: The Lodger Transition."
2016. https://www.leahkardos.com/files/Scary_Monsters_ch1.html.
Leas, Ryan. "Scary Monsters Summed Up Everything about David Bowie." September 2020. https://www.stereogum.com/2097443/david-bowie-scary-monsters
-40th-anniversary/columns/sounding-board.
Legaspi, Althea. *Rolling Stone*, September 24, 2019. https://www.rollingstone.com/
music/music-news/king-crimson-robert-fripp-david-bowie-estate-dispute-heroes
-scary-monsters-890139/
Lindsay, Matthew. "Making David Bowie: Scary Monsters (and Super Creeps)."
September 7, 2021. https://www.classicpopmag.com/2021/09/making-david-bowi
e-scary-monsters-and-super-creeps.
O'Leary, Chris. "A Society of One." Pushing Ahead of the Dame blog. 2020a. https://
bowiesongs.wordpress.com/ashes/notes/chapter-4-a-society-of-one-1980-1982.
———. "The Shore at Pett Level." Pushing Ahead of the Dame blog. 2020b. https://
bowiesongs.wordpress.com/2020/06/11/the-shore-at-pett-level.
Paola, David. "My David Bowie Album Today 'Scary Monsters (and Super
Creeps).'" May 2021. https://paola1chi.blogspot.com/2021/05/my-david-bowie
-album-today-scary.html.
Peebles, Andy. "David Bowie Talks about *The Elephant Man*, *Scary Monsters* LP and More." January 1981. BBC Radio. https://www.youtube.com/
watch?v=HY1oW5fNth4.
Reynolds, Simon. "How David Bowie Came Out as Gay (and What He Meant
by It)." 2017. https://longreads.com/2017/02/22/how-david-bowie-came-out-as
-gay-and-what-he-meant-by-it.
Sullivan, Jim. "Robert Fripp at 75." May 2021. https://rockandrollglobe.com/art
-pop/robert-fripp-at-75.

White, Ben. "David Bowie & Mos Def: The Style Council." January 2003. https://www.complex.com/music/2016/01/david-bowie-mos-def-2003-cover-story.

VIDEOS

Carson, Johnny. *The Tonight Show*. Bowie performance. 1980. https://www.youtube.com/watch?fbclid=IwAR3XZR6OrZeb-fgOrvr1sTwnIDlWvL7H5x8n-Do3FrRLFjk0Mda3UOgEqOU&v=NkefglL9c4c&feature=youtu.be&ab_channel=gracexakane.
Jensen, Kid. "Bowie Interview." 1983. https://www.bbc.co.uk/programmes/p06w6m3y.
Meldrum, Molly. *Countdown*. ABC. 1979. https://www.youtube.com/watch?v=xefm_CZXSrM&ab_channel=Vaxman80.
———. *Countdown*. ABC. November 1980. https://www.youtube.com/watch?v=QqPbTpXw9QU&ab_channel=That%27sEntertainment.
Nicholson, Mavis. "Afternoon Plus." February 1979. https://www.youtube.com/watch?v=LwTFW4kfHl4&ab_channel=ThamesTv.
Nacho Man. "David Bowie in New York." 1980. https://www.youtube.com/watch?v=F1fTtwGqdQw&ab_channel=NachoVideo.
Rice, Tim. "Friday Night, Saturday Morning." September 1980. https://www.youtube.com/watch?v=gp6A7vhfung&ab_channel=Tanaferry.
Saturday Night Live. 1979. https://vimeo.com/557050601.
Walker, Sharon. *The New Romantics: A Fine Romance*. Documentary. BBC. 2001. https://www.bbc.co.uk/iplayer/episode/b007btt3/the-new-romantics-a-fine-romance

BOOTLEGS

Bowie, David. *Strung Out on Heavens High*. https://www.davidbowieworld.nl/mijn-bootlegs-2-2/outtakes-promo/attachment/david-bowie-strung-out-on-heavens.

Index

About the Author

Adam Steiner is the author of *Into The Never: Nine Inch Nails and the Creation of* The Downward Spiral and *Politics of the Asylum*, a fictional nightmare vision of the NHS, and the poetry-film project Disappear Here: Living With Buildings. His next book is a critical examination of the music of Nick Cave and The Bad Seeds. He lives in the UK.
www.adamsteiner.uk
@BurndtOutWard